Time Capsule:
Medieval England

Michelle Caskey

Inquisitive Minds Press®
Caledonia, MI

Time Capsule: Medieval England

Published by *Inquisitive Minds Press*®
Caledonia, MI 49316
www.InquisitiveMindsPress.com

Printed in the United States of America

ISBN-10: 0988544431
ISBN-13: 978-0-9885444-3-7

Cover and Illustrations by Melanie Rankin

Interior page layout by Michelle L. Caskey

Photos used in this book were either taken by Michelle Caskey or Melanie Rankin, or they come from the public domain.

This book is dedicated to my amazing husband. Dennis thanks so much for all of your support. You work tirelessly behind the scenes as family provider, editor, web designer, technology guru, and publisher... among many other things. This curriculum wouldn't have been possible without your love and dedication. I can't tell you how much I appreciate you!

Companion Download

This curriculum contains some supplemental material you will want to download for your child. It includes maps, templates, scripts, logic puzzles, and other items for you to print for your child to use while completing various lessons throughout this course. To download this material, go to the following website:

http://www.InquisitiveMindsPress.com

If you have never registered at *Inquisitive Minds Press* before, then you will first need to create a new user account by selecting the **Register** link and submitting the necessary information.

Once you have an account and are logged in, select the **Register Products** link. Follow the instructions to register your product.

You will need to use the following password: ***Ancientengland***

Make sure you capitalize the first letter of the password (A). Also make sure that there are no spaces in the password. Select **Register**. Once your product is registered, you may go to **Your Resources** in order to access your companion download as well as the supplementary materials section.

If you have trouble downloading the supplemental material, send an email to Admin@inquisitivemindspress.com for further assistance, or use the **Contact** page on the website.

Introduction to Time Capsule: Medieval England – You are There!

You and your children are about to go on the adventure of a lifetime! The best way to learn something and retain the material is to actually experience the lesson firsthand. While I am unable to truly send you back to medieval times, my hope is that these activities will provide as close to a firsthand experience for your family as possible.

The goal of this curriculum is not to learn every fact possible about this time period. Instead, the Time Capsule lessons are bursting with hands-on projects to enable you and your children to not only hear about the medieval times, but also to see, hear, taste, and touch what it would have been like to have lived during this unique time period.

I hope you enjoy your journey. Creating this curriculum has been a blast! It has been incredibly fun to work on these lessons and to experience them with my own children. I hope that you enjoy using this material as much as I have enjoyed creating it. I'd love to hear about your experience!

Michelle Caskey
Michelle@inquisitivemindspress.com

A Few Tips Before You Get Started…

Daily Lessons – The Time Capsule curriculum is set up with 12 full weeks of lessons. The manual contains lists of all of the supplies necessary for each lesson as well as the necessary preparation you will need to do in advance. Each day's lessons also include a variety of options from which you can choose.

Don't feel that you have to complete everything before you move on to the next day's lessons. Each child learns differently and will enjoy different types of projects. Some of the activities are geared more for younger children and some for older ones. Choose a few things you think your child will enjoy as well as a few things that will stretch him or her. If you and your children are having a great time and learning a bunch, however, feel free to dig in and do everything. The choice is completely up to you.

If you have done unit studies in the past that's great; however, this curriculum will be unlike any unit study you have ever done before. Our goal is to expose children to as many different experiences as possible while studying this material. We have included lessons which will teach a variety of subjects including:

- Logic
- History
- Reading
- Literature
- Writing
- Photography

- Social studies
- Drama
- Science
- Math
- Geography
- Arts and crafts
- Drawing
- Art appreciation
- Music appreciation and more

You may decide to use this curriculum exclusively for the 12 week period and let your child completely immerse themselves in this subject material. Or, you may decide to do your regular subjects in the morning and to do your Time Capsule lessons in the afternoon – or on Fridays only – or over summer vacation. There is no right or wrong way to use these lessons. Decide what you think will work best for your family.

Details About Specific Subjects

Writing - Throughout the course of this material, your child should keep a journal of some kind. Depending on the age, interests, and abilities of your child, this journal can take on many different forms. You may decide to have your child write out what they are learning and experiencing as they go. You may decide to have your child draw pictures, take photographs, or print pictures off of the internet. Your child may also want to put some of the flatter objects they create inside of their journal. I recommend you get a 3-ring binder and plastic page protectors for each child who participates in this curriculum to contain their journal entries.

For children who don't enjoy the physical act of writing things down, try to limit what you require from them in this area. This course is about helping your child to experience and enjoy learning about the Middle Ages. If you find that they are resisting you during a certain lesson, feel free to modify the material to make your child more comfortable. A great way to do this is to let your child narrate back to you what they have learned and you can write it down for them.

Photography - Your child will be learning different tips through this course to help them take better photographs. Have your child take pictures while doing the optional activities as well as during other times if they desire. If you have more than one child, have them take pictures of each other as well as their projects. If you have one child, let your child take pictures of YOU performing the above activities and you can take pictures of them. Be sure your child also gets to take pictures of their completed projects if applicable. The best of their photos should be printed and placed inside their journals.

Drama – This portion of the lesson is a great time for you and your children to really ham it up. The more time you take making costumes or props, the more your children will enjoy this piece. Even shy children will come out of their shell if they see you acting with gusto. You may even want to get the whole family involved in these portions of the lesson. That will really thrill the kids!

Depending on how many people will be participating, you may either need to assign multiple parts to each person or take turns reading different parts. You can even change the parts around depending on how many boys and/or girls will be participating. For example, in the first scene of the drama, we changed Thea, the peasant girl into Theo, another peasant boy. We did this to accommodate the fact that we had two boys who needed roles.

We suggest that you run through the script a couple of times and then do a final run through while videotaping (if you have a video camera.) You may decide to set up the camera on a tripod or to have a family member run the camera.

Children will be thrilled to see themselves on screen – and these videos become a wonderful keepsake for helping your child remember their experiences during their Time Capsule lessons. Enjoy this silly time with your kids!

How Do I Get Started? –

Overall:
1. Look through the entire curriculum.
2. Make a list of needed materials which you don't normally have around the house.
3. You may want to give a copy of this list to all of the grandparents – they are usually eager to help out, either with digging up supplies at home or with helping to purchase some of the school supplies for your child.
4. Begin collecting the necessary materials so that you'll have them when you need them. Try to stay at least a week or two ahead on gathering supplies if possible.

Weekly:
1. Familiarize yourself with one week's lessons at a time.
2. Confirm that all of the necessary materials are available.
3. Complete all of the preparations which are necessary for each lesson.
4. You are ready to start the lessons with your children. Have fun!

Table of Contents - Overview

You are a Peasant

in Medieval England

Table of Contents for Peasant Weeks

Week One – You are a Peasant
Day One

Daily Life of a Peasant

Materials: None

Preparation: None

Lesson: Peasants did not have an easy life. They lived on land that was owned by someone else and they spent a lot of time working in the fields. Farming has always been a strenuous activity. Can you imagine how hard it would have been before there were tractors and other heavy farming equipment to help take care of the crops? Many peasants woke up at 3am to start their day!

Peasants were at the very bottom of the social ladder. They were not free to do whatever they wanted to do. They had to obey their local lord. A man named Jean Froissart wrote this description of peasant life back in 1395:

> "It is the custom in England, as with other countries, for the nobility to have great power over the common people, who are serfs. This means that they are bound by law and custom to plough the field of their masters, harvest the corn, gather it into barns, and thresh

and winnow the grain; they must also mow and carry home the hay, cut and collect the wood, and perform all manner of tasks of this kind."

Mr. Froissart called these people "serfs." A serf is a type of peasant. In fact, there were three different types of peasants during the Middle Ages:

1. **Slaves** – These people could be bought and sold.
2. **Serfs** – These people lived and worked on land that was owned by someone else.
3. **Freemen** – These people actually owned all or part of the land they worked. Some freemen were able to make a good living for themselves.

Even though most peasants had a hard life and didn't have much political power they were extremely important to medieval society. They are the ones who grew the food. Imagine how hungry the rest of the people would have been if the peasants decided to stop growing food!

Peasant villages were small and between ten and sixty families lived there. Peasants lived in small, simple houses without much furniture or other possessions inside other than a table, a few stools, and a chest. Their houses were made from wood or straw. The floor was covered with straw or reeds. These were woven together to make mats which covered the floor. They also scattered herbs under the mats so that when they were stepped on, fresh scents werereleased into the air.

The windows of the poorest peasant houses were just holes in the wall as they wouldn't have been able to afford to buy glass.

Houses wouldn't have had any running water. This means no bathtubs, no sinks, and no toilets. There also wasn't any soap or shampoo. You may think it was wonderful not to have to take baths; however, people were covered in dirt and fleas and lice. Their beds were mattresses stuffed with dried leaves or straw which attracted even more bugs. They went to the bathroom in a bucket which they emptied into the nearest river each morning. How would you like for that to be your job?

Peasants were said to be given only two full baths in their lifetime: once when they were born and once when they died. They did wash up their hands and faces, however, using water they had gathered from the river. Unfortunately, this was often the same river where they had just dumped their bathroom buckets. No one understood about germs or bacteria during this time.

Families cooked and slept in the same room. There was a hole in the middle of the ceiling so that smoke could escape through the roof. Children slept in a loft if their house was big enough. Each family also had its own vegetable garden.

At night, the poorest peasants brought their animals inside with them! This was to keep them safe from wolves and bears and to keep them from wandering off. It also prevented others from stealing their valuable livestock! Can you imagine the smell?!? These animals weren't house trained. They also brought in more fleas and flies.

Peasant children lived hard lives. Many of them died from disease before they even reached their first year. Peasant children didn't go to school in these days. They weren't educated much beyond being taught to farm and/or to develop whatever other life skills the parents thought might be necessary for survival. You might think this sounds like fun as well, but these children worked in the fields with their parents as soon as they were able. Often children were used to pick up all of the stones in a field and to chase birds away while their parents were planting seeds. It was back breaking work and the children didn't have much hope that their lives would ever improve. For peasants, life was nasty, rough and short.

For the next two weeks you will pretend to be a peasant living in medieval England. You will get to experience some of the hardships and work that a peasant would have experienced. As you complete these activities and go about your day, try to imagine what it was like to do these things all day every day of your life. Do your best to imagine how a peasant child might have felt knowing that this was their reality. They wouldn't have had much hope that their life was ever going to get better.

Create Peasant Clothes

Materials for Boy Costume (Pick and choose as desired):
- Loose fitting pants, such as black or brown sweatpants with long socks pulled up to the knees
- OR dark jeans rolled up to just below the knees
- A long-sleeved shirt (possibly baggy)
- A long handkerchief tied at the waist
- Tall, black boots or bare feet

Materials for Girl Costume (Pick and choose as desired):
- Long dress made of a simple fabric – usually one color
- OR a baggy, white blouse paired with a long, full skirt – usually one color
- Ballet slippers
- Unmarried girls usually wore their hair loose – but you may want to wrap your head in a handkerchief

Preparation: None

Parent Note: Peasants usually wore clothing that was loose fitting and comfortable. They needed to be able to work in the fields without their clothing getting in the way. For this activity, we are going to create an outfit to wear while acting in the drama as well as while completing their other lessons if your child so desires.

You can make this activity as simple or as elaborate as you and your children will enjoy. There

are many sites on the internet which give you ideas on sewing medieval costumes. We are going to show you simple ways in which you can gather costumes – but you are welcome to take the time to make more elaborate costumes if that is something which interests you.

An easy and inexpensive way to gather the clothing items we recommend is to check out secondhand stores and garage sales.

Feel free to improvise! The most important thing is that your child feels the part – not that they are completely authentic.

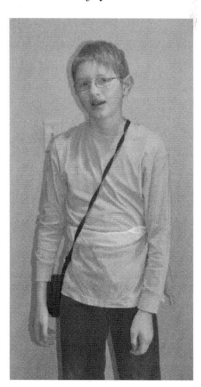

7

Holding the Camera Level and Still

Materials:
- Camera (preferably a digital one)
- Printer (optional – makes it easier to print your child's photos but isn't required)

Preparation: None

Lesson: Whether you have lots of experience using a camera or just a little, there are some very valuable tips you should learn. These tips will help your pictures to look better and more interesting than they ever have before. Every time you take a picture, you should try to visualize the way the entire scene will look. What kind of message are you sending with your photograph? The more you look at your photos and study them, the better you will get at creating compositions which are pleasing to the eye. Remember, it takes time to feel comfortable behind the camera. Take lots of pictures and practice, practice, practice.

The first tip we are going to cover is that you need to be sure you are holding the camera level before you take a picture. This may sound obvious; however, in the excitement of the moment you may not think of this simple tip.

This photo is crooked for no artistic reason.   This photo is nice and straight.

While you are lining up your shot, be sure to check the bottom and top of your viewfinder. You want to be sure that these areas look straight and that they are not tilted to one side. Sometimes artists will purposefully take photographs which are crooked. Right now, we aren't doing this. We are going to practice taking photos which are lined up nice and straight.

The other part of this lesson is to try to hold your camera still. There's nothing more frustrating that spending some time taking pictures only to come home and find that many of them are blurry! Today's photography lesson will help to alleviate that problem. Before taking a picture, it is important for you to stop, slow down for a brief moment, and be still before snapping a picture. In the excitement of the moment, it's easy to snap pictures wildly without performing this essential step. If you forget to do this, however, many of your pictures will be blurry and unusable.

Before taking a picture, do the following:
1. Take a deep breath and let it out. This will force you to slow down.
2. Prepare to take your picture.
3. Before pressing the button, try squeezing your elbows into your sides as much as possible. This will help to steady the camera.

That's it! Using this technique, you should find that more of your pictures are nice and crisp. Go out into your yard and take several pictures of whatever object catches your eye. Do your best to keep the camera straight and still while taking your pictures. You may want to put a few of your nicer photos in your journal.

Write in Your Journal

Materials:
- Your child's journal
- Paper
- Pencil, colored pencils, markers, etc.

Preparation: None

Parent Note: Have your child write down a few key points about what they learned about peasants. Depending on their age and ability, you can require your child to write one sentence or several paragraphs. You can also let them narrate back to you what they have learned. Then, have them draw a picture or print pictures from the internet to add some more insight to their journal page.

Possible Writing Prompt: Pretend you are one of the only peasants in your village who can read and write. Write a letter to your baron describing your family's living conditions. You might decide to make the tone of the letter hostile – or you may choose to be more diplomatic and ask him to make improvements.

Reading

Parent Note: The read aloud suggestions are intended for you to read to your child. The individual reading suggestions are intended for your child to read aloud to you – or to read on their own. Continue reading each selection throughout the peasant weeks until you are finished.

Read Aloud For Younger Children:
Don't Let the Barber Pull Your Teeth: Could You Survive Medieval Medicine? by Carmen Bredeson

Read Aloud For Older Children:
Adam of the Road by Elizabeth Janet Gray

Individual Reading for Grades 2-4:
Roland Wright: Future Knight by Tony Davis

Individual Reading for Older Children:
Dragon Slippers by Jessica Day George

Week One – You are a Peasant
Day Two

Clear a Field of Rocks

Materials:
- One bucket or bowl per child

Preparation: Find an area with many smaller rocks or a few large ones.

Parent Note: Whether you live in the city or the country, you should be able to set up this

experience for your child in some way. If you live near farmland it will be easy. If you have at least a patch of grass or live near a park, take your child there and let them gather up as many stones as they can to clear them out of the area. Have them place their stones in buckets or bowls. The main point of this activity is for your child to experience how hard it was for the peasant children to clear rocks from the fields and to haul them somewhere else.

Some children might object to this activity at first. Encourage them to give it a try so they can experience what it would have felt like to be a peasant child. Taking photos of your child may help encourage them. ☺

Listen to Old English

Materials: Audio clip from the supplement section on our website

Preparation: Go to our website and prepare to play the clip designated for this lesson.

Lesson: In medieval times, most peasants didn't read or write. Even though they lived in England, they didn't speak English as we do today. They spoke a language called Anglo-Saxon or Old English. Old English is very different from modern day English. In fact, if you hear Old English spoken, you won't be able to recognize hardly any words!

For this lesson, listen to the audio clip in Old English from the supplement section on our website so that you can hear the difference between Old English and Modern Day English. Listen closely and see if you can recognize any of the words.

Making a Model House with Wattle and Daub Construction

Materials:
- Craft sticks
- Hot glue
- Straw, long grass, or thin twigs (You can use pipe cleaners if necessary)
- Drinking straws
- Scissors
- Duct tape
- A bucket
- Dirt
- Clay
- Sand

Preparation: None

Lesson: Many peasants and villagers lived in houses which were made with wattle and daub. Wattle was a Middle English word which means 'covering.' It refers to a group of stakes or poles which are interwoven with twigs or sticks in order to become a wall or roof. Daub comes from the Middle English word "dauben" which means 'to whiten or paint.'

In this activity, you will be making a model of a house using a construction method which is similar to the wattle and daub method used by peasants during the early Middle Ages.

Parent Note: If it's too tedious or time consuming for your child to make the entire house, have them at least make a few walls so that they understand how labor intensive it was to construct a house in this manner.

Activity:
1. Lay four craft sticks on a flat surface in the shape of a square.
2. Hot glue the corners together and set them aside to dry.
3. Repeat this process until you have created four squares which will become the walls of your model.
4. Cut the straws to a length that will lie easily across the wall frames. Lay the straws parallel to each other with at least ½ inch between straws. This will form the structure of the wall. Hot glue the straws into place – about 3 per wall.
5. Weave the straw, long grass, or twigs between the drinking straws in a traditional in-out pattern. Continue weaving until the panels are full. There will be gaps between the building materials. We will take care of that later with the daub.

6. Assemble the walls into a house by hot gluing the edges together.
7. Combine equal parts of dirt, clay, and sand to create the daub mixture. Mix thoroughly and add water until it is the consistency of mud.
8. Apply this mixture to the inside and outside of the wall panels. Press the daub into the weaving so that it sticks to the walls.
9. Lay a craft stick on edge across the top of each wall panel. Press it into the daub.
10. Set your model aside to dry.
11. Using the straw or long grass, weave a mat. This will become your roof.
12. Lay the mat across the top of the house and hot glue it into place.

Literature

Materials: *(choose one)*
- Aesop's Fables for Children illustrated by Milo Winter
- The Classic Treasury of Aesop's Fables illustrated by Don Daily

Preparation: None

Lesson: Peasants couldn't read or write. They did, however, listen to oral stories that had been passed down from generation to generation. Some of these stories were fables, which are short stories told to pass on a lesson with moral significance. Aesop's Fables are a collection of fables which were believed to have been written by a slave named Aesop who lived in ancient Greece. These fables were written between 620 and 560 BC.

Parent Note: For the next two weeks, you will be reading fables to your child. Read several fables each day. After you read each fable, discuss it with your child. Be sure they understand the moral. Ask them whether or not they agree with the moral. See if they can come up with a different moral on their own.

Medieval Instruments

Woodwinds	Stringed Instruments	Percussion
Bladderpipe	Harp	Tabor
Zink	Viol	Drum
lizard	Gamba	Cymbals
Recorder	Lute	
Serpent	hurdy-gurdy	
bagpipe	Dulcimer	
crumhorn	Harpsichord	
Racket	Rebec	
Sacbut	Psaltery	

Materials:
- Chart from companion download
- Link from the supplement section on our website

Preparation:
1. Print one copy of the chart for each child.
2. Prepare to use the link from the supplement section on our website.

Lesson: Music was very important to people during medieval times. Songs were sung during festivals as well as just being part of everyday life. The most common instrument in use was the human voice. No money or training was necessary for someone to be able to sing.

Amazingly, there were many diverse musical instruments available during this time period. These instruments can be categorized into three distinct categories: woodwinds, stringed instruments, and percussion instruments. Woodwinds require the player to blow air into them or across an opening in order to generate sound. Stringed instruments produce sounds by either being plucked or played with a bow. Percussion instruments are those where sound is produced by one object striking another or by them being scraped or shaken.

Parent Note: Using the resources in the supplement section on our website, have your child create a chart like the one above which sorts the different medieval instruments into their proper category.

You may want to have your child include a picture of each instrument in their chart as well as the name. Also, be sure you take the opportunity to let your child listen to these instruments as some of them make very different sounds than the ones we're used to hearing in modern times.

Week One – You are a Peasant
Day Three

The Feudal System

Materials: None

Preparation: None

Lesson: During medieval times, people of England lived under a form of government known as the feudal system. This system came about because kings were responsible for vast amounts of land. Yes, kings were rich; but, they also had to find a way to enforce the rules for all of the people who lived on their land as well as to protect those same people from harmful marauders.

A king's job has always been a difficult one. Their job was particularly hard during medieval times because they didn't have TVs, radios, cell phones, or the internet to help them communicate quickly with all of the people. In fact, it often took them several days just to travel from one side of their kingdom to another. Can you imagine having to ride on a horse for a number of days to try to enforce the laws of your land?

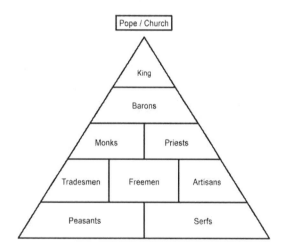

For these reasons, kings figured out a way to distribute some of their power. They appointed a group of men called barons or lords to help them maintain order. The king gave these barons large portions of land in exchange for their help. The barons were then charged with governing that land, paying the king something called homage or taxes, and promising to provide troops who would fight for the king whenever necessary. Some of these soldiers were called knights and we will learn more about them in a few weeks. ☺

Barons also had much more land than they or their family were able to care for on their own… and that's where peasants came into the picture. Barons allowed peasants to live on the land in exchange for them working the land. Peasants became tenants of the barons; but, instead of paying their rent with money, they paid with hard work and the sweat of their brow.

Peasants divided their time between working for their baron, working for the church, and working for themselves. They worked hard and received little for their efforts. The barons did, however, provide protection to the peasants. That was very important to people who were otherwise hard pressed to defend themselves.

People were also told by their local bishop that the harder they worked for the church, the more of a chance they would make it into heaven. You should discuss this as a family to decide whether or not you think this was a true statement.

The feudal system wasn't an equal form of government for all of the people. It favored those in the higher social orders such as the kings and barons. While a peasant was able to work hard to try to better their situation, they knew that they would always be a peasant. Their children would also always be peasants. That's just the way it was.

Literature

Materials: (choose one)
- Aesop's Fables for Children illustrated by Milo Winter
- The Classic Treasury of Aesop's Fables illustrated by Don Daily

Preparation: None

Parent Note: Read several new fables today. After you read each fable, discuss it with your child. Be sure they understand the moral. See if they can come up with a different moral on their own.

Ancient England (886 A.D.)

ANCIENT ENGLAND
866 A.D.

Materials:
- Maps from companion download
- Paper and pencil
- Tracing paper (optional)

Preparation:
1. Print one copy of the maps for each child.

Lesson: If you do a little bit of research, you could find many different looking maps of medieval England. Why is this? It is because the political borders in ancient England didn't remain in one place for very long. This was partly because there were many wars which occurred and different people groups who invaded on a regular basis.

This was also partly because during medieval times, an English king didn't necessarily pass on his power to his descendants. The future ruler could be any relative of the king who was able to convince a large enough group of supporters to help him try to steal the throne. This helps to explain why power changed hands so quickly during these times.

Activity: In this lesson, you will be comparing the political boundaries on an ancient English map to those of modern day England.

1. Trace the outline of the ancient map on a piece of paper. (Either use tracing paper or place a blank piece of paper on top of the map and hold them both up to a window.)
2. Trace the outline of the modern map on the same piece of paper.
3. Compare the political boundaries of the ancient map to those on the modern map. What similarities and differences do you notice? Do any of the ancient borders still exist in England today?

Does Differently Colored Light Affect the Growth of Seeds?

Materials:
- Bean seeds
- Disposable, plastic cups of different colors (must be transparent)
- Disposable, plastic cups that are clear
- Potting soil, seed starter, or dirt
- Tape
- Graph paper (optional)

Preparation: Figure out a sunny place in which to put the plants for several weeks.

Lesson: Sunlight is not white. It actually contains some of every color that exists. If we use an object called a prism, we can separate the light into the different colors of the spectrum. Those colors are red, orange, yellow, green, blue, indigo, and violet. We can remember these colors by taking the first letters of each color to make the name "Roy G. Biv." This is called an acronym.

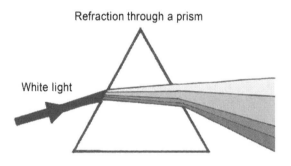

Refraction through a prism

White light

If sunlight contains all colors, then how do we see objects as a specific color? This is what happens. First, all of the colors of sunlight shine on the object. The surface of the object then absorbs all of the colored light rays except for one. It reflects that one color back to our eyes. Our eyes perceive the color that is reflected and send a message back to our brain telling us the color of the object.

Let's use a banana for an example. If you set a banana on the counter, the sunlight will shine on the banana. All of the colors except for yellow will be absorbed by the banana. The yellow light will be reflected back to our eyes and we will perceive the banana to be yellow.

Today, we are going to experiment further with the colors of sunlight. Our objective is to try to determine whether or not exposing a seed to one specific color in the spectrum of light will enable seeds to grow more quickly or slowly than exposing them to all of the colors of the spectrum.

Activity:

1. Use one cup of each color that you have gathered as well as one clear cup as planters. The clear cup will be your control group.

2. Put several inches of potting soil in the bottom of your planters.
3. Put one seed into each planter and poke it about 2" below the top of the soil.
4. Water your seeds.
5. Take another cup which is the same color as your planter and put it upside down on top to make a terrarium. Use a small piece of tape to secure these cups together. Do not tape all the way around because you will need to be able to water your seeds throughout this experiment.
6. You will need to check your seeds every few days to see if they need water. Do not overwater them! Within 7-14 days, your plants should start popping up above the soil.
7. After the plants appear, you should measure the daily amount of growth for each plant. Optionally, you can use your graph paper to make a bar graph similar to the one below. Record the growth of each plant.
8. After several weeks, determine whether all of your plants grew at the same rate or if the various colors made a difference.

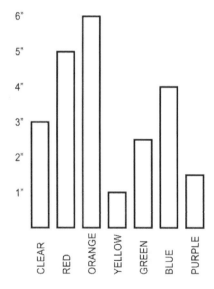

Peasant Problems

Materials:
- Paper and pencil

Preparation: None

Lesson: Peasants might not have been formally educated but they did have to use math to figure out different situations throughout their day. Since they couldn't write, they did all of their ciphering in their head! See how well you can solve these problems. The answers are in the companion download.

1. **Problem 1**: Today is the first day of crop planting for you and your family. If the sun rises at 5:34am and sets at 8:21pm, how much daylight will this day contain?

2. **Problem 2**: Later in the year, you need to figure out how much time you will actually have to plant your crops. If you had 12 hours of daylight that day, subtract 30 minutes for breakfast, 17 minutes for lunch, and 43 minutes for dinner. How much time is left for planting?

3. **Problem 3**: You have 4 fields that you need to plow today. If you have 15 hours of daylight, how much time will you have to plow each field?

4. **Problem 4**: Calculate the perimeter of your field (see diagram below.) Now calculate the area.

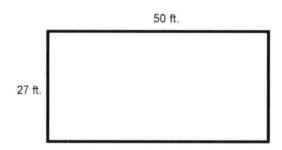

50 ft.

27 ft.

Week One – You are a Peasant
Day Four

The Bayeux Tapestry

Materials:
- Paper and pencil

Preparation: None

Lesson: The Bayeux Tapestry is an important piece of art from medieval times. It is thought to have been commissioned in the 1070s by Bishop Odo of Bayeux, who was the half brother of William the Conqueror. It is 230 feet long and isn't actually a tapestry at all. It is an embroidered cloth. It was rediscovered in 1729 by scholars who found it being displayed in a Cathedral in Bayeux, Normandy, which is how it received its name.

The Bayeux Tapestry contains over fifty different scenes depicting many events in the Middle Ages. They begin with the events leading up to the Norman conquest of England and end with the Battle of Hastings. It is an amazing piece of art.

For this assignment, you will research the Bayeux Tapestry using whatever sources you prefer (library books, internet, etc.) Choose one event illustrated in the tapestry and write a one page paper on **ONE** of the following:
- The importance of that event to Medieval England
- Make up an exciting story to convey the scene you've chosen from the tapestry
- Any other aspect about the Bayeux Tapestry which interests you

Be sure to include your research paper in your journal.

Weaving a Floor Mat

Materials:
- Light cardboard or cardstock
- Choose your weaving material (construction paper, raffia, pipe cleaners, yarn, ribbons, field grasses, metallic wire, fabric, burlap, etc.)

Preparation: (Depending on your child's ability. Some children can do this part themselves.)

1. Fold the cardboard or cardstock in half.
2. Draw a light pencil line across the end opposite the fold, about 1" from the edge.
3. Make a series of cuts one inch apart from the folded edge to this line.
4. Cut the weaving material into strips.

Lesson:

We learned earlier that peasants wove either straw or reeds together to make floor mats for their homes. Today we will be learning to weave mats. You may choose from many different patterns. If you don't have experience weaving, you will want to start with the plain weave. If you have done this before, go ahead and try a more complicated weave – or see if you can make up a unique pattern on your own.

Plain Weave
Pattern: Over 1, Under 1
Under 1, Over 1

Basket Weave
Over 2, Under 2
Under 2, Over 2

Herringbone Pattern

Under 1, Over 2, Under 1, Over 2
Over 1, Under 1, Over 2, Under 1
Over 2, Under 1, Over 2, Under 1
Under 1, Over 2, Under 1, Over 2
Over 2, Under 1, Over 2, Under 1
Over 1, Under 1, Over 2, Under 1

Twill Pattern
Under 1, Over 2, Under 1, Over 2
Over 1, Under 1, Over 2, Under 1
Over 2, Under 1, Over 2, Under 1
Under 1, Over 2, Under 1, Over 2

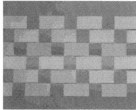

Reading

Parent Note: The read aloud suggestions are intended for you to read to your child. The individual reading suggestions are intended for your child to read aloud to you – or to read on their own. Continue reading each selection throughout the peasant weeks until you are finished.

Read Aloud For Younger Children:
Don't Let the Barber Pull Your Teeth: Could You Survive Medieval Medicine? by Carmen Bredeson

Read Aloud For Older Children:
Adam of the Road by Elizabeth Janet Gray

Individual Reading for Grades 2-4:
Roland Wright: Future Knight by Tony Davis

Individual Reading for Older Children:
Dragon Slippers by Jessica Day George

Learn to Draw a Chicken

Materials:
- Paper
- Pencil with an eraser
- A black marker (optional)
- Colored pencils or crayons (optional)

Preparation: None

Lesson: In this lesson, you will learn to draw a chicken step-by-step.

1. First, draw a circle for the head and an oval for the body. Be sure to draw everything lightly so that you can erase various lines at the end. Also, make sure you leave room for the chicken's legs and feet at the bottom of your paper.

2. Connect the two shapes to make the neck. Draw the tail feathers.

3. Draw the chicken's legs. The top of the legs consist of half circles. Draw the chicken's feet which are sort of star shaped at the bottom. Draw the wing, which is an oval with finger-like feathers. This is similar to what you drew for the tail.

4. Draw the chicken's eye and the comb on the top of its head. Now draw its beak which is an oval with a v-shaped opening. Now draw its waddle, which is a teardrop shape under the beak. You may add detail to the chicken's feathers and feet as well.

5. Use the black marker to trace all of the lines you are keeping. Lastly, erase your construction lines. Your chicken should look something like the one below. You may then use the colored pencils or crayons to add color to your drawing if you would like. Great job!

The Game of Skittles

Materials:
- Something to use for the 9 skittles (bowling pins)
  NOTE: Empty pop or plastic water bottles work great for this.
- Masking tape or a jump rope
- A ball (be sure this is soft if you'll be playing indoors)

Preparation:
1. This game can be played indoors or outside. If playing indoors, you may want to set up the skittles at one end of a longer hallway to help contain the skittles and the ball in one area. (Be sure to shut all of the doors in the hallway for further containment.)
2. Make a starting line on the floor with masking tape or a jump rope. You may want to set up the skittles and try knocking them down yourself so that you get a good idea of what is a fair distance at which to set them up for your kids.
3. The nine skittles should be arranged in a diamond at the end of an alley so that the sides of the square are diagonal to the edges of the alley. A typical diamond size is 45 inches from the middle of the front skittle to the middle of the rear skittle.

Lesson: People in medieval times used to indulge in games and recreation whenever they had an extra bit of time. One of their favorite pastimes was called skittles. This is very similar to what we call bowling. Today, you will get a chance to try playing skittles for yourself.

Activity:
1. Have your child stand behind the starting line.
2. Each turn starts with all of the skittles standing and consists of three throws down the alley. ***The ball must be rolled the length of the alley and not thrown – although, if you find your children having a hard time knocking down the skittles you may want to let them give it a gentle toss.***
3. If the first or second throw is a "sticker," which means that no skittles are left standing, the pins are all reset. So the maximum score in one turn is twenty seven. You can keep track of your scores if desired.
4. Games usually consist of 5 or 10 turns each.
5. The player with the most points at the end of the game wins.

Week One – You are a Peasant
Day Five

If Peasants Were So Poor, What Did They Eat?

Materials: None

Preparation: None

Lesson: Most peasants were farmers and as such, much of their food came from fields and gardens which they cared for themselves. They ate whatever vegetables were ripe at the time. They also gathered acorns to eat and they occasionally ate meat – again from livestock they cared for themselves. In the winter, food was the hardest for them to find. There aren't many crops to harvest in the winter and they didn't have as many ways to store their food as we do in modern times.

Peasants usually cooked using a large cauldron over the fire in the middle of their house. They would generally throw whatever they could find into the pot and call it stew. Sometimes they served this stew with meat or bread. Sometimes they ate something called frumenty, which was a popular type of wheat pudding.

Peasants didn't eat with forks. They usually used their fingers. Occasionally they used a knife but they didn't use it to cut as we do. Instead, they used it like a spear to stab pieces of meat from the shared trencher in the center of the table.

The peasants used trenchers that were made from wood as serving plates. They were often carved from the trunk of a tree. They had one trencher which they placed in the middle of the table. The entire family ate their food from it. The only time spoons were used was if something messy, like a stew, was served. Food on trenchers was eaten with the fingers. Imagine how messy your hands would get if you ate most of your food with your hands!

Much of what peasants ate was made from grain such as wheat, rye, oats or barley. People preferred eating the lighter bread made from wheat flour, which is the same type of bread that we eat today. Wheat could only be grown in fields which had been fertilized heavily, however, so that grain was usually reserved for the richer freeman and barons. Regular peasants also weren't allowed to bake bread in their own houses. They had to pay to use the baron's ovens.

27

Peasants were allowed to catch certain fish from the nearby streams, which added greatly to their food supply. They were not allowed to keep any salmon or trout, however. Those fish were reserved for the barons. Does that seem fair to you? They were also not allowed to fish from the ponds that the lords kept stocked for themselves.

Peasants were allowed to enter the forests to gather things such as acorns, nuts, and honey. They weren't allowed to hunt animals in the forests, however. That privilege was also reserved for kings and barons. Are you noticing a pattern? Does it seem as if the barons kept the best of everything for themselves?

One privilege given to peasants was that they were allowed to let their pigs roam in the forests. This made pork another food that was available to peasants. Pigs forage in the forest and they love to eat things such as acorns, making them one of the cheaper and easier types of livestock for a peasant to keep. Peasants occasionally ate lamb or beef as well. They also ate dairy products such as milk and cheese.

Peasants grew vegetables and herbs in their gardens. Some were even fortunate enough to have a few fruit trees from which they could gather food. If they had a year with a poor harvest, that made things even more difficult for them. A peasant lived or died by the success of their crops.

Peasants didn't understand about germs and bacteria; but, it doesn't take a modern-day scientist to see that wet food attracts bug and begins to smell bad. Drying food was a common way for people to preserve their crops in the Middle Ages. They also knew how to salt and smoke meat to keep it from rotting. In these ways, peasants were able to save certain foods to eat during the long winters.

Write in Your Journal

Materials:
- Your child's journal
- Paper
- Pencil, colored pencils, markers, etc.

Preparation: None

Parent Note: Have your child write down a few key points about what they learned about how and what peasants ate. Depending on their age and ability, you can require your child to write one sentence or several paragraphs. You can also let them narrate back to you what they have learned. Then, have them draw a picture or print pictures from the internet to add some more insight to their journal page.

Possible Writing Prompt: Write a weekly menu for your family using foods eaten by peasants. Try to make the meals as balanced as possible. Be sure to only include foods which the baron would have allowed you to eat.

Make an Olive Oil Lamp

Materials:
- A glass jar with a wide mouth (a ½ pint canning jar or an empty baby food jar works well)
- Extra virgin olive oil
- A piece of scrap paper approximately 3" x 3"
- A fire source – it will be much easier if you use a propane fire starter versus a match
- Hot pad
- A glass or plate which is larger than the opening of your jar for snuffing out the fire
- Graph Paper (optional)

Preparation: None

Lesson: Before the fall of the Roman Empire, people often made candles using olive oil. In the beginning of the Middle Ages, however, olive oil became scarce. People began making candles by melting animal fat and pouring it into a mold. They used rushes (a thin type of grass) to make wicks. In this activity, you will make your own lamp using olive oil.

Activity:
1. Add some olive oil to the jar. You don't need much – just an inch or so is plenty. The more you use, however, the longer you will be able to burn your lamp.
2. Wad up the piece of scrap paper and place it in the middle of your jar. This will serve as your wick.
3. Light the wick. You may need to hold the flame on the paper for several seconds to really get it going. Also, try to get the paper lit before it absorbs too much olive oil. Be persistent. This does work!
4. Your lamp will burn for several hours, especially if you used a larger amount of olive oil. Be very careful because the longer your lamp burns, the hotter the glass will become. **Parent Note:** You may want to place it on a hot pad or on some other surface which is safe to hold hot substances.
5. Optionally, you may want to have your child graph how much oil is burned each hour.
6. To extinguish the flame, **DO NOT pour water onto your lamp**. You will need to cut off the supply of oxygen to your lamp by placing a glass or ceramic object, such as a larger bowl or plate, overtop of your lamp. This will quickly snuff out the fire.

Literature

Materials: *(choose one)*
- Aesop's Fables for Children illustrated by Milo Winter
- The Classic Treasury of Aesop's Fables illustrated by Don Daily

Parent Note: Read several new fables today. After you read each fable, discuss it with your child. Be sure they understand the moral. See if they can come up with a different moral on their own.

Peasant Problems 2

Materials:
- Paper and pencil

Preparation: None

Lesson: Peasants might not have been formally educated but they did have to use math to figure out different situations throughout their day. See how well you can solve these problems. The answers are in the companion download.

1. *Problem 1:* You are raising a flock of 100 sheep. 40 of your sheep are ewes. If half of the ewes will have one lamb this year, what is the total number of sheep you will have in your flock after the ewes have all had their lambs?

2. *Problem 2:* The size of your pasture is 300 acres. You know that 6 ewes and their lambs can graze comfortably on each acre. How many ewes can you have in your flock before there wouldn't be enough grass to feed your flock properly?

3. *Problem 3:* It's time to sheer your sheep. You have 400 sheep in your flock. If each sheep averages 7.3 lbs of wool, how much wool will your flock produce?

4. *Problem 4:* It takes 2 minutes to sheer each of your 300 sheep. You started sheering at 7:15am. What time will you finish sheering your last sheep?

Week Two – You are a Peasant
Day One

Clock the Wind

Materials:
- Five three-ounce disposable cups
- Paper hole punch or sharpened pencil
- Ruler
- Two straws
- Pin
- Stapler
- Pencil with eraser
- Paint or marker (optional)
- Timer (optional)

Preparation:

1. Punch one hole in the side of four of the cups, about half an inch below the rim.
2. For the fifth cup, punch four equally spaced holes in its sides, about one quarter of an inch below the rim. Also punch one hole in the center of the bottom. Be sure this hole is larger in diameter than the pencil so that it will be able to turn freely.
3. Optionally, you may want to paint or somehow mark one of the four cups with one hole so that it is easier to count revolutions later.

Lesson: We have already learned how important farm crops were to a medieval peasant. The success of their crops was extremely dependant on having favorable weather conditions. Warm, sunny days with plenty of rain were essential. Peasants learned as much as they possibly could about weather in order to ensure their livelihood. For this activity, we will be making a wind-speed gauge.

Activity:
1. Take a single-hole cup and push a straw through the hole until about one inch of the straw is inside the cup. Make sure the straw is horizontal and staple it to the side of the cup. Repeat this with another single-hole cup and straw.
2. Push the empty end of each straw into one of the side holes in the five-hole cup and out the one across from it. Turn the cups so that they face the same direction.
3. Push the empty ends of each straw protruding from the fifth cup into the other two single-hole cups until about one inch of the straw is inside each cup. Turn the new cups so all the bottoms of the cups face the same direction. Staple the ends of the straws to the side of each cup like you did for the first two cups.
4. After making sure all cups are about the same distance from the center of the five-hole cup, carefully push the pin through the two straws where they intersect, in the middle of the five-hole cup. Use caution when handling the sharp pin.

5. Push the pencil through the hole in the bottom of the five-hole cup, eraser-end first, until it reaches the straws. Carefully push the pin into the eraser.
6. Try blowing very gently straight into one of the four open cups for a few seconds. If the device rotates, you are now ready to measure wind speeds.
7. Take the gauge outside and set it somewhere level. Count the number of times one cup completely turns around for 15 seconds, then multiply that value by four. This will give you the number of revolutions per minute (rpm.)
8. Take your device to different locations and measure the wind there. Do you come up with the same number everywhere? Why or why not?
9. ***Optional for older kids:*** To actually determine wind speed in miles per hour, you will need to go a bit further.
    a. First, calculate the circumference of the circle made by the rotating cups by measuring the distance around the circle that they make (using a tape measure or a piece of string you can measure with a ruler.)
    b. Then convert this to miles by dividing the number of inches by 12 to get feet.
    c. Then, divide that number by 5,280 to get miles.
    d. Multiply this number by revolutions per minute.
    e. Finally, divide your product by 60 to convert minutes to hours. This will give you an approximation of the velocity at which the wind speed gauge is spinning. There is some friction which slows down your gauge and this isn't accounted for – but your calculation will be close.

Hammer Throwing

Materials:
- A hammer (the bigger the better – if you happen to have a sledge hammer, that would be perfect)

Preparation: None

Lesson: One of the contests that peasants enjoyed was hammer throwing. Their hammers were large with 3 ft. to 3 ½ ft. long handles. The weight of the hammers varied. They threw between 130 and 140 feet. See how far you can throw your hammer.

Parent Note: In medieval times, the hammer was swung around the head and thrown from a standing position. You may need to modify this technique to make it safe for your child. Depending on their age and ability, you may want to let them pick up the sledge hammer to see how heavy it is… but then throw something lighter or softer for safety's sake. ☺

Write a Classified Ad

Materials:
- Paper and pencil

Preparation: None

Lesson: As you have learned so far, the life of a peasant wasn't the most pleasant. You will have your work cut out for you in this lesson. The local lord has hired you to write a classified ad for the local newspaper. Your job is to try to recruit people to come work for him on his manor. Include as many of the positive aspects of being a peasant as you can think of in your assignment. Advertisers don't necessarily stick to the truth when coming up with ads. You may need to exaggerate the truth or hide certain facts to entice people. You may also decide to take a photo or draw a picture to include as well. Have fun with this! ☺

Frumenty

Frumenty is a thick wheat porridge that was traditionally served with venison. It was often made with meat broth or almond milk, depending on whether it was to be served on a meat or meatless day. *NOTE:* You may want to use a double boiler when cooking the frumenty as it has a tendency to burn easily if it is cooked at too high of a temperature.

Ingredients:
- 2 1/2 cups water
- 1 tsp. salt
- 1/2 cup white farina or cream of wheat
- 1/2 cup sugar
- 2 eggs, beaten
- 1 tsp. vanilla
- 1 tsp. nutmeg
- 1/4 cup golden raisins
- 1/4 cup chopped, blanched almonds
- 1 Tbsp. sesame seeds

Directions:
1. Preheat oven to 375° F.
2. Heat water and salt to boil.
3. Stir in farina; cook 1 minute, stirring constantly. Remove from heat.
4. Stir in sugar, eggs, vanilla, and nutmeg.
5. Stir until sugar is dissolved.
6. Add raisins, almonds, and sesame seeds.
7. Pour into greased baking dish.
8. Bake at 375° F for 30 minutes.

Reading

Parent Note: The read aloud suggestions are intended for you to read to your child. The individual reading suggestions are intended for your child to read aloud to you – or to read on their own. Continue reading each selection throughout the peasant weeks until you are finished.

Read Aloud For Younger Children:
Don't Let the Barber Pull Your Teeth: Could You Survive Medieval Medicine? by Carmen Bredeson

Read Aloud For Older Children:
Adam of the Road by Elizabeth Janet Gray

Individual Reading for Grades 2-4:
Roland Wright: Future Knight by Tony Davis

Individual Reading for Older Children:
Dragon Slippers by Jessica Day George

Week Two – You are a Peasant
Day Two

An Increased Food Supply

Materials: None

Preparation: None

Lesson: Because most peasants were farmers, it was very important for them to grow enough food to feed themselves, their families, and everyone else who lived in the area. In the beginning of the Middle Ages this was a hard thing to do. Planting crops took a long time and was back-breaking work!

When planting a field, peasants originally used a farm tool called a simple plow. This was dragged behind an ox or a horse. It cut a thin strip into the ground. Someone else followed behind planting seeds and a third person followed behind them to cover up the seeds individually. Peasant children were also in the fields trying to scare away the birds until the seeds could be safely covered.

Between the years 700-900, a new type of plow was invented. This heavier plow was better designed to work in the dense, wet soils of England. It also contained something called a moldboard which provided several improvements:

- It turned over the soil which slowed the growth of weeds.
- It made furrows, which are long mounds for planting. This helped fields to drain better and caused better growing conditions.
- It made plowing easier and quicker for the peasants, which enabled them to plant larger fields.

Soon after the heavier plow went into use, the harrow was also invented. The harrow was made from several wooden boards that were attached to a horse. It allowed the farmers to plow their field crossways after dropping the seeds. The harrow covered the seeds with dirt without the peasants having to do this task by hand anymore. Can you imagine how much faster it would have been to cover the seeds this way?

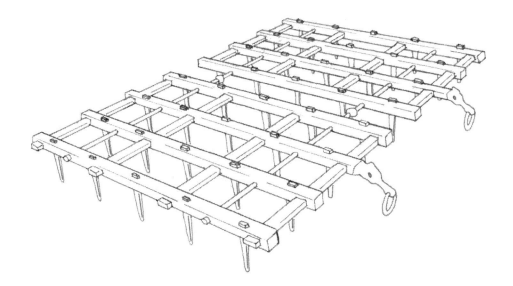

Between the years 1050-1200 there was another innovation which sparked an agricultural revolution. That was when farmers went from using a 2-crop rotation to a 3-crop rotation. For thousands of years, farmers had used the 2-crop rotation which means they planted crops in half of their fields and let the other half remain empty or fallow. Then, the following year, they planted the opposite fields and let the fields which had been planted remain empty. They knew that the soil needed a chance to rest and regain nutrients before it was any good for future planting. (This was especially important during Medieval Times because they didn't have fertilizers to put on their crops the way we do.)

At some point, however, the peasant farmers started planting a third of their fields with one crop in the fall, such as winter wheat or rye. The next spring, they planted a second third of their fields with another crop such as beans, lentils, or peas. The final third of their fields was allowed to rest. This enabled them to have more land planted at any given time increasing their food production.

The more food the peasants were able to harvest the better chance that their families would survive and even thrive! This extra food also enabled the noblemen to be able to hire knights for protection. We will talk more about knights in a future week!

How to Focus the Camera

Materials:
- Camera (preferably a digital one)
- Printer (optional – makes it easier to print your child's photos but isn't required)

Preparation: None

Lesson: Another tip which is very important is to be sure your camera is focused before you take a picture. Modern cameras are usually very easy to focus. You will see a circle or some other object in your viewfinder which you need to point at the subject of your photo. Press down halfway on the picture-taking button for your camera to focus and take your picture. (You may need to consult your camera's manual for more specific info pertaining to your camera model.)

The other part of focusing a picture well is to be sure you hold your camera very still. Sometimes it's hard to keep the camera from shaking. One tip for doing this is to squeeze your elbows into your sides while you are taking a photo. You may also want to use a tripod to take pictures if you want to be sure the camera stays completely still.

An unfocused picture   A focused picture

For this lesson, you will practice taking sharp, well-focused pictures. Take some time documenting other lessons you are completing or find something completely unrelated in which to photograph. You may want to include some of your best photos in your journal.

Literature

Materials: *(choose one)*
- Aesop's Fables for Children illustrated by Milo Winter
- The Classic Treasury of Aesop's Fables illustrated by Don Daily

Preparation: None

Parent Note: Read several new fables today. After you read each fable, discuss it with your child. Be sure they understand the moral. See if they can come up with a different moral on their own.

The Phases of the Moon

Materials:

- Eight Oreo cookies per child
- Plastic knife (optional)

Preparation: None

Lesson: Peasants didn't have any scientific equipment other than their five senses. Their scientific knowledge was extremely limited compared to modern standards. One thing they would have been conscious of, however, was the moon and its different phases.

I'm sure you've looked up at the night sky and have noticed that the moon doesn't always look the same. In fact, you're probably familiar with the terms "full moon" and "crescent moon." But do you know why the moon looks different every few days?

Earth is revolving around the sun. The moon is revolving around Earth. Depending on where the sun and the moon are in relation to Earth, more or less of the moon will actually be "lit up" or reflect the rays of the sun. Look at the following diagram to see the different phases of the moon throughout a typical month.

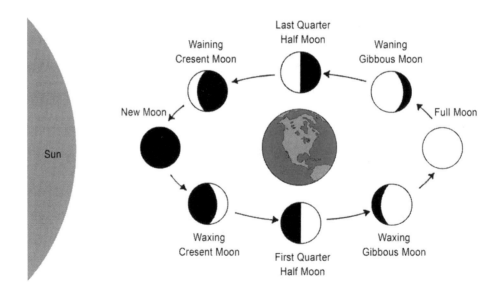

Activity:

1. Using the illustration, have your child create all eight phases of the moon using their Oreos. Have them open the cookies up and scrape off the appropriate portion of frosting for each phase using the plastic knife or their finger.
2. You might want to have them take a photo of their moon phases to recreate the illustration above. They can put a copy of this photo in their journal.

Foot Race

Materials: None

Preparation: None

Lesson: Peasant children didn't have the money to buy lots of toys – but they still enjoyed playing whenever they got the opportunity. One thing they enjoyed doing was running and racing each other. In this lesson you will also get to race each other. You can make this as silly as you'd like. First, try a regular race. Then try running backwards. Try the crab walk. Try crawling. There are many different variations you can try together. Have fun! ☺

Week Two – You are a Peasant
Day Three

What Color is My Hair and My Dress?

Materials: Logic puzzle from companion download

Preparation: Print one copy of the logic puzzle for each child.

Lesson: Solve this logic puzzle by determining the color of each girls dress as well as the color of her hair.

Watching a Seed Grow

Materials:
- 3 or 4 radish seeds
- 2 clear, disposable cups
- Potting soil
- Video clip from the supplement portion of our website

Preparation: None

Lesson: This activity is similar to one you did earlier. You will be planting seeds again; however, this time, the purpose and the method will be slightly different. For this activity, you will get to observe a seed in its various stages of development.

1. Add 3-4" of potting soil to the first cup.
2. Dampen the seeds and put them on the side of the cup next to the plastic. This will allow you to see your seeds as they grow.
3. Poke the seeds into the soil enough that they are covered with dirt.
4. Add water to dampen the soil.
5. That's it! Simply check the seeds every day to watch them grow. Radish seeds come up very quickly so be sure to check their progress each day as you water them. Observe the various changes as they take place – root development, stem growth, leaves appearing, etc.
6. Watch the video clip of a seed growing from the supplement portion of our website. Then, you will know what to be looking for as your seed grows.

Learn to Draw an Ox

Materials:
- Paper
- Pencil with an eraser
- A black marker (optional)
- Colored pencils or crayons (optional)

Preparation: None

Lesson: In this lesson, you will learn to draw an ox step-by-step.

1. First, draw two tapered rectangles for the body and the head. Be sure to draw everything lightly so that you can erase various lines at the end.

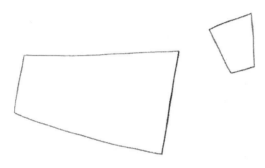

2. Next, round the corners of the smaller rectangle. Add rounded shapes off of the larger rectangle to make the ox's shoulder and bottom. Draw two lines to connect the head to the body.

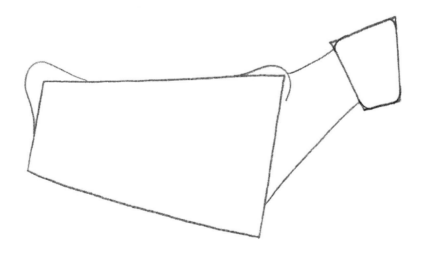

3. Now, we will draw the ox's legs, tail, nose and mouth. The back legs are rounded at the top, curved at the knees, and angled down to the hoof. The front legs are fairly straight and then rounded for the hooves. Draw the tail which is slightly-curvy like an S with a tuft of hair at the bottom. Draw the nose and the bottom of the mouth as shown.

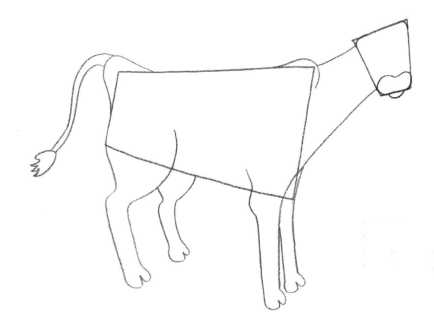

4. Now, we will add some details to our ox. Draw the eyes as shown. Add the hair on the top of the head. Now, add the ears which are squiggly oval shapes. Add the S-shaped horns. Draw the holes for the nose. Add the detail to the hooves as shown.

5. Use the black marker to trace all of the lines you are keeping. The final step is to erase your construction lines. Your ox should look something like the one below. You may then use the colored pencils or crayons to add color to your drawing if you would like. Great job!

Reading

Parent Note: The read aloud suggestions are intended for you to read to your child. The individual reading suggestions are intended for your child to read aloud to you – or to read on their own. Continue reading each selection throughout the peasant weeks until you are finished.

Read Aloud For Younger Children:
Don't Let the Barber Pull Your Teeth: Could You Survive Medieval Medicine? by Carmen Bredeson

Read Aloud For Older Children:
Adam of the Road by Elizabeth Janet Gray

Individual Reading for Grades 2-4:
Roland Wright: Future Knight by Tony Davis

Individual Reading for Older Children:
Dragon Slippers by Jessica Day George

Make a Photo Collage of a Peasant's Life

Materials:
- Photos from the past two weeks
- Paper
- Glue

Preparation: None

Lesson: Hopefully you've been taking pictures during your adventures these past two weeks. During this activity, you will be choosing some of your favorite photos to make a collage of your experience. What would it have been like to be a peasant in Medieval Times? Use your photos to tell the story of a peasant's life. What kind of experiences did you enjoy? Which ones were difficult or unpleasant? Be sure to include a variety of activities so that you give a more accurate picture of a peasant's existence. Feel free to take a few more photos to include if you'd like.

The Black Death

Materials: None

Preparation: None

Lesson: After everything you've learned about a peasant's life these past few weeks, you'd probably agree that their lives were pretty hard. Today, you'll be learning about something which made their lives even harder. It didn't just affect the peasants, however. Within a two year span, this new setback killed 30-45% of all the people in England, from the king's family all the way down to the lowest peasants. It was called The Black Death.

The Black Death was the name given to a disease which was known in the medical community as the bubonic plague and the pneumonic plague. It was nicknamed The Black Death because it caused lumps and black spots to appear on the victims' bodies. Within three days of catching the disease, almost all of the victims died.

Remember a few days ago when we talked about how the average peasant's home was filled with fleas, lice, and flies? Well, guess how The Black Death was passed from person to person. It was caught by getting bitten by fleas; so, you can imagine how quickly the disease spread!

The Black Death struck terror into the hearts of all of Europe. When people discovered that the disease was approaching their village or town, they would panic. There was nothing anyone could do to stop the disease and there was no cure.

The plague also spread rapidly because people in medieval towns and villages lived very closely together and they didn't comprehend anything about contagious diseases. The streets were littered with filth and garbage. People used to dump their chamber pots and garbage into the streets for the waste to be swept away by street sweepers. This created the ideal situation for the flea-covered rats to breed and to spread the disease further.

People didn't realize that flea-infected rats were the culprits. In fact, at one point they blamed the spread of the disease on the many cats that patrolled their villages in search of rats. The people were desperate to stop the spread of this deadly pestilence and they had to try something. Millions of cats and dogs, too, were killed in a futile attempt to end this disease. Their actions actually made things worse because they drastically limited the natural predators of the rats.

The Black Death had a huge impact on society. There weren't enough men to work the fields – and many of them went unplowed. Ripe harvests went to waste as there was no one to bring them in. Animals died because there weren't enough people to take care of them. Even though there were less people, this lack of farm labor still caused food shortages.

The barons who had lost so much of their workforce stopped planting their fields with grain, which was labor intensive, and started raising sheep instead. This caused a lack of bread for the peasants. The less food that existed the higher the prices rose. The cost of food became up to four times as expensive as it had been before. Imagine how hard this was for the peasants on top of everything else they faced!

Write in Your Journal

Materials:
- Your child's journal
- Paper
- Pencil, colored pencils, markers, etc.

Preparation: None

Parent Note: Have your child write down a few key points about what they learned about The Black Death. Depending on their age and ability, you can require your child to write one sentence or several paragraphs. You can also let them narrate back to you what they have learned. Then, have them draw a picture or print pictures from the internet to add some more insight to their journal page.

Possible Writing Prompt: Pretend you have actually travelled back in time to Medieval England. If you could only give one piece of advice for avoiding the Black Death, what would it be?

Literature

Materials: *(choose one)*
- Aesop's Fables for Children illustrated by Milo Winter
- The Classic Treasury of Aesop's Fables illustrated by Don Daily

Preparation: None

Parent Note: Read several new fables today. After you read each fable, discuss it with your child. Be sure they understand the moral. See if they can come up with a different moral on their own.

Field Trip to a Local Farm

Parent Note: This is a wonderful time to visit a farm in your area. If possible, see if your child can participate in some sort of internship or program which allows them to perform farming tasks themselves. As children participate, be sure to capture pictures of them in action for their journal. Also, ask your child questions so that they can compare their experience with what they have learned so far about the life of a peasant.

Cures for the Black Death

Materials:
- Chart from the companion download

Preparation:
1. Print one copy of the chart for each child

Lesson: While the Black Death was running rampant and ravaging the population, there were several cures that were attempted. Some of these cures may have been helpful while others sound quite bizarre. Read through the chart of cures. With what you know about the Black Death, which of these do you think had the best chance at slowing down or stopping the disease? Write a paragraph about each cure you would like to try and discuss why you think it would be beneficial. You may also write about a cure that you would definitely NOT want to try. ☺

49

Week Two – You are a Peasant
Day Five

Bucket Race

Materials:
- Two buckets
- Two large cups or bowls
- An outdoor source of water

Preparation: None

Lesson: Peasants didn't have running water and they had to gather their water daily from either a stream or well. Today, you will get to see what it felt like to have to gather the water.

Parent Note: Depending on how many children will be participating, set up a race where your children fill up a bowl with water, run several yards, dump the water into the bucket, and run back to fill up their bowl again. The first one to fill their bucket to overflowing wins. Don't be surprised if your kids turn this into a contest to see who can get who the wettest! ☺

Make a Flyer Warning People about Black Death

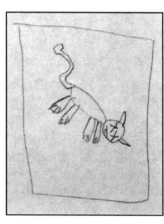

Materials:
- Paper and pencil
- Markers or colored pencils (optional)

Preparation: None

Lesson: You've learned what a deadly and terrifying disease the Bubonic Plague was to people in Medieval Times. For this activity, imagine you have just learned that the plague has reached your village. Create a flyer that you can hang on the village gate warning people to stay away. You may decide to list facts that will help people to avoid the disease. You may decide to use illustrations or photos of people with the disease to caution people to turn around and go home. What method you use is up to you. Just do your best to keep people away!

Quiz Bowl

Parent Note: See how well you and your children can answer questions about the material that has been covered concerning peasants.

1. Did peasants own their own land? (no)

2. What type of work did most peasants perform? (farming)

3. What were the three types of peasants during the Middle Ages? (slaves, serfs, and freemen)

4. Were peasants important to medieval society? Why or why not? (Yes - they grew most of the food)

5. How many full baths did most peasants take in their lifetime? (2 – one at birth, one at death)

6. How many rooms were in a typical peasant cottage? (1)

7. How did peasants keep their livestock safe at night? (They brought it into their house)

8. Did peasant children go to school? (no)

9. What types of jobs did peasant children perform? (Cleared stones from the field, chased away birds, helped plant and take care of the animals.)

10. Under what system of government did the people of England live during the Middle Ages? (The feudal system)

11. Why was the feudal system put into place? (To help the king distribute some of his power)

12. Was the feudal system an equal form of government for all of the people? (no)

13. What was the name of the wooden object which was placed in the middle of the table and filled with food? (A trencher)

14. What did peasants usually eat with? (Their fingers)

15. Were peasants allowed to keep all of the fish they caught? (No - salmon and trout were reserved for the barons.)

16. Were peasants allowed to get food from the forests? (Yes, they could gather acorns, nuts, and honey from the forest; but, they couldn't hunt animals in the forests.)

17. How did peasants preserve food? (They dried food. They also salted and smoked meat to keep it from spoiling.)

18. How many people did it take to plant a crop when a simple plow was used? (Three - one to use the plow, one to plant the seeds, and one to cover up the seeds)

19. What invention allowed farmers to stop covering up the seeds by hand? (A harrow)

20. What other innovation allowed farmers to plant additional crops on their land? (Changing from the 2-crop rotation to the 3-crop rotation)

21. What killed 30-45% of the entire population of England within a two year span? (The Black Death)

22. How long did it take for someone to die once they caught the disease? (Three days)

23. How did people catch this disease? (It was caught by getting bitten by fleas, usually brought into the house on rats.)

24. What did people mistakenly think was the cause of the disease? (Cats)

25. What impact did The Black Death have on society? (There weren't enough workers in the fields, there was a food shortage, and the cost of food went up dramatically.)

Reading

Parent Note: The read aloud suggestions are intended for you to read to your child. The individual reading suggestions are intended for your child to read aloud to you – or to read on their own. Continue reading each selection throughout the peasant weeks until you are finished.

Read Aloud For Younger Children:
Don't Let the Barber Pull Your Teeth: Could You Survive Medieval Medicine? by Carmen Bredeson

Read Aloud For Older Children:
Adam of the Road by Elizabeth Janet Gray

Individual Reading for Grades 2-4:
Roland Wright: Future Knight by Tony Davis

Individual Reading for Older Children:
Dragon Slippers by Jessica Day George

Medieval Adventure, Scene One

Materials:
- Script from companion download
- Costumes which were made/gathered in a previous lesson
- Whatever other props you create during your lessons and/or have laying around the house to add excitement to this adventure.

Preparation:
1. Photocopy the script so that each actor has their own copy.
2. Read through the script a few times so that you know what to expect and can help to direct the kids.

Parent Note: Choose roles for yourself and your children. Remember, the more dramatic you act the more your kids will as well – and the more value they will gain from this assignment. If you are planning to videotape the play, you may want to do it while on your field trip to the farm so that the background looks more authentic. ☺

Activity Suggestions for Further Learning and Fun

Below is a list of further suggestions which have not been incorporated into the two weeks of learning that you may also want to try. The more you immerse your child in these types of activities, the more they will learn and enjoy this experience. ***Warning:*** You child will probably most enjoy some of the suggestions are the messiest or the most out of the ordinary! ☺

Food
- Gardening – plant seeds, weed, harvest vegetables
- Food storage – wash fresh food, learn to can, learn to freeze, dry herbs
- Gather acorns or mushrooms in the woods
- Cook a meal over a campfire
- Eat an entire meal with your fingers

Lifestyle
- Get up at 3am and start your day
- Sleep in a barn
- Take a bath in a barrel
- Wear the same clothes for a week – and don't take a bath

Livelihood
- Take care of farm animals
- Chase birds out of a garden
- Weave an actual rug
- Observe a beekeeper harvesting honey
- Go fishing

You are a Tradesman

in Medieval England

Table of Contents for Tradesman/Tradeswoman Weeks

Week Three – You are a Tradesman/Tradeswoman
Day One

Daily Life of a Medieval Tradesman

Materials: None

Preparation: None

Lesson: The last few weeks we learned about rural peasants, who generally farmed for a living. This week we are going to learn about a community who were a step up from the farmers. These people usually lived in villages and performed some type of labor that wasn't agricultural. We will refer to this group of people as tradesmen or tradeswomen.

There were lots of people who lived in the cities or villages and provided goods and services for others. Some of these people were quite skilled and could even be classified as artisans. Blacksmiths, carpenters, wheel wrights, weavers, coopers, butchers, cheese mongers, spice-grocers, and glassblowers all fit into this category.

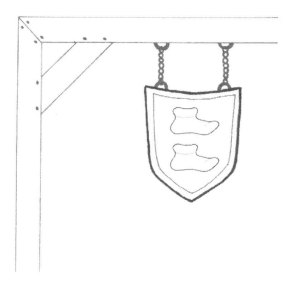

Like peasants, some of these tradesmen owned their own businesses and some worked for others. They often worked in shops that had large windows through which they could display their wares. They also advertised with colorful signs. These signs usually had pictures on them instead of words because most of the people at this time couldn't read. Can you imagine living in a village where almost no one knew how to read?

Once someone had trained in their craft for many years, they were considered an expert and were called a master. Some people trained for up to 14 years to reach this level. Once someone became this skilled, they could also join a guild. They presented their finest pieces to the guild to be judged. If they were deemed worthy, the guild declared the work to be a "master's piece" and they were allowed to join the guild. That is how the term masterpiece came about.

Guilds were similar to the unions of today. They set the prices on their member's goods. They determined people's wages. As time went on, guilds also began to play a larger role in government, taking over some of the duties that had previously been performed by the baron or his officials.

Artisans had the chance to make a name for themselves and to earn a descent living. The more prestigious their customers, the higher their reputations were as well. For instance, a goldsmith had a higher social standing than a blacksmith.

Also, the more skill that was necessary for one's trade, the more highly they were regarded. Carpenters worked on larger projects such as houses and wagons. A furniture maker worked with wood as well; however, their craft required more attention to detail and more expertise to perform their job well. This meant that a furniture maker often garnered more respect than did a carpenter.

For the next two weeks you will pretend to be a tradesman or tradeswoman living in a medieval village. You will get to experience some of the tasks that a villager would have experienced. As you complete these activities and go about your day, try to imagine what it would have been like to do these things all day, every day of your life. Do your best to imagine how it would have felt to be an artisan during this time period.

Write in Your Journal

Materials:
- Your child's journal
- Paper
- Pencil, colored pencils, markers, etc.

Preparation: None

Parent Note: Have your child write down a few key points about what they learned about medieval tradesmen. Depending on their age and ability, you can require your child to write one sentence or several paragraphs. You can also let them narrate back to you what they have learned. Then, have them draw a picture or print pictures from the internet to add some more insight to their journal page.

Possible Writing Prompt: You are a tradesman in need of an apprentice. Write a Help Wanted ad which includes details about the position they will fill. Be sure to promote the open position to try to attract as many applicants as possible.

Literature

Materials:
- Stories from Shakespeare by Geraldine McCaughrean

Preparation: None

Parent Note: Read this book aloud and discuss it with your child.

Creating Tradesmen Costumes

Materials for Boy Costume (Pick and choose as desired):
- A long vest or shirt which can be worn as a tunic
- A long-sleeved, baggy shirt
- Tights or leggings, believe it or not. Medieval people called it hose.

Materials for Girl Costume (Pick and choose as desired):
- Long, trailing dress with puffy sleeves
- OR a baggy, white blouse paired with a long, full skirt – usually one color
- Pointed shoes
- An elaborate headdress or braided hair

Preparation: None

Parent Note: For this activity, we are going to create an outfit to wear while acting in the drama as well as while completing their other lessons if your child so desires.

You can make this activity as simple or as elaborate as you and your children will enjoy. There are many sites on the internet which give you ideas on sewing medieval costumes. We are going to show you simple ways in which you can gather costumes – but you are welcome to take the time to make more elaborate costumes if that is something which interests you.

An easy and inexpensive way to gather the clothing items we recommend is to check out secondhand stores and garage sales. Feel free to improvise! The most important thing is that your child feels the part – not that they are completely authentic.

Choose Your Content

Materials:
- Camera (preferably a digital one)
- Printer (optional – makes it easier to print your child's photos but isn't required)

Preparation: None

Lesson: One of the first choices you have to make as a photographer is how much of a scene you want to show. Whether you are taking a picture of a person, a tree, or a building, beginning photographers are often reluctant to show anything less that the entire subject. A picture of Grandpa is taken from head to toe even though his head is so small that you can't see the details of his face clearly.

Try to get in closer to your subject. Take one picture of the entire person if you'd like – then go in closer to get a picture of just their head. You'll be amazed at how much more expressive your photos will be when you zoom in. Robert Capa, a famous war photographer says, "If your pictures aren't good enough, you aren't close enough." Getting closer to your subject eliminates distracting objects from your image. It lets you focus on the main subject.

Before you take a picture, try to decide what you want your photo to be about. Take one picture of the entire scene and then zoom in on a few details. Be sure you hold your camera still and straight when you are taking your pictures as well.

This picture is of an entire person.   Notice how much more impact there is when you zoom in on your subjects.

For today's lesson, you will practice consciously taking close-up photos of the subject of your choice. Be sure you zoom in more closely than normal and try to capture the emotion of the moment. You may want to include a few of your better photos in your journal.

Week Three – You are a Tradesman/Tradeswoman
Day Two

Old English Words Which Still Exist Today

Materials:
- Sheet of words from companion download

Preparation:
1. Print one copy of the worksheet for each child.

Lesson: We learned in a previous activity that Old English was very different from the modern English spoken today. As different as it was, however, there were some words from medieval times that are still in use. Some of these words have very different meanings than in the past, however. In this lesson, you will discover some of these words and will learn how their meaning has changed over time.

On the worksheet from the companion download, you will find examples of some words as well as with their meaning from the Middle Ages. Look these words up in the dictionary to see what they mean today. Try to determine how the old meaning relates to the new meaning.

For instance, the modern meaning of the word ***achievement*** is "something accomplished, especially by superior ability, special effort, great courage, etc." In medieval times this word meant "a full display of an entire coat of arms." A coat of arms contained pictures detailing the triumphs and courageous acts of a person and/or their family. So it's easy to see how the older meaning of this word relates to the new one. Some of these words will be easier to figure out than others. You may want to include your findings in your journal.

Learning to Whittle

Materials:
- A bar of soap (Ivory or another softer soap works well)
- Either a jackknife or a popsicle stick (depending on the age and skill of your child)
- Line art from the companion download
- Newspaper
- Paper towel

Preparation: Print a copy of the line art from the companion download.

Lesson: You learned earlier than tradesmen hung wooden signs outside of their shops to advertise their wares. Some of these signs had designs carved on them. Woodcarving and whittling can be difficult skills to learn. For this activity, you will begin learning how to whittle using a bar of soap.

Activity:
1. Have your child choose which line art they'd like to use for their carving.
2. Spread newspaper out on your work surface so that cleanup will be easier.
3. Unwrap your bar of soap and hold it so that any words on the soap are face up. Scrape off the lettering using your knife or popsicle stick.
4. Either trace or print a copy of the design you'd like to use on a piece of paper.
5. Using your knife or popsicle stick, trace over the outline of your design. Be sure to press hard enough that your design will show up on your soap.
6. Hold your bar of soap tightly.
7. Begin to whittle away at the unwanted parts of your soap. **Use slow, small strokes which ALWAYS go away from your body.** You don't want to attempt to remove too much soap with any one cut. The deeper you try to cut the more likely you will be to cut yourself.
8. Continue to whittle until your soap resembles the design you have chosen.
9. Smooth away unwanted marks with a paper towel.

Reading

Parent Note: The read aloud suggestions are intended for you to read to your child. The individual reading suggestions are intended for your child to read aloud to you – or to read on their own. Continue reading each selection throughout the tradesman/tradeswoman weeks until you are finished.

Read Aloud For Younger Children:
<u>Who Was Leonardo da Vinci</u> by True Kelley and Roberta Edwards

Read Aloud For Older Children:
<u>The Door in the Wall</u> by Marguerite De Angeli

Individual Reading for Grades 2-4:
<u>The Adventures of Sir Givret the Short</u> by Gerald Morris

Individual Reading for Older Children:
<u>Dragon Spear</u> by Jessica Day George

Prisoner's Base

Materials:
- 2 jump ropes or chalk (optional)

Preparation: Mark a "home base" for both teams on opposite sides of the area where you will be playing. This will also serve as a prison for the opposing team. You can use the jump ropes or the chalk for this if you'd like.

Lesson: Prisoner's Base is a fun version of tag that has been around since before the time of William Shakespeare. It is easier to play with a larger group – but you can adapt the game for use with a smaller group of kids as well. ☺

1. Divide the players up evenly. If playing with a large group, choose a prison guard for each team. If playing with a smaller group, have all of the kids be regular players.
2. Let the children play tag. If someone is tagged by the opposing team, they must go to prison (which is the opposing team's home base.)
3. A player may escape from prison if someone from their team is able to make it to prison to rescue them without being tagged first. If a teammate is tagged while attempting to bust a player out of prison, they must join them in prison.
4. The game is played until all of one team's players are in prison.

Bake a Tartys In Applis (Medieval Apple Pie)

Ingredients for Tart crust:
1 1/2 cups flour
4 Tbsp. butter
2 egg yolks
1/2 tsp. salt
pinch saffron
water, about 3/8 cup

Ingredients for filling:
4 - 5 apples
6 figs, chopped
1/4 cup raisins
½ tsp ginger
½ tsp sugar
¼ tsp cinnamon
1/8 tsp cloves
1/8 tsp nutmeg
1/4 tsp. salt
pinch of saffron

Directions for tart crust:
1. Mix flour, salt, and saffron together in a large bowl.
2. Cut or rub the butter and eggs into the flour mixture until it forms fine crumbs.
3. Add water a little at a time until it just sticks together - too much water will make the dough too soft and sticky.
4. Cover with a towel and let rest for 30 minutes.
5. Roll out on a well floured surface.
6. Put crust into pie pan and pinch edges with fingers to make them look nice.

Directions for filling:
1. Peel, core, and grate apples.
2. Add figs, raisins, and spices.
3. Mix well and put into tart crust.
4. Bake at 350° until done - about 40 minutes.
5. Serve warm or cold.

Week Three – You are a Tradesman/Tradeswoman
Day Three

Life in a Medieval Village

Materials: None

Preparation: None

Lesson: Medieval villages usually included several things in common. First, somewhere in the village there was an open, grassy area called the "green." Most villages also had a well that was shared by everyone. The most important buildings in the village were the parish church, the parsonage where the priest lived, and the blacksmith shop. If a stream ran through the village then a mill was also essential. Villages were small and usually didn't contain more than 100 people. This was similar to the amount of people in a small neighborhood or subdivision today. Every village had a lord or baron in charge. His manor house was near the village but it wasn't usually inside.

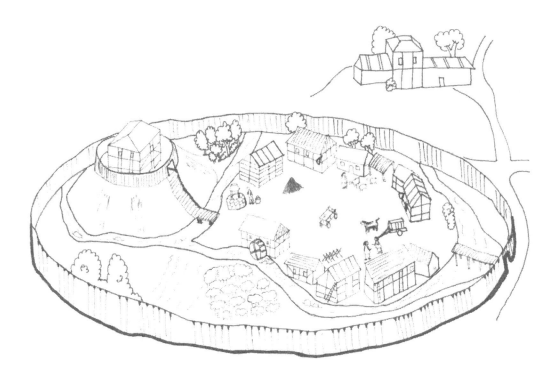

The larger the village, the more it smelled. People went to the bathroom in buckets. Later, they threw the contents of these buckets into deep holes called cesspits or into gutters that drained into the streams and rivers. There was also animal dung in the streets. And butchers threw the remains of slaughtered animals in the open street sewers. Imagine the stench that would have made!

Villages were also noisy places. There was the sound of hooves and cart wheels passing by, peddlers selling their wares, church bells ringing, geese hissing, roosters crowing, dogs barking, blacksmiths hammering, and villagers talking.

Most of the villagers lived in one-roomed houses. They had a yard and a garden in front as well as behind. Their yard was also surrounded by either a fence or a ditch to keep their animals inside.

Living in a village provided protection for the peasants and their families. First, villages were built on hills and they were surrounded by enormous stone walls as well. Men were required to practice their archery skills in the village green. During times of conflict, they manned the walls to defend the village against invaders. They launched arrows, rocks, hot oil, and burning wood on anyone who dared attack.

The inhabitants also banded together to complete other tasks which benefitted the village as a whole. Because their homes and buildings were built with wood and straw, they were highly flammable. Villagers kept water barrels near the front door of each building. The men participated in fire brigades, where they worked together to hurl many buckets of water on fires in order to put them out and protect the rest of the village. They also had fire hooks they used to pull burning thatch and wood off of roofs.

Villagers did whatever they needed to do to be self-sufficient. They grew their own food. They used the wood and grasses around them to make their houses and furniture. They used wool from their sheep, flax they grew, and leather from animal hides to make their own clothes. The village blacksmith made all of the tools necessary for daily life. The local mill ground their grain into flour.

There were some items, however, that villagers wouldn't have been able to provide for themselves. These products had to be traded for with other nearby villages or with peddlers who went from town to town selling their wares. Imagine how important your garden and animals would be if you didn't have a grocery store at which you could shop. Medieval villagers had to work hard to survive. Almost everything they had was made by their own hands or the hands of their neighbors.

Literature

Materials:
- Stories from Shakespeare by Geraldine McCaughrean

Preparation: None

Parent Note: Read this book aloud and discuss it with your child.

Play Draughts (Medieval Checkers)

Materials:
- Checkerboard (was played on a 100 square board if you can find one. Modern day checkers is played on a 64 square board)
- 12 colored discs per player

Preparation: None

Lesson: Draughts was the ancestor of the game we commonly refer to as checkers. Draughts has been traced back to the 1300s and was probably played well before that. (People in England still call the game draughts today.) The rules in the Middle Ages were slightly different than those of modern days. Try the game both ways and see which way you prefer. **Medieval differences are in bold below.**

Activity:
1. Each player places his or her pieces on the 12 dark squares closest to him or her.
2. Black moves first because "charcoal starts a fire." Players then alternate moves.
3. Moves are allowed only on the dark squares, so pieces always move diagonally. Single pieces are always limited to forward moves (toward the opponent.)
4. A piece making a non-capturing move (not involving a jump) may move only one square.
5. A piece making a capturing move (a jump) leaps over one of the opponent's pieces, landing in a straight diagonal line on the other side. Only one piece may be captured in a single jump; however, multiple jumps are allowed on a single turn.
6. When a piece is captured, it is removed from the board.
7. **If a player is able to make a capture, there is no option -- the jump must be made.** If more than one capture is available, the player is free to choose whichever he or she prefers. **(If the opponent sees that the jump wasn't made, they can remove your piece from the board themselves.)**
8. When a piece reaches the furthest row from the player who controls that piece, it is crowned and becomes a king. One of the pieces which had been captured previously is placed on top of the king so that it is twice as high as a single piece.
9. Kings are limited to moving diagonally, but in modern rules they may move both forward and backward. **In medieval rules, the king may jump backward when capturing an opponent but otherwise may not move backward.**
10. Kings may combine jumps in several directions, forward and backward, on the same turn. Single pieces may shift direction diagonally during a multiple capture turn, but must always jump forward (toward the opponent.)
11. A player wins the game when the opponent cannot make a move. In most cases, this is because all of the opponent's pieces have been captured, but it could also be because all of his pieces are blocked from moving.

Make a Water Clock

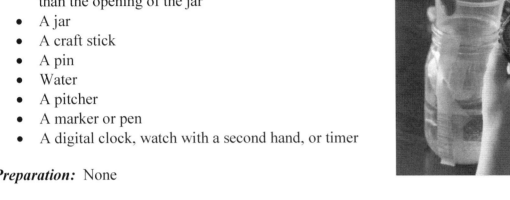

Materials:
- Paper
- Scissors
- Scotch tape
- A disposable cup which is slightly wider at the top than the opening of the jar
- A jar
- A craft stick
- A pin
- Water
- A pitcher
- A marker or pen
- A digital clock, watch with a second hand, or timer

Preparation: None

Lesson: In medieval times, most people determined what time it was by listening to their own internal body clock or by observing where the sun was in the sky. Even so, there were more sophisticated methods of telling time which had been invented. One of these methods was called a water clock. Some medieval water clocks were quite elaborate! For today's activity, however, you will be making a very simple water clock.

Activity:
1. Cut a strip of paper to use as a gauge. Tape the gauge to your jar so that the gauge goes from the top of your jar to the bottom.
2. Poke a hole in the bottom of the cup with the pin. You may need to use the side of the scissors as a thimble to get the pin to go through the cup. Also, you will want to wiggle the pin somewhat so that your hole is just a little bit larger than the width of the pin.
3. Place the cup inside the jar so that it rests in the rim. Be sure the bottom of the cup is raised above the bottom of the jar.
4. Stick the craft stick into the jar as well so that that cup is resting on it. This will allow air to escape from inside the jar as it fills with water.
5. Fill the cup with water.
6. Using the digital clock and the marker, draw lines on the gauge showing where the water level was at 1 minute intervals. Do this for 15 minutes.
7. You can now empty your clock of water and refill it.
8. Try using your water clock to estimate how long it takes to complete certain tasks such as brushing your teeth, running a lap around the house, or making toast. Use your digital clock or timer as well to record the actual time. How close were you able to estimate the time with your water clock? You may want to take pictures of your water clock and record your estimates and actual times in your journal.

Tradesmen Problems

Materials:
- Paper and pencil

Preparation: None

Lesson: Tradesmen also used math to figure out different situations throughout their day. See how well you can solve these problems. The answers are in the companion download.

1. You are the blacksmith in a medieval village. Last week you made 137 horseshoes. This week you made 95 horseshoes. Next week you are scheduled to make 54 horseshoes. How many horseshoes will you have made during this three week span?

2. Your baron has put the men of the village in charge of refilling all of the water barrels in the village. There are 90 barrels which need to be filled. You filled 38 barrels the first day and 17 barrels the second day. How many barrels do you have left to fill?

3. Your neighbor, the weaver, made 30 rugs. She sold 2 rugs to each of her 6 friends. How many rugs did the weaver have left?

4. The baker was extremely busy today. It was 98 degrees and he sold 67 loaves of bread. He sold 15 more rolls than loaves of bread. How many rolls did he sell?

Week Three – You are a Tradesman/Tradeswoman
Day Four

<u>Rivers in England</u>

Materials:
- Map from the companion download
- Paper and pencil
- Tracing paper (optional)

Preparation: Print one copy of the map for each child.

Lesson: England is a very lush, green island. It has many rivers which flow through the landscape. Since it isn't an especially large island, its rivers aren't very long – however, they are extremely important.

The longest river in England is the river Severn, just 220 miles in length. It begins in Wales and enters the Atlantic Ocean near Bristol in England. Among the most important rivers in England are the Trent and Mersey rivers, which drain rainfall from large areas of central England.

The Thames, however, is probably the most important river in England. It flows through Oxford and London and is the deepest river in Britain. It's 215 miles long and is navigable from the North Sea all the way to London, which is the capital of Great Britain.

The Thames has played a central role in British history for some 2000 years. From the Roman invasions of 43 BC to the turn of the millennium in AD 2000, some of the most famous events in British history have taken place on or near the Thames. These include the signing of the Magna Carta in 1215, the plot to blow up the houses of Parliament in 1605 and the Great Fire of London in 1666.

For this activity, trace the map of England that you printed. Either use tracing paper or hold regular paper and the map up to a window to trace. Be sure to trace and label the main rivers as well. When your map is finished, you may want to include this map in your journal.

Listen to Medieval Music

Materials: Link from the supplement section on our website

Preparation: Prepare to use the link from the supplement section on our website.

Lesson: Music was important to people during medieval times. It played a significant role in the lives of the people. Music was especially popular during times of celebration and festivities. There were even people called minstrels, troubadours, and bards whose job it was to entertain people with stories and songs.

As you already discovered in an earlier lesson, there were many different types of medieval instruments, including recorders, horns, trumpets, whistles, bells, and drums.

During holidays, music was an integral part of the celebration. On Mayday, dancers frolicked to specially-prepared, high-pitched music. It was believed that by doing so, the hibernating spirits were awakened and forewarned that spring had arrived. During Christmas, the sound of bells brought the good news of Jesus' birth to the listeners.

For this activity, you will be listening to examples of medieval music. Listen for some of the different instruments you learned about previously.

Reading

Parent Note: The read aloud suggestions are intended for you to read to your child. The individual reading suggestions are intended for your child to read aloud to you – or to read on their own. Continue reading each selection throughout the tradesman/tradeswoman weeks until you are finished.

Read Aloud For Younger Children:
Who Was Leonardo da Vinci by True Kelley and Roberta Edwards

Read Aloud For Older Children:
The Door in the Wall by Marguerite De Angeli

Individual Reading for Grades 2-4:
The Adventures of Sir Givret the Short by Gerald Morris

Individual Reading for Older Children:
Dragon Spear by Jessica Day George

Make a Court Jester Jumping Jack

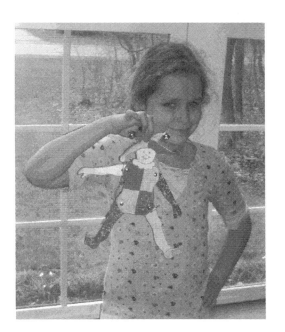

Materials:
- Cardstock
- Brads
- String
- Hole punch
- Small bead
- Markers, glitter and sequins (optional)
- Small bells (optional)
- Jester from companion download

Preparation:
1. Using cardstock, print a copy of the jester for each child.

Lesson: Court jesters were people whose job it was to tell jokes and provide entertainment for the king. Jesters often wore brightly colored clothes. Their hats were floppy with three points, each of which had a bell at the end. Medieval children didn't have many toys; however, some children did have something called a jumping jack, which was a representation of a court jester. For this activity, you will be making your own jumping jack.

1. Have your child cut out the pieces of their jester.
2. Using the hole punch, make holes where shown.
3. Tie a string horizontally from arm to arm (use the top holes for this.) Be sure the string is taut after it is tied.
4. Tie a string vertically from the left arm hole to the left leg hole (use the bottom holes for this.) Repeat for the right arm and leg. Be sure the string is taut after it is tied.
5. Tie a string to the center of the arm string. Attach a bead to the top of this string.
6. Pulling the string should now make your court jester dance.
7. Have your child decorate their jester using the markers, glitter, sequins, etc. They may also decide to attach bells to the corners of their jester's hat.

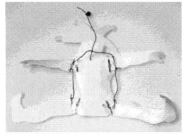

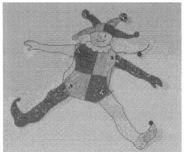

Learn to Draw an Anvil and Hammer

Materials:
- Paper
- Pencil with an eraser
- A black marker (optional)
- Colored pencils or crayons (optional)

Preparation: None

Lesson: In this lesson, you will learn to draw an anvil and hammer step-by-step.

1. First, we will draw the anvil. To do this, draw a triangle on its side with a flat top. Then, give it thickness to make it into a three dimensional wedge.

2. Next, draw a partial triangle underneath the first shape you drew. Give it the same three dimensional thickness as the first shape. Then, draw a cone shape on the end of the wedge as shown.

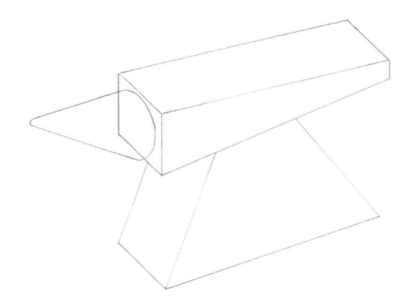

74

3. Next, we will draw the hammer. Start by drawing a rectangle with a triangle at the end which is perpendicular to the top wedge. Give it some thickness to make it three dimensional. To draw the handle of the hammer, draw a cylinder which is perpendicular to the head of the hammer.

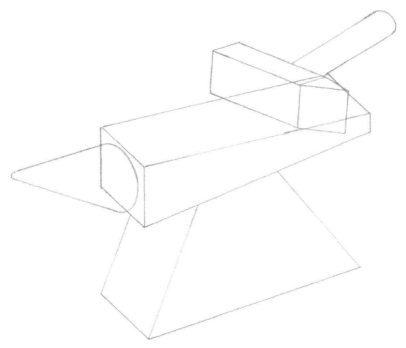

4. Next, draw arcs as shown to attach the wedge of the anvil to the bottom triangle. Draw a small square on the wedge. Draw an ellipse on the head of the hammer which lines up with the handle.

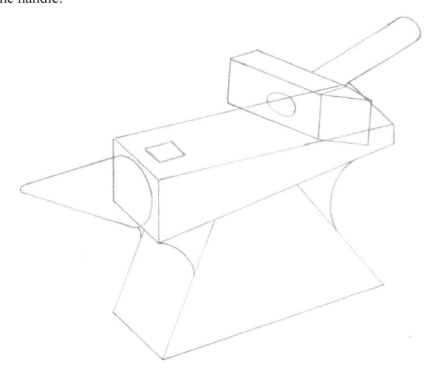

5. Lastly, trace all of the lines that you will be keeping with the black marker. Now you can erase all of the construction lines. You may then use the colored pencils to color in your drawing if you would like. You should have a hammer and anvil similar to the one that's shown below. Great job!

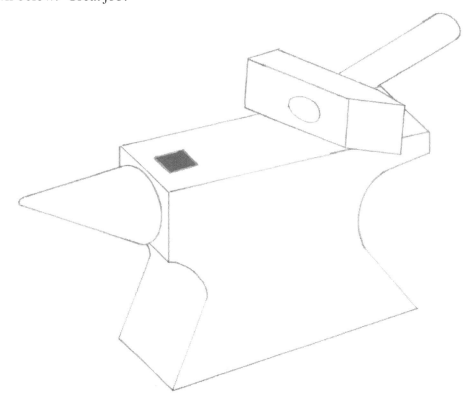

Week Three – You are a Tradesman/Tradeswoman
Day Five

Women in Medieval Times

Materials: None

Preparation: None

Lesson: Women who lived in medieval towns and villages didn't have very many rights. They were thought to be inferior to men. Females were expected to obey their fathers and husbands instantly or they were severely punished.

You may think this meant that all women stayed at home and were only allowed to raise children and clean their houses. That was certainly not the case. Although women were responsible for raising their children and completing the housework, they were also given various other duties.

If a woman's husband was a farmer, she often worked in the fields alongside her husband and children. If a woman's husband was a tradesman, she often worked in the shop with him – or even was a tradeswoman in her own right. Women were allowed to be weavers and to perform an assortment of tasks related to the making of clothing such as sewing and spinning. They were also allowed to be involved with tasks related to food preparation such as being a baker or a cheese maker. The guilds that protected these types of craftsmen, however, were usually closed to women.

Women often did various other tasks such as foraging in the forest for food, gardening, weeding, hay making, animal tending, and cleaning. If a woman performed a job for someone, however, she was usually paid less than was a man performing that same job. For example, if a man earned 8 pence a day for reaping, a woman only earned 5 pence. If a man earned 6 pence a day making hay, a woman only earned 4 pence. This is just the way it was. Not many people complained or thought that this treatment was unfair. Do you think this is fair?

Women were also given less freedom than men in other areas of their lives. They weren't allowed to marry unless their parents gave their consent. They couldn't own a business without being given special permission. They couldn't own property of any kind unless they were a widow and the property had been left to them by their husband. If their parents passed away, they couldn't even inherit the land if they had any surviving brothers. Once a woman was married, any rights she did have came under the control of her husband.

It was important for women of all social classes to have children. The poorer families needed children to help with the work. The richer families needed children so that they would have heirs (someone to which they passed down their property and power after they died.)

Due to the importance of having children, many women were pregnant for a great deal of their lives. Because medical knowledge was so limited during medieval times, having a baby was quite dangerous. As many as 20% of all women died while giving birth to their babies. Childbirth was the number one cause of death among young women. Life was difficult for women during medieval times.

Write in Your Journal

Materials:
- Your child's journal
- Paper
- Pencil, colored pencils, markers, etc.

Preparation: None

Parent Note: Have your child write down a few key points about what they learned about women in the Middle Ages. Depending on their age and ability, you can require your child to write one sentence or several paragraphs. You can also let them narrate back to you what they have learned. Then, have them draw a picture or print pictures from the internet to add some more insight to their journal page.

Possible Writing Prompt: Pretend you are a married woman living in medieval times. Write a letter to your sister about your present situation. Either tell her how wonderful things are between you and your husband – or lament about how hard things are for you.

What is My Profession?

Materials: Logic puzzle from companion download

Preparation: Print a copy of the logic puzzle page for each child.

Lesson: Solve this logic puzzle by determining the full names of each of the attendees along with their current and previous professions.

Literature

Materials:
- <u>Stories from Shakespeare</u> by Geraldine McCaughrean

Preparation: None

Parent Note: Read this book aloud and discuss it with your child.

Dragon Slime

Materials:
- Glue (most kinds of white craft glue will work)
- 2 disposable cups
- Food coloring (you pick the color)
- 1 cup of water
- 1 tsp. borax powder (available at most large grocery stores near the laundry detergent)
- A plastic spoon (for stirring)
- A tablespoon (for measuring)
- Video about dragons from the supplement section on our website (optional)

Preparation: None

Lesson: Dragons are amazing creatures which appear in many medieval fairy tales and myths. Around the world, there are numerous pieces of artwork, sculptures, and artifacts depicting dragons. Epic poems written in the Middle Ages tell of knights battling dragons. The respected Greek explorer and historian, Herodotus, described small, flying reptiles resembling pterodactyls in Egypt and Arabia. Science books about animals described dragons right along with elephants and other animals of the day. Aristotle said that it was common knowledge that these creatures existed in his day. Marco Polo even wrote that the Chinese emperor had dragons which pulled his chariot on special occasions!

Today, we call these animals dinosaurs instead of dragons. The word dinosaur wasn't coined until the year 1841 by Sir Richard Owen, a biologist and paleontologist. The word dinosaur literally means "terrible, powerful, wondrous lizard." Dragons fit that description, don't you think? For this activity, you will be making "Dragon Slime."

Activity:

1. Fill one disposable cup with water. Add a spoonful of borax powder and stir it up. Then set it aside.
2. Fill the other disposable cup with about 1 inch (2.5 cm) of the glue.
3. Add three tablespoons of water to the glue.
4. Add a few drops of the food coloring and stir until mixed.
5. Now comes the fun part...Add one tablespoons of the borax solution you made earlier and stir well. Watch the slime form!
6. After the slime forms let it sit for about 30 seconds. Then pull it off the spoon and play with it!
7. You can continue to add additional tablespoons of the borax solution until you're happy with the consistency. The more you add, the more rubbery your slime will become.
8. Keep your slime in a tightly closed plastic bag when you are not playing with it.

Week Four – You are a Tradesman/Tradeswoman
Day One

Look at the Stars

Materials:
- Telescope or binoculars (optional)

Preparation: None

Lesson: Richard of Wallingford (1292-1336) was the son of a blacksmith; but, his parents died when he was a child. The local priest took pity on the young orphan and took him into the priory to raise him. Because Richard was brought up in the church, he was given a more extensive education than he ever would have received as the son of a blacksmith. He became a medieval mathematician and astronomer.

Richard is best known for creating the most sophisticated astronomical clock that existed in the British Isles at that time. He also constructed a device called an equatorium, which could be used to calculate lunar, solar, and planetary longitudes and could predict eclipses.

For this activity, choose a clear night to go outside and observe the stars. If you have a telescope or binoculars, you may use them. Otherwise, just look up. It is helpful if you choose a location which is as far away from light pollution as possible. Point out any constellations you observe. Enjoy the beauty of the stars with your children.

Who Were the Anglo-Saxons?

Materials:
- Paper
- Pencil
- Colored pencils (optional)
- Tracing Paper (optional)
- Map from the companion download

Preparation: Print a copy of the map for each student.

Lesson: Anglo-Saxons were the English-speaking people who lived in Britain until 1066, when they were conquered by the Normans. The Anglo-Saxon people were not native to the area; but, they had initially conquered Britain themselves. According to the *Ecclesiastical History of the English People*, which was written by the Venerable Bede in 731, they came to the island of Britain in A.D. 449.

Prior to the arrival of the Anglo-Saxons, Britain was inhabited by a blend of Celtic tribes. The Scots and the Picts lived in the northern areas. Various other people groups lived in the south. They were called Britons and were united by the fact that they were under Roman rule.

Britain had been ruled by Rome since A.D. 43. By the beginning of the fifth century, however, the Roman Empire was being attacked more and more by various people groups that they referred to as "barbarians" because they weren't Romans. Because their troops were needed closer to home, the Romans soldiers withdrew and left the Britons to defend themselves.

Who were the Britons defending themselves against? They faced the Picts and the Scots as well as Germanic invaders from the east. The Britons made the incredibly bold decision to hire one of their enemies to fight the others. They hired the German mercenaries to attack the Picts and the Scots. These mercenaries were from three different Germanic nations located in Europe. They were called the Angles, the Saxons and the Jutes. The mercenaries quickly defeated the Picts and the Scots.

Unfortunately, however, Briton's plan backfired. As the Germanic mercenaries looked around at the incredibly fertile land they had conquered, they sent word home to their families to come join them. They also viewed the people of Briton as cowards since they hadn't been able to fight their own battles.

The Jutes settled in the northern area of Britain, known as Scotland today. The Angles and the Saxons settled in the southern area of Britain, known as England and Wales today. These Angles and Saxons intermingled to become the Anglo-Saxons.

Activity: For this activity, trace the map of Britain which shows where the different Germanic tribes settled. Either use the tracing paper or use regular paper and hold your map up to a window to trace. You may also want to color your map. Once you are happy with the results, put your map inside your journal.

Reading

Parent Note: The read aloud suggestions are intended for you to read to your child. The individual reading suggestions are intended for your child to read aloud to you – or to read on their own. Continue reading each selection throughout the tradesman/tradeswoman weeks until you are finished.

Read Aloud For Younger Children:
Who Was Leonardo da Vinci by True Kelley and Roberta Edwards

Read Aloud For Older Children:
The Door in the Wall by Marguerite De Angeli

Individual Reading for Grades 2-4:
The Adventures of Sir Givret the Short by Gerald Morris

Individual Reading for Older Children:
Dragon Spear by Jessica Day George

Making Waffres (Waffles)

Ingredients:
- 12 beaten eggs
- 3 cups wheat flour
- 1/3 cup sugar
- 1 tbsp minced ginger
- 1 1/2 cup grated cheddar cheese
- 1/2 tsp salt
- butter or oil
- honey (for topping)

Directions:
1. Mix all of the ingredients together and use a normal waffle iron to cook.
2. When ready, they will be golden brown.
3. Serve warm or cold topped with honey.

Blind Man's Bluff

Materials:
- A blindfold

Preparation: None

Lesson:
1. Pick one person to be it. That person is blindfolded and stands in the middle of the room.
2. Twirl this person around 3 times and then have them try to touch the other players who run away from them.
3. The other players should try to get as close as possible to the person who is it without being caught.
4. When the player who is it catches another player he must try to guess who it is by touching their face and hair.
5. If he doesn't guess on the first try the other players can give hints. When he correctly guesses the name of the person he has caught, that person is now it.
6. The game continues until all players have had a chance to be it.

Week Four – You are a Tradesman/Tradeswoman
Day Two

Day Laborers, Peddlers, and Pilgrims

Materials: None

Preparation: None

Lesson: During the Middle Ages, it was rare for people to leave their homes and venture abroad. Because travel was so infrequent, not much energy was put into the building of proper roads. Most medieval roads were made from hard packed dirt or cobblestones. They were often littered with potholes from the weather and from people digging up the stones to use for other purposes, such as building walls. Any travel attempted on these roads was painstakingly slow. It took about two days to travel 60 miles by horse. That same distance takes modern people about an hour by car.

Most medieval peasants weren't even permitted to travel, as they had too many responsibilities to manage with taking care of their lord's land. There were peasants, however, who lost their lands, or who came to a village landless in the first place. These people earned their living as hired hands, moving from one village to another. They were often called cotters or day laborers, which literally means someone who was paid by the day.

Quite often these workers stayed longer than one day, however, helping with harvesting or planting. They might also serve as laborers on a construction project. They were hired to sheer sheep, weave wattle, dig ditches, make thatch, and even to guard prisoners. They were typically very poor and were never far from a run of bad luck and/or starvation.

There were also people who made their living as peddlers. These people were merchants who sold their wares from village to village and town to town. They stopped at the village gates to sell gloves, buckles and other items. Food peddlers also went through the town going from door to door selling bread, freshly baked pies, and ale.

Another set of people who traveled about were known as pilgrims. In the Middle Ages, the church encouraged people to make pilgrimages to special holy places called shrines. It was believed that if you prayed at these shrines you might be forgiven for your sins and you would then have more of a chance of going to heaven. Other people went to shrines hoping to be cured from illnesses from which they were suffering. Often these pilgrims were barons, although sometimes the wealthier nobles paid others to make the pilgrimage for them.

The most popular shrine in England was the tomb of Thomas Becket at Canterbury Cathedral. When Becket was murdered, local people managed to obtain pieces of cloth soaked in his blood. Rumors soon spread that, when touched by this cloth, people were cured of blindness, epilepsy and leprosy. It was not long before the monks at Canterbury Cathedral were selling small glass bottles of a substance which was supposedly Becket's blood to visiting pilgrims.

At other shrines, people went to see the teeth, bones, shoes, combs, etc. that were said to have once belonged to important Christian saints. The most common relics at these shrines were nails and pieces of wood that the keepers of the shrine claimed came from the cross which was used to crucify Jesus.

When people arrived at the shrine they paid money to be allowed to look at these holy relics. In some cases, pilgrims were even allowed to touch and kiss them. The keeper of the shrine also gave the pilgrim a metal badge that had been stamped with the symbol of the shrine. These badges were then fixed to the pilgrim's hat so that people knew they had visited the shrine. It sounds silly; however, for people who didn't have much hope of having medicine that would cure them it was one of the only hopes they had. Imagine how desperate some of these people were to travel for days or even weeks to visit these shrines!

Literature

Materials:
- <u>Stories from Shakespeare</u> by Geraldine McCaughrean

Preparation: None

Parent Note: Read this book aloud and discuss it with your child.

Make a Pilgrim's Badge

Materials:
- Cardstock
- Scissors
- Aluminum foil
- Masking tape
- Badge template from companion download
- Black marker (optional)

Preparation:
1. Using the cardstock, make a copy of the different pilgrim badges for your child.

Lesson:
1. Choose which badge template you would like to use.
2. Cut out your badge.
3. Using the aluminum foil, tightly wrap your badge so that it resembles the lead badges worn by medieval pilgrims.
4. Optionally, you may draw details on your badge using the marker – or you may want to use the scissors to press details into the foil.
5. Tape your badge onto your shirt or a floppy hat.

Check Your Background

Materials:
- Camera (preferably a digital one)
- Printer (optional – makes it easier to print your child's photos but isn't required)

Preparation: None

Lesson: Another photography tip to keep in mind is to check your background. If you want to take a picture of an object, you need to look at the object to be sure it looks the way you want it to in the photo. Before you snap the picture, however, be sure to look behind the object to be sure there isn't anything unsightly in your picture. Items like garbage cans, people sticking out their tongues, or anything else unwanted will distract from the quality of your picture. If background objects don't add anything to a picture except for visual clutter, do what you can to eliminate them. Move your feet – try taking a picture of your subject from a different location to give yourself a better background.

You aren't always going to want to get rid of the background in your picture, however. There are times when having a beautiful setting for your subject will make your photo come alive. Backgrounds can give scale to a subject as well as a sense of place. Sometimes the background in a photo is what the real picture is all about!

This simple tip will make a world of difference in the quality of your photos. For this activity, take some photos and carefully choose the background before taking your shot. You may want to include a few of your better photos in your journal.

Obstacle Course

Materials: These will vary – see lesson below

Preparation: Set up the course for your child.

Parent Note: Tell your child that running through obstacle courses was a common way for men to prove their worthiness for becoming a knight. You don't have to purchase anything fancy for this activity. You can set up an obstacle course in your backyard with whatever items you happen to have on hand. Here are some suggestions:

- A board laid on the ground becomes a balance beam
- A table or bench becomes a tunnel to crawl under
- A sprinkler becomes a great obstacle to run through
- Hats or shoes scattered in an area become a great slalom course for your child to weave through
- A jump rope laid on the ground becomes a tightrope for your child to walk across or rings for your child to step through
- Have your child do jumping jacks, walk backwards, or walk heel to toe in a straight line
- Set up a wading pool or a slip and slide for them to run through
- Have your child toss water balloons, shoot baskets, toss beanbags, throw a Frisbee, etc.

Come up with as many obstacles as you like. A complicated course can provide hours of fun for your child.

Week Four – You are a Tradesman/Tradeswoman
Day Three

Creating Condensation

Materials:
- Small metal can (an empty vegetable can works well)
- Water
- Salt
- Measuring spoon
- Crushed ice

Preparation: None

Lesson: People in the Middle Ages had an extensive knowledge of the weather. The success of their crops depended upon them being able to successfully understand the changes in temperature and its effect on their food supply.

For this activity, we will be learning about one result of temperature change called condensation. Condensation occurs when liquid drops of water are produced from water vapor. It is the process which creates clouds, so it is necessary for rain and snow formation as well.

If you go outside in the early morning, you will find dew on the grass. Dew is condensation. It is formed when the temperature outside drops low enough to cause the water vapor in the air to turn into a liquid.

Condensation occurs on hard surfaces as well. Water condensing on a glass of ice water, or on the inside of windows during winter, is the result of those glass surfaces' temperature cooling below the dew point of the air which is in contact with them, causing the water in the air to change from a vapor to a liquid and to stick to the glass.

Activity:
1. Fill a small, metal can about ¼ full with water.
2. Stir 4 tablespoons of salt into the water.
3. Add enough crushed ice to fill the can and stir.
4. Observe what happens on the outside of the can.
5. Wait 15 minutes or so and observe the can again.
6. Rub your finger on the side of the can and you will feel the condensation.

Tradesmen Problems 2

Materials:
- Paper and pencil

Preparation: None

Lesson: Tradesmen also used math to figure out different situations throughout their day. See how well you can solve these problems. The answers are in the companion download.

1. Duncan had 50 loaves of bread. He gave 3 loaves of bread to each of his 6 friends. How many loaves of bread did Duncan have left?

2. Evan and Brin are building a wall around the village with stones. Evan's part of the wall was 3 stones high and 6 stones long. Brin's part of the wall is 5 stones high and 4 stones long. How many more stones did Brin use?

3. Mrs. Bloom baked a cake in the baron's community oven. She ate 1/12 of the cake and gave 7/12 of the cake to her neighbor. What fraction of the cake was left?

4. A peasant's house, which is square shaped, has an area of 100 ft². What is the house's perimeter?

Polyhedron

Materials:
- A box of toothpicks
- A bag of mini marshmallows
- A lotion bottle or some other object with which to prop up your creation until it hardens (see step 7)

Preparation: None

Lesson: Leonardo da Vinci was an amazing artist, scientist, and inventor. He was born in 1452, which was near the end of the Middle Ages. When he was 15 years old, he was sent off to be an apprentice to Andrea del Verrocchio, one of the most famous artists in Florence, Italy.

Leonardo had an incredible imagination. He filled more than 100 notebooks with his ideas. He came up with inventions in his desire to make everyday life easier for his fellow man. These included designs for a "perfect" city, innovative weapons, and flying machines. He also came up with new mathematical theories and he painted some amazing paintings such as the Mona Lisa.

Leonardo drew illustrations for mathematical books that were widely read. His illustrations were very different than anything people had ever seen. When he drew polygons (many-sided figures) he drew them three-dimensionally and with "open" faces. This meant that people could see through the sides of the polygon and better understand the shapes they were studying.

For this activity, we will be constructing a polyhedron, which is a three-dimensional figure like the ones Leonardo illustrated. Specifically, we will be making a rhombicuboctahedron, which is a 26-faced figure.

Activity:

1. Attach four marshmallows and four toothpicks to make a square.
2. Add additional marshmallows and toothpicks so that there are four more squares attached to the top, right, bottom, and middle of the original square.
3. Repeat steps 1-2 to create another half for your rhombicuboctahedron.

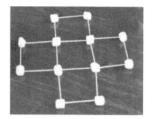

4. Attach toothpicks to the corners of each square on both halves.
5. With one of the halves, stick a toothpick in the bottom of each marshmallow on the outside edge.

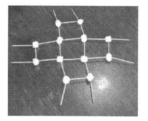

6. Attach these toothpicks to the outside edges of the other half. You'll have to bend the toothpicks down to make them fit.

7. You will probably have to find something to use to prop up your polyhedron until the marshmallows dry.

8. Your result should look just like a soccer ball.

Learn to Draw a Shepherd

Materials:
- Paper
- Pencil with an eraser
- A black marker (optional)
- Colored pencils or crayons (optional)

Preparation: None

Lesson: In this lesson, you will learn to draw a shepherd step-by-step.

1.   First, draw the bottom half of an oval for the head. Draw a flat-topped triangle with a square underneath it for his body. Now, draw an even flatter-topped triangle to finish the body.

2.   Draw two vertical lines through the top two shapes of the body as shown below. Draw a curved line to complete the top of the head. Draw the shepherd's eyes, eyebrows, and nose

3. Draw the neck, hands and feet. Extend two lines upward to make the shepherd's sleeves. Erase unnecessary lines, as shown below, to complete his tunic.

4. Draw the head covering as shown below. Then, draw his beard and mouth.

5.   Finish the details by drawing the cord for the head covering and belt. Draw his sandals and shepherd's hook. Use the black marker to trace all of the lines you are keeping. Lastly, erase your construction lines. Your shepherd should look like this. Great job!

Reading

Parent Note: The read aloud suggestions are intended for you to read to your child. The individual reading suggestions are intended for your child to read aloud to you – or to read on their own. Continue reading each selection throughout the tradesman/tradeswoman weeks until you are finished.

Read Aloud For Younger Children:
Who Was Leonardo da Vinci by True Kelley and Roberta Edwards

Read Aloud For Older Children:
The Door in the Wall by Marguerite De Angeli

Individual Reading for Grades 2-4:
The Adventures of Sir Givret the Short by Gerald Morris

Individual Reading for Older Children:
Dragon Spear by Jessica Day George

Week Four – You are a Tradesman/Tradeswoman
Day Four

Shepherds, Woodcutters and Outcasts

Materials: None

Preparation: None

Lesson: In medieval times, people who lived outside of the boundaries of the village were considered to be living in the wild. These people who lived in the wild were looked at with suspicion and were often scorned. There were three groups of people who most often fit into this category. They were the shepherds, the woodcutters, and the outcasts.

Shepherds might have a small shack in or near the village; but, they spent much of their time living in ramshackle huts in the hills and sometimes even living in caves. They usually grazed their sheep in marshes and pastures during summer and fall. During the winter, however, they put their sheep in the manor fold so that the lord's fields benefitted from their manure.

Woodcutters spent much of their time in the forest cutting down trees for lords. Peasants did enter the forest to gather branches and to tend to their animals; but, forests were spooky places for medieval people. Anyone who spent the majority of their time in the woods was looked down upon.

Outcasts were basically beggars who were oftentimes physically disabled or mentally unbalanced. They had either been forced to leave society because of social pressure or had left civilization of their own free will. Not much is known about this group of people other than that they wandered from village to village looking for day work and/or handouts.

People felt they could treat these ill-fated outsiders however they saw fit. They were often treated with contempt by the villagers. Sometimes they were fortunate and were able to find a generous soul who gave them a bite of food and a place to sleep. Sometimes they were chased out of town.

Some outcasts were actually individuals who had broken the law. These degenerate people rarely came around the villages unless they were going to try to steal or perform some other type of treachery. If an outlaw was noticed, it was within the rights of the villagers to capture or even kill him.

Write in Your Journal

Materials:
- Your child's journal
- Paper
- Pencil, colored pencils, markers, etc.

Preparation: None

Parent Note: Have your child write down a few key points about what they learned about shepherds, woodcutters and outcasts. Depending on their age and ability, you can require your child to write one sentence or several paragraphs. You can also let them narrate back to you what they have learned. Then, have them draw a picture or print pictures from the internet to add some more insight to their journal page.

Possible Writing Prompt: Pretend you are a local tradesman who has just encountered an outcast wandering through the village. Describe the encounter. What did he do? How did you treat him?

Making Yarn Sheep

Materials:
- Wooden clothespins with springs
- Paint
- A paintbrush
- Cardboard
- Yarn
- Black felt
- Hot glue
- Embellishments such as ribbon, lace, bells, etc. (optional)

Preparation: Using the cardboard, cut a kidney bean shape for each child. (Depending on your child's ability, they should be able to do this part themselves.)

Lesson:
1.   Paint the clothespins whatever color you would like. Realistic colors are white, black or brown.
2.   While your clothespins are drying, paint the cardboard pieces. You don't need to paint all of the cardboard – just the part which will be the sheep's head.
3.   When everything is dry, clip the clothespins onto the appropriate spots for them to become legs. You may want to hot glue the legs into place.
4.   Wrap the cardboard with the yarn. Be sure you cover the springs and all of the cardboard except for the face. Add enough layers of yarn until your sheep is nice and fat. Either tuck the end of the yarn or hot glue it into place to keep it from unraveling.
5.   Cut ears and a tail out of the felt and hot glue them onto your sheep.
6.   You can embellish your sheep with a ribbon collar, lace, or even bells. Anything goes.

Reading

Parent Note: The read aloud suggestions are intended for you to read to your child. The individual reading suggestions are intended for your child to read aloud to you – or to read on their own. Continue reading each selection throughout the tradesman/tradeswoman weeks until you are finished.

Read Aloud For Younger Children:
Who Was Leonardo da Vinci by True Kelley and Roberta Edwards

Read Aloud For Older Children:
The Door in the Wall by Marguerite De Angeli

Individual Reading for Grades 2-4:
The Adventures of Sir Givret the Short by Gerald Morris

Individual Reading for Older Children:
Dragon Spear by Jessica Day George

Field Trip to see a Craftsman

Parent Note: This week is a great time to visit a historical site in your area which features artisans or craftsmen such as those about which we have been learning: a blacksmith, a weaver, a shoemaker, a candle maker, a shepherd, etc. If the site features techniques used in medieval times, that would be awesome; however, even places which detail techniques used in more recent time periods, such as Colonial America, will still give your child a sense of how traditional hand crafts were done.

If possible, have your child participate in any hands-on activities which are offered. No other type of learning can come close to being as valuable as actually doing something yourself. Be sure to ask your child questions so that they can compare their experience with what they have learned so far about the life of a medieval tradesman.

Week Four – You are a Tradesman/Tradeswoman
Day Five

Create Your Own "Woodcut" Print

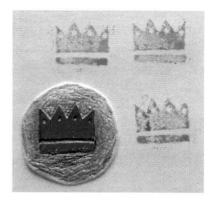

Materials:
- Heavy, Styrofoam plate
- Newspaper
- Permanent marker
- Pencil
- Ink pad(s) – You can use multiple colors of inkpads if you would like
- Paper

Preparations: None

Lesson: Near the end of the Middle Ages, one way that artisans put designs onto fabric or inside of books was by using woodcuts. When an artisan created a woodcut print, he first drew an image onto a block of wood. Then he cut away the background. That caused the image he had designed to be raised up above the background on the wood block.

The artisan then rolled ink onto the woodblock. The ink coated the image and left the background clean. Finally, the woodblock was pressed onto paper or cloth and the image he had created appeared, exactly as shown on the woodblock only in reverse. For this activity, you will be using the same technique as a medieval woodcutter; however, you will be using Styrofoam instead of wood.

Activity:
1. Protect your workspace with newspaper.
2. Cut any curled edges off of the Styrofoam plate to create a flat surface.
3. Decide what you'll want your image to look like by sketching it on a scrap piece of paper. Be sure the lines in your image have some thickness to them in order for this project to work.

4. Next, draw your image onto the Styrofoam plate with a permanent marker. Don't press too hard.
5. Use your pencil to color in everything you didn't mark with your marker. This time you should press hard. This will leave the marker lines raised above the background. You want this to happen so that your design will pick up the ink and the part you pressed down with pencil will not.

6. Press your ink pad onto the Styrofoam. Be sure to mark all the raised portions with the ink.
7. Quickly but carefully press the Styrofoam onto your piece of paper.

8. You now have a simple and safe "woodcut" print of your own. You can make as many copies of your print as you like in as many colors as you like. Have fun with it.

Literature

Materials:
- <u>Stories from Shakespeare</u> by Geraldine McCaughrean

Preparation: None

Parent Note: Read this book aloud and discuss it with your child.

Play Game Ball (American Football)

Materials:
- Football
- 1 Handkerchief per child (optional)

Preparation: None

Lesson: The word 'game' was an Old English word which meant 'fight' or 'battle.' In medieval times, people played a game called game ball which was much like American football only there weren't any rules to be followed. The object was to get your ball to the opposing team's goal using whatever means necessary.

In medieval times, the ball was made from a pig's bladder which was either stuffed with dried peas or inflated with air. This explains why we still call an American football a "pigskin," even though modern footballs are made from cowhide.

For this activity, you will play a game of touch football or flag football, if you have handkerchiefs to use as the flags. Have fun!

Quiz Bowl

Parent Note: See how well you and your children can answer questions about the material that has been covered concerning tradesmen and tradeswomen.

1. Where did tradesmen usually live? (In villages - above their shops)

2. Name at least two examples of specific types of tradesmen. (Blacksmith, carpenter, wheel wright, weaver, glass maker, cooper, butcher, cheese monger, spice-grocer, glassblower, sewer, spinner, baker, cheese maker)

3. What words were often used on a tradesman's advertising signs? (None. They used pictures instead of words because most people couldn't read.)

4. Explain the process for joining a guild. (Train for up to 14 years to perfect your craft. Present your finest pieces to the guild to be judged. If they were deemed worthy, you were able to join the guild.)

5. How did the term "masterpiece" come about? (When a tradesman tried to join a guild and they presented their finest pieces of work, these pieces were judged. If they were considered worthy, the tradesman was considered a master craftsman - and his work was considered master's pieces. This term eventually turned into the word masterpiece.)

6. How many people lived in an average medieval village? (100 or less)

7. Name at least two examples of things which made villages less than sanitary. (Going to the bathroom in buckets and throwing the waste into cesspits or gutters. Animal dung in the streets. Butchers throwing the remains of slaughtered animals into the street sewers.)

8. Name at least two ways that a village provided protection for the people. (Surrounded by walls. Built on hills. Men were required to practice archery skills. Water barrels kept near the front door of each building. Fire hooks.)

9. Name at least two ways that villagers were self-sufficient. (Grew their own food. Made their own houses and furniture. Made their own clothes. Their blacksmiths made necessary tools. Their local mill ground their grain into flour.)

10. Did medieval women have as many rights as medieval men? (No)

11. Did medieval women stay at home all day? (No, they either worked alongside their husbands - in the fields or shops where they worked - or were tradeswomen themselves.)

12. What are some of the trades that women frequently held on their own? (Weaver, sewer, spinning woman, baker, cheese maker, etc.)

13. What was considered to be one of the most important tasks performed by women in the Middle Ages? (Having children)

14. Was it common for people to travel in the Middle Ages? (No)

15. What types of work were day laborers usually hired to perform? (Harvesting, planting, construction projects, sheering sheep, weaving wattle, digging ditches, making thatch, and guarding prisoners)

16. What was a medieval peddler? (A merchant who went from village to village selling their goods.)

17. What was a medieval pilgrim? (Often wealthier people who were traveling to some religious shrine hoping to be forgiven of their sins or healed from illness.)

18. Were shepherds highly trusted in medieval times? (No)

19. How were outsiders typically treated? (With contempt. Sometimes chased out of town.)

20. If an outlaw was noticed, what was within the rights of the villagers to do to him? (Capture or even kill him.)

Medieval Adventure, Scene Two

Materials:
- Script from companion download
- Costumes which were made/gathered in a previous lesson
- Whatever other props you create during your lessons and/or have laying around the house to add excitement to this adventure.

Preparation:
1. Photocopy the script so that each actor has their own copy.
2. Read through the script a few times so that you know what to expect and can help to direct the kids.

Parent Note: Choose roles for yourself and your children. Remember, the more dramatic you act the more your kids will as well – and the more value they will gain from this assignment. If you are planning to videotape the play, you may want to do it while on your field trip to see the craftsman so that the background looks right. ☺

Activity Suggestions for Further Learning and Fun

Below is a list of further suggestions which have not been incorporated into the two weeks of learning that you may also want to try. The more you immerse your child in these types of activities, the more they will learn and enjoy this experience. ***Warning:*** You child will probably most enjoy some of the suggestions are the messiest or the most out of the ordinary! ☺

Lifestyle
- Visit a historic village
- Visit a flour mill, a cider mill, or a saw mill
- Try to have the entire family stay in one room of the house for the entire day
- Participate in a water brigade to put out a fire
- Have the females of the family strictly obey the males
- Try cleaning the house without modern conveniences (i.e., wash dishes by hand, scrub the floor on hands and knees, wash clothes in a sink or barrel)
- Go on a walk down a dirt or gravel road
- Cut wood with an axe

Livelihood
- Participate in a carpentry project
- Learn glass blowing
- Observe a butcher at work
- Whittle with wood
- Do a craft with leather
- Watch someone spin wool
- Try to peddle something door to door
- Serve someone as a day laborer
- Help take care of some sheep

You are a Knight

in Medieval England

Table of Contents for Knight/Lady-in-Waiting Weeks

Week Five – You are a Knight/Lady-in-Waiting
Day One

The First Stage of Knighthood - Page

Materials: None

Preparation: None

Lesson: Knights were almost always the sons of barons and other nobility. Only the rich could afford to buy all of the gear necessary to protect themselves in battle. There were three steps to becoming a knight. Completing these steps took someone about fourteen years to accomplish.

When a boy turned seven, his parents sent him off to live in the home of a knight. The boy became his page. Pages had many duties which might not seem very knight-like to us. They were required to wait on their master and to do errands for him. Why did they have to do these things? To be a successful knight, you needed to be humble and obedient. These very important character qualities were being taught to the young men who were in this stage of their training.

Pages also started some of the physical training that they needed to be proficient in as a knight. They were taught the first steps of sword fighting by using blunt, wooden swords. They also learned how to wrestle and how to ride a horse while wielding a sword.

Another very difficult thing pages learned how to do was to joust. Jousting was extremely dangerous. If these boys had practiced jousting against each other, there probably wouldn't have been any pages left to grow into knights! Instead, they learned to joust with the help of a quintain.

A quintain was a swinging pole which held a shield on one end and a dummy or sandbag on the other. When the page charged and hit the shield, the entire apparatus rotated. The page's goal was to avoid the rotating arms so as not to get knocked out of their saddle.

When first learning how to joust, the page mounted a wooden horse on wheels while holding a lance. Two other pages pulled the horse toward the target allowing the page to concentrate on aiming the lance without having to worry about controlling a real horse at the same time.

Pages were also taught accuracy with the lance by practicing a task called Running at the Rings, where they aimed their lance at small rings that were hung from the quintain. These rings were much harder to lance than it was to hit a man in a real battle; so, becoming good at this skill made the future knight extremely accurate with his weapon.

For the next two weeks you will pretend to be a knight or a lady-in-waiting living in medieval England. You will get to experience some of the tasks, food, and chores that a knight or a lady-in-waiting would have experienced. As you complete these activities and go about your day, try to imagine what it would have been like to do these things all day, every day of your life.

Write in Your Journal

Materials:
- Your child's journal
- Paper
- Pencil, colored pencils, markers, etc.

Preparation: None

Parent Note: Have your child write down a few key points about what they learned about pages. Depending on their age and ability, you can require your child to write one sentence or several paragraphs. You can also let them narrate back to you what they have learned. Then, have them draw a picture or print pictures from the internet to add some more insight to their journal page.

Possible Writing Prompt: Pretend you are a page. Write a letter back home about your training experiences thus far.

Literature

Materials:
- Beowulf as told by Michael Morpurgo

Preparation: None

Parent Note: Read this book aloud and discuss it with your child.

Build a Castle Using Sugar Cubes

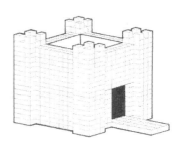

Materials:
- Boxes of sugar cubes
- Elmers liquid glue or a hot glue gun
- Craft sticks for making a portcullis, drawbridge, ladders
- Piece of plywood or thick cardboard for the base of the castle (2'x2')
- Paint (optional for painting a moat or ground on the base)
- Cardboard or construction paper for making turrets, arrow slots etc.

Preparation: None

Lesson:
1. Prepare your base. Paint it, if desired, and allow the paint to dry.
2. Start building the first layer of castle on your base. You should glue the first layer directly to the base itself. (Be sure to leave a gap for your door.)
3. Build the second layer of your castle and so on.
4. You can add towers to the sides of your castle by adding more cubes at the corners of your structure.
5. To create battlements at the top, put a cube on top of every other cube.
6. Allow your castle to sit for several hours to let the glue harden.

Create Knight and Lady-in-Waiting Costumes

Materials for Knight Costume (Pick and choose as desired):
- A long vest or shirt which can be worn as a tunic. Knights quite often had a red cross on their tunic. (We will be making a tunic later in the week.)
- A long-sleeved, baggy shirt
- A sword and shield
- A belt to wear over the tunic
- Boots
- Sword and shield (We will be making these later on as well.)

Materials for Lady-in-Waiting Costume (Pick and choose as desired):
- Long, trailing dress with puffy sleeves
- OR a baggy, white blouse paired with a long, full skirt – usually one color
- Pointed shoes
- Braided hair covered with a veil or wimple

For this activity, you will assemble an outfit to wear while you are acting in the drama as well as while completing the other lessons if you so desire.

Week Five – You are a Knight/Lady-in-Waiting
Day Two

Pictures of Patterns

Materials:
- Camera (preferably a digital one)
- Printer (optional – makes it easier to print your child's photos but isn't required)

Preparation: None

Lesson: Sometimes the subject of your photo is one object. Sometimes what catches your eye is a group of objects which all relate to each other to create a pattern. One flower can be beautiful. A field full of flowers can be much more dramatic. One umbrella may not seem very interesting; however, if you group several umbrellas together into one shot, it makes for a very arresting image.

Sometimes you will find objects which are naturally repetitive and are visually striking without having to modify them in any way. Sometimes, you will need to do some work to set up your shot before you take your picture. For instance, if you are walking through the woods in the fall and see a pile of bright yellow leaves with just one red leaf sitting on top, that could be an appealing image to try to capture on film. If you see a pile of yellow leaves and decide to add one red leaf yourself before taking the picture that is also fine. You don't have to take photos of things exactly as you see them. Feel free to modify the scene before taking your shot.

For this lesson, you are going to practice looking for patterns which already exist as well as creating some patterns you think might be interesting to photograph. Try experimenting with several different objects to see what kind of results you can come up with. You may want to include some of your better photos in your journal.

Giotto di Bondone

Materials:
- Plaster of Paris
- Giotto black line artwork from companion download
- Disposable cup
- Plastic fork
- Plastic or aluminum plate with at least a half inch well
- Pencil
- Tempera paints
- Paint brushes
- Acrylic glaze or varnish

Preparation:
1. Prepare the Plaster of Paris. Use a ratio of equal parts of plaster to water. Start by putting about one cup plaster in the cup and then add one cup of water.
2. Stir with a plastic fork until all the powder is liquefied and then pour it onto the plate.
3. Let the plaster set up for about half an hour or so. You want to paint on it while it is still a bit wet; but, don't wait much longer than that.
4. Print a copy of the Giotto black line artwork for each child.

Lesson: Giotto (jee-OTT-oh) was an artist during the late Middle Ages. He mainly created fresco paintings. A fresco is a painting which is produced on a moist plaster surface. He is also known for being the first artist to use natural backgrounds in his landscapes and for painting people who looked three dimensional rather than flat. For this activity, you are going to create a mini fresco.

Activity:
1. Tape your black line picture to the outside edge of the plate.
2. Using the pencil, trace over the image in the black line with a firm hand. Don't push too hard or it will crack the plaster. Push just hard enough that you feel the pencil pushing into the soft plaster a bit. When you are all done you will have a relief of the black line image on the plaster.
3. Paint your fresco.
4. Once the paint has dried, you can add an acrylic glaze or some varnish to protect the piece and make it shiny.

Reading

Parent Note: The read aloud suggestions are intended for you to read to your child. The individual reading suggestions are intended for your child to read aloud to you – or to read on their own. Continue reading each selection throughout the knight/lady-in-waiting weeks until you are finished.

Read Aloud For Younger Children:
The Princess and the Three Knights by Karen Kingsbury

Read Aloud For Older Children:
Shakespeare Can Be Fun: Hamlet for Kids by Lois Burdett

Individual Reading for Grades 2-4:
The Dragon in the Sock Drawer by Kate Klimo

Individual Reading for Older Children:
The Squire's Tale by Gerald Morris

Create a Sword

Materials:
- 1 Pool noodle
- 1 PVC pipe with a ½" diameter
- 1 PVC cap with a ½" diameter (the kind that slides on, not screws on)
- 1 Sheet of thick craft foam
- Hack saw (or other saw for cutting the pipe and the pool noodle)
- Scissors
- Marker
- Colored duct tape (optional)

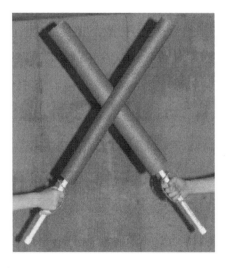

Preparation: None

Lesson: For this activity, you will create swords using swimming noodles and PVC pipe.
1. Cut the pool noodle to the proper length (30" is a great length for a sword blade.)

2. Cut the PVC pipe to the proper length (40" is a great length for the blade plus handle put together.) It is extremely helpful to have someone hold the opposite end of the PVC pipe in place while it is being cut.

3. Carefully push the PVC pipe through the middle hole of the pool noodle. Go slowly! If you go too quickly, the noodle may bend and the pipe might get pushed through the side of the noodle. (Hint: If you are having difficulty, wet the PVC pipe to lubricate it first.) Continue pushing until the pipe is about near the end of the noodle without popping through.

4. Cut a piece of craft foam which is approximately 2" by 8".

5. With the scissors, poke a hole near each end of the foam. Be careful not to poke your hand!

6. Cut a plus shape to enlarge the holes you just made. This will allow you to thread the PVC pipe through the hole. Be careful not to cut it too wide. It's better if it fits snugly.

7. Slide the PVC pipe through one hole in the craft foam.

8. Bend the craft foam up and slide the PVC pipe through the second hole in the craft foam.

9. Firmly press the PVC end cap over the bottom of the pipe to make it nice and smooth.

10. Slide the foam into whatever position you want it to end up as your hand guard.

11. Optionally, you may use the duct tape to secure the hand guard into place. You may also wish to cover all or part of the pool noodle to keep it from wearing down. Ours were sturdy enough that we left it uncovered.

12. You are now all set to use your sword. It's much softer than a Nerf sword so it's fun and safe. ☺

Sword Fight

Materials:
- Sword you just created

Preparation: None

Lesson: Use the swords you created earlier to have a sword fight. There aren't any rules in a medieval sword fight other than to defeat your opponent as quickly as possible. One tip you may want to remember is to keep your elbows bent and close to your body. Your instinct may be to stretch out your arms in an attempt to keep your opponent further away from you. If your arms are stretched out, it will make it difficult for you to thrust and parry quickly. Keep your sword extended toward your opponent but keep your arms close to your body.

Parent Note: You will need to remind your children to take it easy on each other and to use self control when using their swords. Real knights were extremely chivalrous. When mock fighting their fellow knights, they aimed for their swords and not their friend's body so as to avoid hurting their opponent. ☺

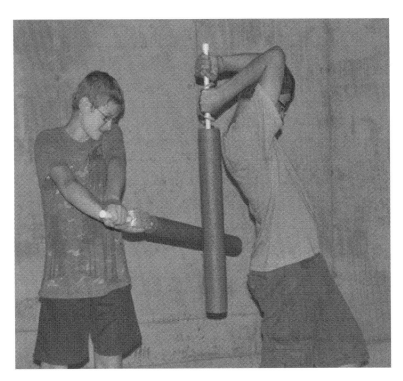

Week Five – You are a Knight/Lady-in-Waiting
Day Three

The Second Stage of Knighthood - Squire

Materials: None

Preparation: None

Lesson: After a boy had been a page for about seven years, he was then sent to the home of a different knight to become his squire. A squire's main duties were to help his knight mentor put on his armor before battle. Squires also spent long hours developing sword fighting and jousting skills.

Squires were required to learn the rules of chivalry. These rules weren't specifically spelled out for knights – it was more a way of life and of how the person was expected to treat other people in his day to day life. The specific ideals of this code were spelled out in "The Song of Roland," a poem written in the early 11th Century. The duties of a knight were described as follows:

- To fear God and maintain His Church
- To serve his feudal lord in valor and faith
- To protect the weak and defenseless
- To give aid to widows and orphans
- To refrain from the pointless giving of offence
- To live by honor and for glory
- To despise financial reward

- To fight for the welfare of all
- To obey those placed in authority
- To guard the honor of fellow knights
- To have nothing to do with unfairness, meanness or deceit
- To keep faith
- At all times to speak the truth
- To persevere to the end in any enterprise begun
- To respect the honor of women
- Never to refuse a challenge from an equal
- Never to turn your back upon a foe

It took a squire approximately another seven years of training before they were ready to become an actual knight.

What Does It Mean?

Materials:
- Dictionary
- Pencil and paper

Preparation: None

Lesson: Look back over the rules of chivalry that we just covered. Be sure you understand all seventeen rules. Look up any words with which you are unfamiliar. Choose five of the above rules and see how well you can keep them throughout the coming week. Write down your commitment to keep these ideals to the best of your ability. You may want to post your pledge somewhere prominent to help you remember them.

Literature

Materials:
- Beowulf as told by Michael Morpurgo

Preparation: None

Parent Note: Read this book aloud and discuss it with your child.

Make a Knight's Tunic

Materials:
- 1 yard of felt or flannel (whatever color you prefer)
  OR ½ yard for a shorter tunic
- 1 smaller piece of felt or flannel (of a different color)
- Template for emblem (choose one from companion download)
- Scissors
- Tacky or fabric glue

Preparation: None

Lesson:
1. Fold the yard of felt in half. Cut a neck hole from the folded edge. You may want to use a t-shirt for a guide on cutting the neck hole. Cut it slightly larger than their normal neck hole as this fabric won't stretch.
2. Choose which template you'd like to use for the front of your tunic.
3. Cut it out and use it to trace the shape onto the small piece of felt.
4. Cut out the emblem.
5. Glue the emblem to the chest of the tunic.
6. Your tunic is now done. Wear it with a belt around the waist and you will look even more like a knight!

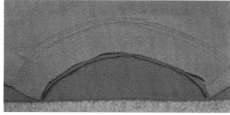

Design Your Own Castle

Materials:
- Paper and pencil
- Clay (optional)

Preparation: None

Lesson: Many castles were built in England during the Middle Ages. These castles were often built on high ground, which enabled its owners to be able to defend them more easily. Castles were often built with many defensive features including:

- **Curtain Walls** - These walls were thick, making it hard for battering rams to cause any damage. They also built battlements on top of their walls with crenellations, which gave the defenders something to hide behind. Walls also had walkways on top of them called parapets, which allowed soldiers to patrol the castle and have a great view of what was going on outside of the walls.
- **Concentric Walls** - Castles usually had several outer walls in concentric circles. These walls got taller as they moved farther into the castle. This allowed defenders to fire on attackers from all of the walls at the same time, as they could see outside of the castle from any wall.
- **Moats** – Deep ditches which were filled with water or stakes. The moats protected from invaders as well as from those who attempted to tunnel under the castle walls or set fire to the walls.
- **Circular Towers** - Circular towers were also a line of defense as castle builders realized that they had more strength than square towers. One way that attackers tried to breach a castle was for them to dig a tunnel underneath a corner of one of the towers, fill the end of the tunnel with anything that would burn, and thereby cause the tunnel and the tower to collapse. Circular towers didn't have corners making this form of attack obsolete. Circular towers also contained winding staircases which forced attackers to ascend single file. This made them easier to defend than to attack.
- **Barbican** - The main gate had a barbican, which was a forward defensible structure jutting out or set in front of the main castle defenses or walls. In many cases the barbican formed part of the castle gatehouse complex, giving added strength to this potential point of weakness.
- **Drawbridges** – Bridges which crossed the moat and allowed passage into the castle. These bridges could be raised or lowered.
- **Loop Holes** – Holes in the castle walls which enabled the defending archers to shoot at the enemy outside the castle while they remained unseen and safe from attack behind the walls.
- **Portcullis** – The portcullis was a latticed gate made of wood or iron which was located at the entrance to the castle. This door could be rapidly lowered at the first sign of attack. Sometimes castles contained two portcullises at the main entrance. This allowed the defenders to trap the enemy between them. This area was called a death trap.

- **Death Traps** – An area at the front of the castle inside which invaders could be trapped. Holes in the walls of the death trap area allowed defenders of the castle to shoot arrows at the enemy, killing them before they could invade the castle.
- **Murder Holes** – Holes in the ceiling of the gateway that allowed defenders to drop heavy or dangerous objects such as burning wood, fire-heated sand, or hot oil on the attackers. Even parts of dead bodies were rained down upon attackers.

For this activity, you will have a chance to design your own castle. You may decide to build a model of a castle using clay. You may draw your castle instead if you would rather. Be sure to use some of the defensive features that you learned about above as well as coming up with some new features on your own.

After you've come up with your best fortifications, let someone test your design by trying to penetrate your defenses. This is a great way to come up with the best design possible and to discover any flaws you might not have seen otherwise.

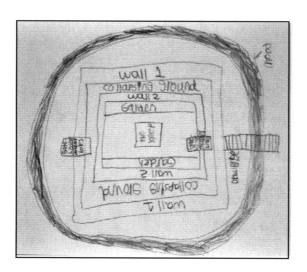

Week Five – You are a Knight/Lady-in-Waiting
Day Four

Knightly Problems

Materials:
- Paper and pencil

Preparation: None

Lesson: Knights also used math to figure out different situations throughout their day. See how well you can solve these problems. The answers are in the companion download.

1. The length of a rectangular field is 75 meters. Its width is 15 meters. Sofie ran around the perimeter of the field 3 times. How far did she run?

2. Molly and Ted are going to build pens for their sheep. Molly wants to build a pen which is 12 meters by 8 meters. Ted wants to build a pen that is 15 meters by 6 meters. Who will need more fencing to build their pen?

3. Tim is buying a horse from the baron. The usual cost of a horse is 180 shillings. The baron has decided to charge him 20% less because Tim is training to be one of his knights. How much money will Tim save? How much will he need to spend to purchase the horse?

4. Alex and Kyle cleaned 27 horse stalls. Kyle cleaned half as many as Alex. How many stalls did Kyle clean?

Learn to Draw a Castle

Materials:
- Paper
- Pencil with an eraser
- A black marker (optional)
- Colored pencils or crayons (optional)

Preparation: None

Lesson: In this lesson, you will learn to draw a castle step-by-step.

1. First, draw a big square. Then draw a long rectangle on either side of the square. Be sure to draw lightly so that unwanted lines can be erased later.

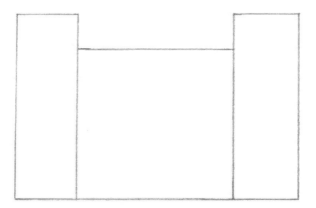

2. Next, draw a small square on top of the large square. Make the width of this new square the same width as that of the long rectangles you drew previously (towers.) Then, draw thin rectangles on top of all three towers with beveled edges on the bottom.

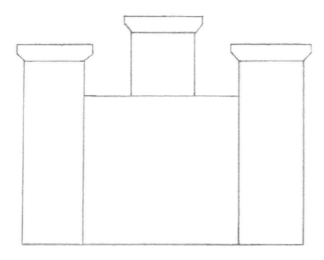

124

3. Now, draw another small rectangle on the middle tower. Then, draw small rectangles on the tops of the towers and wall to create the crenellations as shown.

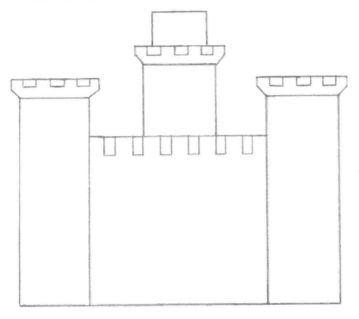

4. Above the rectangle you just drew, draw a small arc with a triangle on top. Now, draw diagonal lines to attach it to the tower. Draw windows and a door as shown.

5. Lastly, trace the lines you want to keep with the black marker. Erase any unwanted lines. Now you can decorate your castle with flags, stonework, and anything else you can think of. If you'd like, you can use the colored pencils to color in your castle. Great job!

Minstrels

Materials:
- A pan (optional)
- Wooden spoons (optional)
- Paper bowl (optional)
- Dried beans (optional)

Preparation: Gather together whatever makeshift instruments you can find around the house. A pan can become a drum, two paper bowls stapled together with dried beans inside can become a tambourine, etc.

Lesson: Minstrels provided much entertainment to people during the Middle Ages. (If your family has read Adam of the Road, as suggested earlier, you will be familiar with minstrels.) They sang and played songs telling of great battles, honor, chivalry, and myths. Minstrels played many different instruments such as the harp or flute. Sometimes they could also play bagpipes, a trumpet, or a guitar.

Most minstrels traveled all around the country, wandering wherever they pleased. However, some also permanently stayed with a certain person, like a king or a baron. The traveling minstrel usually traveled primarily between different castles or manors. He performed there and expected to be fed and sometimes given gifts of clothes.

Minstrels often paid the lord so that he could get permission to perform for the local villagers as well. The songs they sang while inside the castle or manor walls were very different from those performed outside.

For this activity, gather together and assemble whatever makeshift instruments you can find around the house. March around your house or neighborhood making music and singing.

Reading

Parent Note: The read aloud suggestions are intended for you to read to your child. The individual reading suggestions are intended for your child to read aloud to you – or to read on their own. Continue reading each selection throughout the knight/lady-in-waiting weeks until you are finished.

Read Aloud For Younger Children:
The Hero Beowulf by Eric A. Kimmel

Read Aloud For Older Children:
Shakespeare Can Be Fun: Hamlet for Kids by Lois Burdett

Individual Reading for Grades 2-4:
The Dragon in the Sock Drawer by Kate Klimo

Individual Reading for Older Children:
The Squire's Tale by Gerald Morris

Jousting Tournament

Materials:
- Swimming noodles to use as a lance (or something else soft like a cardboard wrapping paper tube)

Preparation: None

Lesson: Jousting was a popular sport for knights. It consisted of two men on horseback trying to use their lances to knock each other off of their horses. Knights were extremely honorable and were disqualified if they killed a horse or if their lance touched any part of their opponent's body other than his chest. For this activity, you will be holding a jousting tournament of your own.

Activity:
1. Both opponents should pretend to be on horseback. Have them walk to opposite ends of the yard and turn to face each other. Each should be holding their lance.
2. At the signal, the opponents should gallop toward each other.
3. Try to hit your opponent squarely in the chest as you gallop past.

Week Five – You are a Knight/Lady-in-Waiting
Day Five

Being Dubbed a Knight

Materials: None

Preparation: None

Lesson: At the age of 21, when he was deemed ready, a squire could finally become a knight. The evening before, the squire underwent a ceremony of purification. First, he received a ritual bath to purify his body. Afterward, the squire was dressed in white clothing, which symbolized purity. He was covered in a red robe which symbolized nobility. He wore black shoes and hose to symbolize death. The squire then placed his sword and shield on the altar where it was blessed by the priest. He spent the entire night in church praying and kneeling before the altar to purify his soul.

In the morning, the squire listened to a lengthy sermon about his new duties as a knight. A sponsor took his sword and shield from the altar and gave it to the lord who was conducting the knighthood ceremony. The new knight was presented to the lord by two sponsors in a public ceremony.

He then took a vow to "fear God, serve the King, protect the weak, and live honorably." This knightly vow was taken very seriously. If a man broke his vow in any way, it was seen as him committing a crime against God and causing his eternal damnation.

In full armor, he then knelt before a local knight, a lord, or the king. The new knight's sword and shield was presented to him. He was then pronounced a knight by the lord saying, "I dub thee Sir Knight" and tapping him on each shoulder with the side of his sword. This was called dubbing and it was considered an essential part of the knighting ceremony.

After the dubbing ceremony, the man was a full-fledged knight. Music and fanfare followed along with a feast which was attended by fellow knights, nobles, and even royalty. Women and ladies of the court also joined in these feasts.

Often, a tournament was arranged for the following day so that the new knight could demonstrate his skills. Can you imagine how excited and proud a knight would have been during this special time in his life?

Write in Your Journal

Materials:
- Your child's journal
- Paper
- Pencil, colored pencils, markers, etc.

Preparation: None

Parent Note: Have your child write down a few key points about what they learned about becoming a knight. Depending on their age and ability, you can require your child to write one sentence or several paragraphs. You can also let them narrate back to you what they have learned. Then, have them draw a picture or print pictures from the internet to add some more insight to their journal page.

Possible Writing Prompt: Pretend you are a brand new knight. Either write a letter back home describing the knighthood ceremony or the tournament that followed. Try to convey your excitement to your loved ones.

Which Knight Won What?

Materials: Logic puzzle from companion download

Preparation: Print one copy of the logic puzzle for each child.

Lesson: Solve this logic puzzle by determining which place the knights came in for each event in the tournament.

Literature

Materials:
- Beowulf as told by Michael Morpurgo

Preparation: None

Parent Note: Read this book aloud and discuss it with your child.

Castle Desk Organizer

Materials:
- 4 cardboard tubes
- Small box
- Gray spray paint (optional)
- Paint brush
- Markers
- Scissors
- Glue

Preparation: None

Lesson: By now, we should all be aware of how important the castle was to people in the Middle Ages. For this activity, you will be making a castle desk organizer. This craft will give you a great place to store your pencils and other desk items. It's also easy and fun.

Activity:
1. Cut any flaps off of the box.
2. Cut the tubes, if necessary, so that they are only a couple of inches taller than the box.
3. Optionally, you may paint the box and the tubes with the grey paint and leave them to dry.
4. With the markers, draw turrets around the top of the castle. Older children may prefer to cut out the turrets.
5. Glue one tube in each corner of the box and leave it to dry.
6. Using the markers, draw windows, doors and stone work.

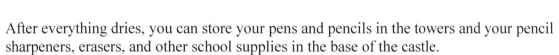

After everything dries, you can store your pens and pencils in the towers and your pencil sharpeners, erasers, and other school supplies in the base of the castle.

Week Six – You are a Knight/Lady-in-Waiting
Day One

Build a Solar Water Purifier

Materials:
- A big bowl (glass works great)
- A glass cup which is at least 1'' shorter than the sides of the bowl
- Clear plastic wrap
- Small rock or weight
- Water
- A handful of dirt

Preparation: None

Lesson: We learned earlier about how unsanitary the drinking water was during the Middle Ages. Unfortunately, they didn't know how to purify their drinking water. Many of them got sick as a result of drinking dirty water.

When we remove salt and other impurities from water it is called distillation. A solar water purifier uses the Greenhouse Effect to trap energy from the sun. It also demonstrates the water cycle that naturally occurs on earth: evaporation, condensation and precipitation. For this activity, we will learn how to purify water by making our own solar water purifier.

Activity:
1. Put water in the bowl.
2. Put a handful of dirt into the water.
3. Place the empty cup in the center of the bowl.
4. Cover the bowl with plastic wrap. Make sure the plastic wrap is tight. If it doesn't stay firmly attached to the bowl, use tape or a rubber band to secure it.
5. Put the small rock or weight on top of the plastic wrap centered over the cup. The extra weight in the center will ensure that the evaporated water will drop into the cup.
6. Place the bowl in the sun and observe how distilled water starts to accumulate inside the plastic cup.
7. Check the cup every hour or so. The more intense the sun is, the faster distillation will occur.
8. When there is enough water in the cup, open the plastic wrap and observe your purified water.
9. Does the water in the cup look different than the water in the bowl? Can you explain why?

Making a Wind Wheel

Materials:
- Cardstock
- Scissors
- Ruler
- Pencil
- Push pin
- Stick or straw

Preparation: None

Lesson:
1. Remove the eraser from the pencil. Set it aside as you will be using it later.
2. Cut your cardstock so that it is a square shape instead of a rectangle.
3. Mark the center of your cardstock with a dot.
4. Use your pencil and ruler to draw diagonal lines from the corners of your cardstock to the dot in the middle.
5. Cut along the diagonal lines, stopping about an inch away from the center of your cardstock.
6. Gently bend one of the corners over until it is over the center dot. Use your fingers to hold it in place.
7. Repeat step five until each corner is bent into the center.
8. Carefully insert the pushpin through each corner as well as through the center dot on the cardstock.
9. Press the tip of the push pin firmly through the stick or straw.
10. Push the eraser onto the sharp end of the push pin. Be sure not to do it too tightly or the wind wheel won't be able to turn.
11. Save your wind wheel for an upcoming activity.

Reading

Parent Note: The read aloud suggestions are intended for you to read to your child. The individual reading suggestions are intended for your child to read aloud to you – or to read on their own. Continue reading each selection throughout the knight/lady-in-waiting weeks until you are finished.

Read Aloud For Younger Children:
How to Become a Perfect Knight in Five Days by Pierrette Dubé

Read Aloud For Older Children:
Shakespeare Can Be Fun: Hamlet for Kids by Lois Burdett

Individual Reading for Grades 2-4:
The Dragon in the Sock Drawer by Kate Klimo

Individual Reading for Older Children:
The Squire's Tale by Gerald Morris

Making Gyngerbrede

Ingredients:
4 cups honey
1 lb. unseasoned bread crumbs
1 tbsp. ginger
1tbsp. cinnamon
1 tsp. ground white pepper
pinch saffron
whole cloves (optional)
red food coloring (optional)

Directions:
1. Bring the honey to a boil and skim off any scum.
2. Keeping the pan over very low heat, stir in the breadcrumbs and spices. You may also add a few drops of red food coloring if you'd like.
3. When it is a thick, well-blended mass (add more bread crumbs if necessary), remove from heat and let cool slightly.
4. Lay mixture out on a flat surface and press firmly into an evenly shaped square or rectangle, about ¾" thick.
5. Let cool. Then cut into small squares to serve.
6. If you'd like, you can garnish each square by sticking a whole clove in the top center.

Tilting Wind Wheels

Materials:
- Wind wheel made previously

Preparation: None

Lesson: For this activity, each player will hold the wind wheels they made in a previous activity. As the wheel turns, each player charges forward toward another player, attempting to stop their opponent's wheel from spinning, while still keeping their own wheel turning. Players cannot use anything to accomplish this except the wind wheel itself.

Week Six – You are a Knight/Lady-in-Waiting
Day Two

The Duties of a Medieval Lady-in-waiting

Materials: None

Preparation: None

Lesson: A medieval lady-in-waiting was a female who acted as the personal assistant to a queen, a princess, or some other noble woman such as a baron's wife. Quite often, a lady-in-waiting was the relative of the woman for whom she worked. She was seen as more of a companion and a confidant than as a servant.

A lady-in-waiting often came from a noble family which was highly thought of – just as knights came from nobility. She served a woman from an even higher rank than herself.

Ladies-in-waiting did not perform menial tasks. These were performed by servants. The duties of a lady-in-waiting included the following:

- Embroidery
- Horseback riding
- Instructing her mistress in matters of etiquette, languages, and dancing
- Keeping her mistress informed about activities and people who were at court
- Music making (either singing or playing an instrument)
- Painting
- Relaying messages discreetly

- Secretarial tasks such as reading to her mistress and writing letters on her behalf
- Supervising the servants
- Taking care of her mistresses' clothing

As you can see, a lady-in-waiting needed to be a well-rounded and educated person. She dressed in a similar fashion as her mistress, since she was considered as more of a friend than an employee. Quite often, ladies-in-waiting ended up marrying high ranking men such as kings, princes, or barons. They were an important member of the household and they also played an important role in entertainment for the family for which they worked.

Make a Kite Shield

Materials:
- Large piece of cardboard per child
- 2 colors of duct tape OR spray paint
- Masking tape (if using paint)
- Markers
- Scissors

Preparation: None

Lesson:
1. Using the markers, draw the shape of your shield on the cardboard.
2. Cut out the shape.
3. Decorate your shield using either the colored duct tape or by painting it. A tip when it comes to painting is that you can use masking tape to mask off sections. You may want to paint the entire shield one color, let it dry and then paint your details. Using masking tape, you can mark off an area for a cross or any other symbol you desire. Then, you can easily spray the second color of paint on your shield. After it dries, remove the masking tape.
4. Add the handles to your shield by making them out of cardboard strips and taping them to the back of the shield. Make one handle large and one smaller. The large one is what you will fit your arm inside and the small one is the one you will grasp with your hand.
5. Have your child try the handles before you tape them down too much. When they are comfortably placed, use lots of tape on them so they are strong. Remember, if you are left-handed hold the shield in your right hand. If you are right-handed hold the shield in your left hand.

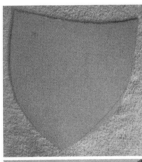

6. You may now use your shield. Enjoy!

Cloud in a Bottle

Materials:
- Candle in a holder
- Match
- Glass jar such as a quart canning jar (narrow mouthed jar)

Preparation: None

Lesson: Clouds form when warm, particle-rich air meets cool, moist air. For today's activity, we will be making our own cloud. This experiment needs to be done inside with air conditioning or outside on a cool day with little or no wind.

Activity:
1. Find a level surface on which you will be able to set your lit candle.
2. Light the candle.
3. Hold the jar upside down over the candle for about 10 seconds. Don't set the jar down on top of the candle because that will cause all of the oxygen in the jar to be used up and the flame to be extinguished.

4. Once the jar's mouth has cooled a little, form a seal around the jar with your mouth and blow. Once you pull your mouth away, you should see a cloud form inside the bottle. *Note: It will be a thin, wispy cloud.*
5. If you're inside with the air conditioning on, try placing the bottle overtop of an air conditioning vent versus blowing into it.
6. Experiment with going from cold to hot versus hot to cold. Which one creates a better cloud?

Literature

Materials:
- Beowulf as told by Michael Morpurgo

Preparation: None

Parent Note: Read this book aloud and discuss it with your child.

Color Changes Throughout the Day

Materials:
- Camera (preferably a digital one)
- Printer (optional – makes it easier to print your child's photos but isn't required)

Lesson: You may have noticed that the time of day in which you are taking your photographs will have a big impact on the color of your pictures. For this lesson, try taking several photos of the same object at different times of the day to see how the different light affects the result. ***Use the following chart to help guide you.***

Before sunrise	The world appears to be much more black and white. Colors are muted. The light has a cool, shadowless quality.
Just after sunrise	The light warms up and becomes much more red or orange because the blue hues are filtered out by the air. Shadows may appear to be blue, however, because they reflect the blue from the sky.
Around noon	There will be the most contrast between. Each color will stand out in its own, true hue. Shadows will appear to be black.
As the sun goes down	The light begins to warm up and become more reddish again. This occurs gradually so you need to remember to watch for it. Objects can begin to take on an unearthly glow. Shadows lengthen and surfaces will become strongly textured.
After sunset	There is often a good deal of light left in the sky. This light is often tinted by sunset colors. The shadows will again disappear and the contrast between colors will again lessen.

You may want to include a few of your better photos in your journal.

Week Six – You are a Knight/Lady-in-Waiting
Day Three

Ladylike Dilemmas

Materials:
- Paper and pencil

Preparation: None

Lesson: Ladies-in-Waiting also used math to figure out different situations throughout their day. See how well you can solve these problems. The answers are in the companion download.

1. During the summer, the lady-in-waiting has 21 dresses to iron. She can iron 6 dresses in one hour. How long will it take her to iron all 21 dresses?

2. Four ladies are eating mince meat pie. Jane has ¾ left, Jill has 3/5 left, Cindy has 2/3 left, and Jeff has 2/5 left. Who has the most amount of mince meat pie left?

3. What are the next three numbers in the following pattern: 320, 160, 80, 40…

4. The queen's age divided by 15 is 5. How old is the queen?

Reading

Parent Note: The read aloud suggestions are intended for you to read to your child. The individual reading suggestions are intended for your child to read aloud to you – or to read on their own. Continue reading each selection throughout the knight/lady-in-waiting weeks until you are finished.

Read Aloud For Younger Children:
Sir Ryan's Quest by Jason Deeble

Read Aloud For Older Children:
Shakespeare Can Be Fun: Hamlet for Kids by Lois Burdett

Individual Reading for Grades 2-4:
The Dragon in the Sock Drawer by Kate Klimo

Individual Reading for Older Children:
The Squire's Tale by Gerald Morris

Knightly Journey

Materials:
- Map from companion download
- Ruler
- Paper and pencil
- Distance calculator link from supplement section of our website (optional)

Preparation:
1. Print a copy of the map for each child.

Lesson: As an important knight, you have been sent on a mission by your king. You are currently serving him in London; however, he wants you to check on several of his outposts to see how loyal the lords in those areas are behaving.
1. First, draw the shortest route between the following cities on your map:
    a. London to Nottingham
    b. Nottingham to Bristol
    c. Bristol to Stonehenge
    d. Stonehenge to Oxford
    e. Oxford to London
2. Using your ruler, measure the distance to each of these cities and record each distance on a sheet of paper. Remember that 1 inch equals approximately 50 miles.
3. Determine the actual distance you would need to travel to each of these destinations.
4. Calculate the total distance of your trip. Remember that your calculations are approximate. See how close you can get to the actual distance from place to place (as the crow flies.)
5. The answers are in the companion download.

Learn to Draw a Knight

Materials:
- Paper
- Pencil with an eraser
- A black marker (optional)
- Colored pencils or crayons (optional)

Preparation: None

Lesson: In this lesson, you will learn to draw a knight step-by-step.

1. First, draw an ellipse for the knight's head. Now, draw construction lines for his body as shown.

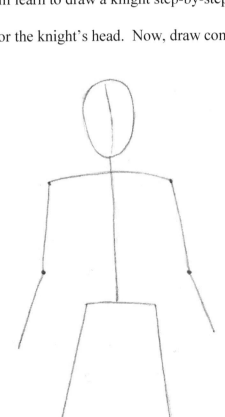

2. Next, draw the shape of the helmet around his head. Draw the sheath on his torso and upper legs as shown. Draw the chain mail armor over his neck and draped onto his shoulders.

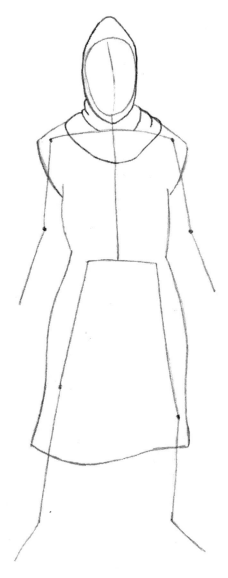

3. Next, draw the helmet design. Draw the knight's boots, arms, and gloves as shown. Draw the hands in such a way that they can hold a sword and shield. *Note:* Try holding something yourself and looking at the position of your fingers to get a better idea of how they should look.

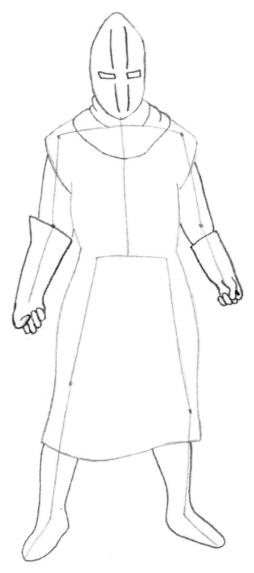

4. Next, draw the knight's sword and shield as shown.

5. Lastly, draw a belt on your knight. Add any other details you'd like to add such as crosshatches for the chain mail. Trace the lines you want to keep with the black marker. Then, erase your construction lines. You may now use the colored pencils to color your drawing if you would like. Great job!

Running Long Jump

Materials:
- A stick, jump rope, or some other way of marking the start line
- A measuring tape OR
  Small sticks for marking each child's jump distance

Preparation: None

Lesson: Knights needed to be able to scale walls and spring over ditches while wearing all of their armor. One way they practiced these feats was to perform a running long jump. In today's activity, you will be practicing the running long jump.

1. Take a running start and see how far you can jump.
2. ***Parent Note:*** You may want to measure their distances so they can compete with themselves or with each other.
3. If you step over the start line before jumping, it is called a foul and you will receive no score for that jump.
4. Jumps should be measured from the furthest back point. For example, if you jump 15 feet but you fall backward and your hand goes back 2 feet, the jump counts as being 13 feet long.
5. The person who jumps the furthest wins the competition!

Week Six – You are a Knight/Lady-in-Waiting
Day Four

The Battle of Hastings and the Norman Conquest

Materials: None

Preparation: None

Lesson: King Edward III, also called "The Confessor" because he had built Westminster Abbey, was the king of England for 23 years. On January 5, 1066, he died leaving no children as heirs. Because of this unfortunate circumstance, the throne of England was up for grabs.

At this time in history, England didn't have strict rules about who was next in line to become king. Either the crown passed to someone with some sort of blood claim, or to someone who could grab the crown before anyone else. When Edward died, there were four different people who felt they deserved to be the next king of England.

First was Edgar the Atheling. As Edward's nephew, he was the closest blood relative. Unfortunately, he was only fourteen years old and was quite sickly. No one seriously considered handing him the crown.

Second was Harold Godwinson, who was a soldier and a politician. He was also from England's noble class and was very popular with the people; but, he was not related to King Edward in any way. Nevertheless, it was thought that Harold was the wisest choice for succeeding Edward to the throne. It was even thought that Edward had wanted Harold to be king after him. Harold told people that it had been Edward's dying wish! Interestingly, there were no other witnesses who heard Edward say this.

Third was William, Duke of Normandy. William was a distant cousin of Edward and he wanted to be the next king. William said that Edward and Harold had promised to make him king – but no one else was able to confirm his story, either.

Fourth was Harald Hardrada, the Viking king of Norway. Believe it or not, Harald was a direct descendant of the kings of England. In fact, England had been ruled by Norwegian kings up until 1042 when Edward the Confessor had snatched the throne back from them. Harald was very unpopular but he was very powerful.

The day after Edward died, Harold Godwinson was crowned king. This caused Harald Hardrada to race in and try to take the throne for himself. He and his brother invaded England with a massive army. They conquered the city of York and then Harald declared himself King of England.

Harold Godwinson wasn't going to stand for that. He gathered up as large of an army as he could muster and marched north to face the usurper. The two armies met at Stamford Bridge on September 25, 1066. It was a bloody battle, but Harold Godwinson's army was the victor. Harald Hardrada and his brother were killed and most of the Viking army was also killed.

King Harold wasn't able to celebrate his victory for long. He soon received news that William, Duke of Normandy, and the Normans were invading the south coast of England – and there was no one to stop him since the entire English army was up north with him! Harold and his men raced south to the Hastings area to face William's army. They must have been battle weary; however, they met their foe head on.

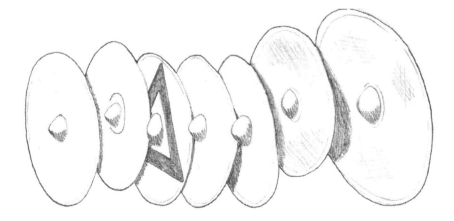

At first, the English infantry held strong against the Norman archers. They linked shields to create a shield wall, which the Norman arrows couldn't pierce. The English appeared to be winning this battle.

Then the English Saxons made their fatal mistake. Late in the afternoon, the Normans appeared to be retreating down a large hill. Some of Harold's men broke their shield wall to chase them.

No sooner had the Normans reached the bottom of the hill then they turned around and cut the English to bits. The Norman cavalry rode among the English, cutting them down. As soon as the shield wall was broken, William's archers were able to have better luck. The Battle of Hastings only lasted for six hours. After William won, he began to be known as William the Conqueror. He marched his army to London and was crowned King at Westminster Abbey on December 25, 1066.

The Norman victory changed much about England and the way it was ruled. Under Saxon leadership, England had considered its noble families to be as important as the king. Under William's rule, however, the king was the supreme ruler of the land. William is the one who set up the feudal system, which we learned about earlier.

William also wanted to be sure he maintained control of England for some time to come. Castles were at the heart of William's strategy for the conquest of England. As he captured strategic towns, villages and river fords, he secured these acquisitions by building castles. The castles provided his troops with strong defensive structures to guard against any upstart Saxons who might have been bold enough to attempt to put a stop to William's ambitions. They also served as central points of supply and assistance for the pillaging bands of Norman soldiers that roamed the countryside terrorizing and subduing the native people. Two of William's most famous castles are the Tower of London and Windsor Castle.

Write in Your Journal

Materials:
- Your child's journal
- Paper
- Pencil, colored pencils, markers, etc.

Preparation: None

Parent Note: Have your child write down a few key points about what they learned about The Battle of Hastings and the Norman Conquest. Depending on their age and ability, you can require your child to write one sentence or several paragraphs. You can also let them narrate back to you what they have learned. Then, have them draw a picture or print pictures from the internet to add some more insight to their journal page.

Possible Writing Prompt: Imagine you were a soldier during one of the battles. Choose to be from whichever country you'd like. Write a journal entry describing what you heard and how you felt. Did you talk with any other soldiers? What did you say? How do you feel about William being crowned king?

In What Order Did the Knights Arrive?

Materials: Logic puzzle from companion download

Preparation: Print one copy of the logic puzzle for each child.

Lesson: The baron had a very important message to deliver to the king. He wanted to be sure his message got through, so he sent out 10 of his best knights with the same message. All 10 knights went by various routes and arrived safely at the king's castle. Your job is to determine in which order the knights arrived.

Literature

Materials:
- Beowulf as told by Michael Morpurgo

Preparation: None

Parent Note: Read this book aloud and discuss it with your child.

Field Trip to a Medieval Festival

Parent Note: This week is a great time to attend a medieval festival in your area. More and more of these types of events are being held around the world. Even if you can't attend one this week, try to research when one will be held in your area so you can mark it on your calendar.

Quite often, visitors to these festivals are given the opportunity to dress in period costumes. They are also allowed to participate in knightly duties such as sword fighting, axe throwing, and jousting. You may even get to sample some medieval food! Be sure to ask your child questions so that they can compare their experience with what they have learned so far about the life of a knight. And have your child take lots of pictures for their journal.

Week Six – You are a Knight/Lady-in-Waiting
Day Five

Quiz Bowl

Parent Note: See how well you and your children can answer questions about the material that has been covered concerning knights and ladies-in-waiting.

1. From what class of people did knights and ladies-in-waiting usually come? (Nobility)

2. How long did it typically take a knight to complete their training? (14 years)

3. How old was a boy when he started his knight training? (Age 7)

4. What are some examples of physical training that a knight underwent? (Sword fighting, wrestling, riding a horse while wielding a sword, and jousting)

5. What was the name of the object which was used to teach a knight to joust more safely? (A quintain)

6. What are the different levels of knighthood? (Page, squire, knight)

7. What were the duties of a squire? (To help his knight mentor dress for battle, to develop fighting skills, and to learn the rules of chivalry)

8. Typically, how old was a man when he became a knight? (21 years old)

9. What vow do knights take? (To fear God, serve the King, protect the weak, and live honorably)

10. If a knight broke his vow, was this seen as a big issue or a small one? (A big one. It was considered that he had committed a crime against God and would suffer eternal damnation.)

11. What two celebratory events followed the knighting ceremony? (A feast that night and a tournament the next day)

12. Was a medieval lady-in-waiting considered to be a servant? (No, she was more like a friend)

13. Was a lady-in-waiting educated? (Yes, she needed to have a well rounded education to perform her duties)

14. What was the nickname of King Edward III? (The Confessor)

15. During medieval times, did England have strict rules about who became the next king? (No. Either the crown passed to someone with some sort of blood claim, or to someone who could grab the crown before anyone else.)

16. How long did the Battle of Hastings last? (6 hours)

17. What was William, Duke of Normandy's nickname after he became the King of England? (William the Conqueror)

18. What system of government did William the Conqueror put into place? (The feudal system)

19. William built many castles in England. Name at least one of them. (Pevensey Castle, Hastings Castle, Dover Castle, The Tower of London, Windsor Castle, Colchester Castle, Rochester Castle and Guildford Castle)

20. Why did William build so many castles? (As William conquered cities and villages he built castles in order to protect and fortify these areas.)

Make a Medieval Battle Axe

Materials:
- Large dowel approximately 1/2 inch thick and 3 feet long
- Cardboard
- Box cutter or sturdy scissors
- Hot glue gun
- Metallic silver spray paint
- Axe blade template from companion download

Preparation: None

Lesson:
1. Using the template of your choice, cut two identical axe blades from cardboard using a box cutter or the scissors. *Parent Note:* Depending on the age of your children, you may need to do this part for them.
2. Spray paint what will be the outsides of both axe blades with silver paint. Allow the paint to dry completely before going any further.
3. Place one of the blade cutouts on a table top. Use the glue gun to draw a thick line of glue up the center of the cutout, between the two blades.
4. Place one end of the dowel onto the hot glue, and allow the glue to cool and harden.
5. Squeeze hot glue around the edges of the blade and onto the end of the dowel.
6. Press the second blade over the first. Squeeze the two into shape around the shaft, and line up the edges of the blades to meet.
7. Allow the glue to dry. You now have your own medieval battle axe!

Throwing Your Battle Axe

Materials:
- Paper plate
- Battle axe you made earlier
- Marker
- Tape or tack

Preparation: None

Lesson: Axes were used in medieval times for chopping wood just as they are today. Their use in warfare probably began quite naturally. Soldiers on the move carried axes for non-warfare purposes such as chopping firewood, logging trees to build defensive fortifications, and other such non-combat uses. Picking up an axe to swing in combat would have been a logical extension as men already had an axe with them.

Also, a lot of medieval-era soldiers who were not knights or archers may have been peasants who were drafted into battle. These peasants wouldn't have been as well equipped as professional soldiers. These types of soldiers may have been given axes instead of swords since they were cheaper to make. Or, they may have even had to bring their own weapons from home. Peasants, who were usually farmers, were more likely to have an axe lying around than a sword.

For this activity, you will be throwing the battle axe that you made earlier.

Activity:
1. Using the marker, draw a bull's-eye on the plate.
2. Hang your bull's-eye up using the tape or the tack.
3. Have your child try to throw their axe to hit the target. If you have more than one child, let them compete to see who is able to hit the target the most accurately.

Reading

Parent Note: The read aloud suggestions are intended for you to read to your child. The individual reading suggestions are intended for your child to read aloud to you – or to read on their own. Continue reading each selection throughout the knight/lady-in-waiting weeks until you are finished.

Read Aloud For Younger Children:
Saint George and the Dragon by Geraldine McCaughrean

Read Aloud For Older Children:
Shakespeare Can Be Fun: Hamlet for Kids by Lois Burdett

Individual Reading for Grades 2-4:
The Dragon in the Sock Drawer by Kate Klimo

Individual Reading for Older Children:
The Squire's Tale by Gerald Morris

Medieval Adventure, Scene Three

Materials:
- Script from companion download
- Costumes which were made/gathered in a previous lesson
- Whatever other props you create during your lessons and/or have laying around the house to add excitement to this adventure.

Preparation:
1. Photocopy the script so that each actor has their own copy.
2. Read through the script a few times so that you know what to expect and can help to direct the kids.

Parent Note: Choose roles for yourself and your children. Remember, the more dramatic you act the more your kids will as well – and the more value they will gain from this assignment. If you are planning to videotape the play, you may want to do it while on your field trip to the medieval festival so that the background looks right. ☺

Activity Suggestions for Further Learning and Fun

Below is a list of further suggestions which have not been incorporated into the two weeks of learning that you may also want to try. The more you immerse your child in these types of activities, the more they will learn and enjoy this experience. *Warning:* You child will probably most enjoy some of the suggestions are the messiest or the most out of the ordinary! ☺

Knight
- Make chain mail
- Find someone to be your mentor for the day (or longer)
- Practice being humble and obedient
- Build a quintain
- Participate in a dubbing ceremony
- Wear armor and carry a sword all day to see how it feels
- Practice skills with weapons – archery, sword, etc.

Lady-in-waiting
- Practice being humble and obedient
- Try helping someone to get dressed
- Style someone else's hair
- Wait on someone for the day
- Embroidery
- Entertain the family with a musical instrument
- Iron clothes

You are a Monk

in Medieval England

Table of Contents for Monk/Nun Weeks

Week Seven – You are a Monk/Nun
Day One

Daily Life of a Monk/Nun

Materials: None

Preparation: None

Lesson: Medieval monks and nuns made the conscious decision to renounce living a worldly life and instead to spend their lives working for God. When they entered a monastery or a convent, they gave up everything they owned and vowed to remain poor their entire lives.

Monastic life was guided by the use of something called *The Book of Hours*. This was the main prayer book which was meant to be read at specific times of each day. It was divided into eight sections which contained prayers, psalms, hymns, and other readings. These readings were designed to help a monk to secure salvation for himself. All work immediately stopped during times of daily prayer. No matter what they were doing, they stopped to attend prayer services. Do you think it was possible for them to do anything which would help them to become saved? You should discuss this as a family.

Each day contained the following eight separate times of prayer:

- *Matins* – Midnight
- *Lauds* – 3am – Reminds the Christian that the first act of the day should be prayer and that one's thoughts should be of God before facing the cares of the day.

162

- *Prime* – 6am
- *Terce* – 9am
- *Sext* – Noon
- *Nones* – 3pm
- *Vespers* – 6pm
- *Compline* – 9pm – After this time, they observed silence until the next morning's prayer.

With these many times of prayer throughout the day, you might think that they did nothing but pray and worship God their entire lives. That is certainly not true. Monks and nuns performed many other functions as well. The following were jobs performed within the abbey/monastery/convent:

- **Abbot/Abbess** - The head of an abbey.
- **Almoner** - An officer of a monastery who gave money and food to the poor and sick.
- **Barber Surgeon** - The monk who shaved the faces and heads of the monks. He also performed light surgery as did all barbers during this time.
- **Cantor** - The monk who led the choir during the worship service.
- **Cellarer** - The monk or nun who made sure the monastery had enough supplies to run properly and efficiently.
- **Infirmarian** - The monk or nun in charge of the infirmary or hospital.
- **Lector** - A monk entrusted with reading the lessons in church or in the dining hall.
- **Sacrist** - The monk or nun responsible for the safekeeping of books, clothes and other items used during the worship service. He or she was also in charge of the maintenance of the monastery's buildings.
- **Prior/Prioress** – Second in charge after the abbot/abbess.

Monks and nuns were also responsible for the following necessary physical tasks:

- Washing and cooking
- Growing vegetables and grain
- Reaping, sowing, plowing, haymaking and threshing crops
- Gathering honey
- Binding and thatching
- Producing wine and ale
- Medical care for the community
- Educating boys and novices
- Copying and illuminating the manuscripts of classical authors
- Providing hospitality for pilgrims

As you can see, monks and nuns had quite a bit of work to do. They were busy all the time helping to care for the needs of others. These menial tasks were also a form of worship for them.

For the next two weeks you will pretend to be a monk or a nun living in medieval England. You will get to experience some of the chores, tasks, and responsibilities that a monk or a nun would have experienced. As you complete these activities and go about your day, try to imagine what it was like to do these things all day, every day of your life.

Write in Your Journal

Materials:
- Your child's journal
- Paper
- Pencil, colored pencils, markers, etc.

Preparation: None

Parent Note: Have your child write down a few key points about what they learned about the daily lives of monks and nuns. Depending on their age and ability, you can require your child to write one sentence or several paragraphs. You can also let them narrate back to you what they have learned. Then, have them draw a picture or print pictures from the internet to add some more insight to their journal page.

Possible Writing Prompt: Imagine you are a monk who is writing a training manual for brand new monks. Describe one aspect of monastic life to the new monks so that they will know how to behave.

Literature

Materials:
- The Adventures of Robin Hood by Roger Lancelyn Green

Preparation: None

Parent Note: Read this book aloud and discuss it with your child.

Make Your Own Stained Glass

Materials:
- A glass jar
- Acrylic paint
- White glue
- A squeeze bottle with a small nozzle (empty glue bottle, etc)
- Food coloring (several colors)
- Liquid dish soap
- Paint brush
- A paper plate to use as a palette

Preparation:
1. Make the "lead" outliner for your child's design by mixing two parts white glue with one part black acrylic paint. Mix thoroughly and put into squeeze bottle for your child. (***Parent Note***: Black Puffy Paint can be used for outlining their project if you would rather.)

Lesson:
1. Think of a design for your stained glass jar before proceeding.
2. Create the outline of your design with the "lead."
3. Allow the outline to dry completely.

4. Create several colors of glass paint by putting white glue on your palette, adding 1-2 drops of dish soap and 1-2 drops of food coloring. Mix well.
5. Test the mixture's color on a small section of glass. Add a few more drops of food coloring to the mixture if you want the paint to be a richer color.
6. Paint in between the outlines you created earlier. If you made the homemade paint and you notice that the paint recedes or "bubbles", simply paint over these areas and they should disappear.

7. After the paint dries, you can use your jar as a candle holder, a pencil holder, or simply as a decorative jar.

Be Careful of Backlighting

Materials:
- Camera (preferably a digital one)
- Printer (optional – makes it easier to print your child's photos but isn't required)

Lesson: When taking pictures, you always need to be aware of the type of light with which you are working. If you are taking pictures inside, take notice of where the windows are located. Try to stand with the windows to your back or side if possible. If you take a picture with the camera pointed toward a window, you will find that the subjects of your photo will often be black or at least darker than what they appeared in real life.

If you are taking pictures outside, take notice of where the sun is located. Try not to point the lens of your camera toward the sun. You will want to take pictures with the sun either behind you or to the side of your subject. One downside of this is that if you are taking pictures of people, they may need to look into the sun too much, which could cause them to squint on a sunny day. In this situation, you will want to put the sun on the side of your subject so that they will be more comfortable and the light from the sun will still benefit your photo. You might also want to try having your subject stand in the shade and use a flash.

For this lesson, try taking some photos of the same subject with either windows or the sun in front of your subject, behind your subject, and to the side of your subject. Notice how different your photos turn out depending on the position of the lighting. You may want to include a few of your better photos in your journal.

See how the window washes out this photo?

This photo is better because the subject isn't backlit by a window

166

Week Seven – You are a Monk/Nun
Day Two

Westminster Abbey and Statues

Materials:
- An empty 2-liter pop bottle
- Newspaper
- Aluminum foil
- Craft sticks
- Tissue paper
- Tape
- Flour
- Water
- Paint (optional)

Preparation:
1. Combine 1 cup of water and 1 cup of flour in a pan.
2. Heat the mixture until it bubbles. Remove from heat and let it cool completely.

Lesson: Westminster Abbey was originally founded in 960AD. It was a small Benedictine monastery at the time. In the 1040s, King Edward I decided to greatly enlarge this monastery in honor of St. Peter the Apostle. There was already a large church (also called a minster) in honor of St. Paul on the east side of London known as the "east minster." This new church became known as the "west minster."

Westminster Abbey has a lot of history. What we are going to focus on for this activity, however, is the large amount of sculpture within its walls. The abbey contains statues of many famous people such as William Wilberforce, Martin Luther King Jr., and Elizabeth Nightingale. There are also statues of Biblical heroes such as Moses, St. Peter, St. Paul, and King David. Statues fill the abbey, helping us to remember to honor the lives of many important people from history.

Activity: For this activity, you will be making your own paper mache statue. You may find a picture of a sculpture that you'd like to recreate or come up with your own design using your imagination. Be sure to take a photo of your finished sculpture for your journal.
1. Remove the cap from the bottle and stuff a ball of aluminum foil into the bottle opening. This will become your statue's head.
2. Tape craft sticks onto your bottle to become arms.
3. Make whatever shapes you prefer using the craft sticks, tissue paper, and tape. Don't feel like you have to make a statue of a person if this is too difficult.
4. Once your statue is ready, you will cover it with paper mache.
5. Tear the newspaper into strips.
6. Dip the strips of newspaper into the paper mache mixture and apply them to your statue. Cover the entire structure completely with three layers of paper mache.
7. Allow your statue to dry completely. You may now paint your statue if you would like.

Jean Pucelle and The Book of Hours

Materials:
- Paper
- Tracing paper (optional)
- Colored pencils or markers
- Examples of illuminated letters from companion download

Preparation: Print the illuminated letters for your child to use as patterns. Have your child choose one that they like or search for a different example on the internet.

Lesson: Jean Pucelle was a French artist who lived during the Middle Ages. Little is known of his life. Pucelle was an exceptionally good painter of miniatures and a manuscript illuminator (or illustrator.) Did you know that books during the Middle Ages needed to be copied by hand? Jean Pucelle was an artist who illustrated books during this time period so he was a skilled artist.

One of the most well-known of Pucelle's works was a book he illuminated for the Queen of France, which still survives. It is called *Hours of Jeanne d'Evreux* (see the above illustration.) It was the queen's private prayer book or in English her Book of Hours.

The Book of Hours was a very popular devotional to have during the Middle Ages – especially for women. In fact, a personalized copy was often given as a wedding present from a husband to his bride. Women of means were able to afford elaborately illuminated copies of the text such as the one you see in the picture above. Poorer women often had a Book of Hours which was smaller and had little or no illumination making it much more affordable.

Other than the beautiful illuminations, the Book of Hours contained information that was useful to its owner for the worship of God. It contained a calendar of church feasts, excerpts from the gospels, several psalms, and various other prayers.

Activity: For this activity, you will be trying your hand at creating an illumination. Try using one of the patterns that your parent has printed off for you – you may even decide to hold the illumination up to the window for easy tracing. Be sure to take your time in decorating your illumination. See how your final version compares to a medieval illumination.

Create Monk and Nun Costumes

Materials for Monk Costume (Pick and choose as desired):
- A long robe with a hood – brown or black is best
  OR a long, black garbage bag with a head hole cut in the bottom
- A rope to use as a belt
- Sandals or bare feet

Materials for Nun Costume (Pick and choose as desired):
- Long dress or robe – white, brown, or black if possible
- Full apron worn over dress
- Huge cross necklace (can make this with cardboard and string if desired)
- Head covered with a long veil or wimple (long piece of fabric)

Parent Note: For this activity, we are going to create an outfit to wear while acting in the drama as well as while completing their other lessons if your child so desires.

You can make this activity as simple or as elaborate as you and your children would enjoy. There are many sites on the internet which give you ideas on sewing medieval costumes. We are going to show you simple ways in which you can gather costumes – but you are welcome to take the time to make more elaborate costumes if that is something which interests you.

An easy and inexpensive way to gather the clothing items we recommend is to check out secondhand stores and garage sales. Feel free to improvise! The most important thing is that your child feels the part – not that they are completely authentic.

Reading

Parent Note: The read aloud suggestions are intended for you to read to your child. The individual reading suggestions are intended for your child to read aloud to you – or to read on their own. Continue reading each selection throughout the monk/nun weeks until you are finished.

Read Aloud For Younger Children:
You Wouldn't Want to Work on a Medieval Cathedral : a Difficult Job that Never Ends by Fiona Macdonald

Read Aloud For Older Children:
Cathedral: The Story of its Construction by David MacCauley

Individual Reading for Grades 2-4:
The Big Book of Knights, Nobles and Knaves illustrated by Adria Fruitos

Individual Reading for Older Children:
Crispin: The Cross of Lead by Avi

Hopscotch

Materials:
- Chalk
- A sidewalk, driveway, or other hard surface
- One stone per player

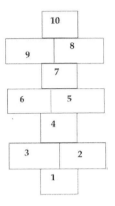

Preparation: You may want to draw the hopscotch court in advance, choosing from the options seen here or creating a design of your own.

Lesson: In modern society, we often think of the game of hopscotch as being a girl's game. Surprisingly, the game actually began as a military training exercise. In ancient Britain, during the early Roman Empire, hopscotch courts were over 100 feet long. Roman soldiers ran the course in full armor carrying field packs to improve their footwork. This is similar to the way that modern football players run through rows of truck tires today.

Roman children began drawing their own smaller hopscotch courts to imitate those of the soldiers. They also added a scoring system to turn the exercise into a game. Each player has a marker, usually a stone. The first player tosses his marker into the first square. The marker must land completely within the designated square without touching a line or bouncing out. If the marker lands in the wrong square, the player loses his turn.

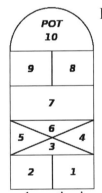

If the marker toss is successful, the player hops through the court beginning at square one. Side by side squares are straddled, with the left foot landing in the left square and the right foot in the right square. Single squares must be hopped into on one foot. For the first single square, either foot may be used. Subsequent single squares must alternate feet.

When the player reaches the end of the court, he turns around and hops back through the court, hopping through the squares in reverse order and stopping to pick up his marker on the way back. Upon successfully completing the sequence, the player continues his turn by tossing his marker into square two and continuing in a similar fashion.

If, while hopping through the court in either direction, the player steps on a line, misses a square, or loses his balance and falls, his turn ends. He does not get credit for completing the current sequence and must start that sequence again on his next turn. The first player to complete one course for every numbered square on the court wins.

Week Seven – You are a Monk/Nun
Day Three

Miracle Plays

Materials: None

Preparation: None

Lesson: During the Middle Ages, mass or church service was often spoken in Latin, which is a language that was not understood by the majority of the people in England. Remember that during this time, many people didn't know how to read, either. So they would have been unable to read the Bible, even if they had been able to get their hands on a copy. Because of this, many people didn't understand very much about the message of the church or about how God wanted them to live their lives.

The local priests knew this was a problem so they created something called Miracle Plays or Mystery Plays. These plays were originally acted out during mass in English. They took stories from the Bible and acted them out so that people could more easily learn important Biblical principles.

Originally, all of the actors were clergy from the church. Over time, however, the plays became more and more elaborate and the entire town became responsible for putting on the production. One scene might take place at the church; but, other scenes took place throughout the village. The stages were erected all along one side of the street representing the different settings throughout the play. As visitors walked down the street, they saw heaven portrayed at one end and hell portrayed at the other.

Guilds took responsibility for building the stages. This was an early form of advertising for them as they could show off their skills while building the intricate sets and props. They also built two-level horse drawn carts called pageants. The bottom level of the pageant was used as a dressing room. The top level was where actors performed. These pageants were pulled down the street to the various settings while the actors said their lines. They were very similar to the modern day floats that you might see in a parade.

Each large town was responsible for portraying a different set of Biblical events called a cycle. Each cycle told a complete story, such as the life of Christ or the creation of the world. Some of these cycles consisted of more than 40 plays and took two or more days to perform. Imagine how much time and effort was spent creating and producing these plays! This was obviously a valued form of entertainment as well as an education for the people. It was similar to how we watch TV and movies today.

Over time, the church stopped overseeing the miracle plays and left their content up to the townspeople. Once that happened, the plays started to include more comic and rowdy elements such as Noah trying to force his wife to board the ark – or people dressed up as demons running around and taunting the crowd. The devil also began to take on a larger role in the plays. His assistant, named Vice, performed mischievous pranks on the virtuous characters. This role was the forerunner of what would become the court jester or the clown.

Learn to Draw St. Paul's Cathedral

Materials:
- Paper
- Pencil with an eraser
- A black marker (optional)
- Colored pencils or crayons (optional)

Preparation: None

Lesson: In this lesson, you will learn to draw St. Paul's Cathedral step-by-step.

1. First, draw a large rectangle. Draw a small triangle centered on top. Now, start the towers by drawing smaller rectangles with small arcs centered on top.

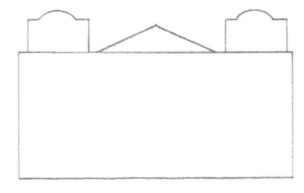

2. Continue drawing the end towers by adding three rectangles with a bell-shaped dome on top. Draw the center tower with a cross on top as shown.

3. Next, draw a horizontal line through the large rectangle making the bottom half slightly larger than the top. Then, draw the windows and circles on the towers as shown.

4. Draw two more horizontal lines just below the top two horizontal lines of the rectangle. Now, draw the columns and the stairs as shown.

5. Lastly, add details to your cathedral as shown. Using the black marker, trace all of the lines. Then, you may color in your cathedral with the colored pencils if desired. Great job!

Make an Astrolabe

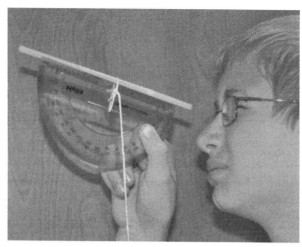

Materials:
- String
- Plastic protractor
- Straw
- Tape
- Weight (washer, rock, or fishing weight)
- Pen and paper

Preparation: None

Lesson: About 140 BC, the Greek astronomer Hipparchus of Rhodes figured out that you could use an imaginary right triangle whose corners were the sun, the earth, and the planets or stars, to calculate the movements of the planets and stars. To measure the angles of these right triangles accurately, Hipparchus invented a metal tool called an astrolabe. An astrolabe is a type of manual calculator, like a slide rule.

Over the next 1,000 years, scientists gradually improved the astrolabe. They added markings so that you could find out how far away from due north you were. This allowed sailors to use the astrolabe, along with a compass, to navigate on the ocean when they weren't in sight of land.

Activity: For this activity, you will be making a modern version of an astrolabe and using it to note the positions of certain stars in the night sky.

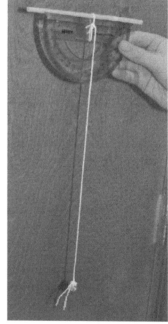

1. Tie a 12-inch piece of string to the hole in the middle of the crossbar on the protractor. Tie a weight to the other end of the string.
2. Using the tape, carefully attach the drinking straw along the straight edge of the protractor. This will act as a sighting guide for looking at stars and planets.
3. Hold the protractor so that the curved part is down and the zero degree mark is closest to you.
4. Sit on the ground, and look along the flat edge of the protractor with your eye at the zero mark. Point the flat edge at the star whose position you want to measure.
5. Once you have the star at the end of your sight, hold the string against the side of the protractor.
6. Note which degree mark the string crosses. Write this down on your paper. This number tells you how many degrees the star is above the horizon.
7. Take readings for several stars and record your observations.
8. Return every 30 minutes, and take new readings. Notice the pattern in which the stars seem to move across the sky as the earth turns.

Literature

Materials:
- The Adventures of Robin Hood by Roger Lancelyn Green

Preparation: None

Parent Note: Read this book aloud and discuss it with your child.

Monk Math

Materials:
- Paper and pencil

Preparation: None

Lesson: Monks also used math to figure out different situations throughout their day. See how well you can solve these problems. The answers are in the companion download.

1. Ivan is putting books on the monastery bookshelves. He started out with 225 books and he has already put 74 books onto the shelves. How many more books does he still need to put on the shelves?

2. Alexis has 36 beads to sew onto 4 dresses. If she sews an equal number of beads on each dress, how many will each dress receive?

3. John needs to earn $48.50 to buy a horse. He has $12.54. How much more money does he need to earn to buy the horse?

4. How many hours are there in 1 week and 3 ½ days?

Week Seven – You are a Monk/Nun
Day Four

All Hallows-by-the-Tower

Materials: Clip from the supplement section on our website

Preparation: Go to our website and prepare to play the clip designated for this lesson.

Lesson: All Hallows-by-the-Tower is the oldest surviving church in London. It was founded in 675 and it was built on the site of a former Roman building. Because of its proximity to the Tower of London, it has often been the site where executed criminals were buried. In fact, the heart of Richard I is said to be buried somewhere in the All Hallows Churchyard.

In 1650, there was a large explosion which badly damaged the church. Some barrels of gunpowder, which were being stored in the churchyard exploded. During the blast, the west tower as well as about 50 houses near the church were destroyed. The explosion also killed many people in the area.

In 1666, the church narrowly escaped the Great Fire of London. It was saved by Admiral William Penn, the father of the founder of Pennsylvania. Admiral Penn ordered his men to demolish the buildings which surrounded the church to create a large firebreak.

All Hallows was also gutted by German bombers during The Blitz in World War II. Despite all of these close calls, the church survived. It remains in operation as a church today.

For this activity, you will be watching a video which gives a brief tour of All Hallows. Be sure to observe the old Roman Road under the church as well as the various ancient chapels.

Reading

Parent Note: The read aloud suggestions are intended for you to read to your child. The individual reading suggestions are intended for your child to read aloud to you – or to read on their own. Continue reading each selection throughout the monk/nun weeks until you are finished.

Read Aloud For Younger Children:
Marguerite Makes a Book by Bruce Robertson

Read Aloud For Older Children:
Cathedral: The Story of its Construction by David MacCauley

Individual Reading for Grades 2-4:
The Big Book of Knights, Nobles and Knaves illustrated by Adria Fruitos

Individual Reading for Older Children:
Crispin: The Cross of Lead by Avi

Write and Act Out Your Own Miracle Play

Materials:
- Pen and paper

Preparation: None

Lesson: We recently learned about miracle plays and how important they were to people during the Middle Ages. For this activity, you will be writing your own miracle play. Choose whichever Bible story you like, such as Noah's Ark, Daniel and the Lion's Den, David and Goliath, or any other event from the Bible. Using that story as a backdrop, write a script for your miracle play giving the people in your family acting and/or speaking parts. After you have finished writing your script, have your family act out the play. You may want to videotape this as well.

Make Your Own Illuminated Letter

Materials:
- Pencil
- Paper
- Ruler
- Waterproof or archival pen (optional)
- Colored pencils, markers, or paint

Preparation: None

Lesson: Near the end of the Middle Ages, books became more popular as an increasing number of people learned how to read. Until the printing press was invented, however, each book had to be reproduced by hand which made them very expensive. Only people of means could afford to buy them. These illuminated manuscripts became very valuable possessions.

Illuminated letters are beautiful. You will still see them appear in books occasionally. The ability to draw and paint these letters is a fun skill to have. You can use them to dress up letters that you write to friends or to create monograms for personalizing gifts. For this activity, you will be designing and creating your own illuminated letter.

Activity:
1. Choose which letter you'd like to illuminate. You might decide to choose one of your initials.
2. Sketch the basic shape of your letter lightly in pencil. A good working size is 2 to 3 inches wide and/or tall. Widen the outlines of your letter at certain points to make it look like calligraphy.
3. Measure a boundary line around your letter in whatever shape you choose. This line can be one that is used as a visible border if you desire. Squares and rectangles are most common.
4. Fill the space with decorations, still working in pencil. Leaves and ivy are fairly simple designs with which to start.
5. Outline your letter and decorations using the waterproof pen, if desired. Otherwise, use a regular marker.
6. Erase all of your pencil marks.
7. Paint or color in the base colors of your letter as well as the decorative elements.
8. After this layer of paint has dried, add highlights.
9. Once everything has dried, touch up any outlines that may have gotten covered with paint.

Carry My Lady to London

Materials: None

Preparation: None

Lesson: During medieval times, children didn't have as many toys as they do today. They needed to find ways to occupy themselves with whatever free time they were given. One of the games they played from time to time was called "Carry My Lady to London."

In this game, two children grasped each other's wrists (or hands) to form a "seat." A third child sat on this "seat" to be carried around by the other two. The goal of this game was to see how far they could go before dropping the child. The children chanted various verses while they wandered about. (see below)

Give me a pin to stick in my thumb, to carry my lady to London.
Give me another to stick in my other, to carry her a little bit farther.

OR

London Bridge is broken, and what shall I do for a token?
Give me a pin to stick in my thumb, and carry my lady to London.

OR

Give me a pin to stick in my chin, to carry my lady to London
London Bridge is broken down and I must let my lady down.

Week Seven – You are a Monk/Nun
Day Five

The Church as a Place of Learning

Materials: None

Preparation: None

Lesson: During the Middle Ages, the majority of children were educated at home. Depending on the social status of their parents, families taught their children vastly different types of information. Most peasants didn't know how to read or write. They mainly taught their children how to farm and to do the daily chores which were required for farming and housework. Tradesmen and craftsmen taught their children how to perform the specialized crafts for which they themselves were trained. Some nobility sent their boys off to learn at the hands of a fellow knight.

During the 800s, the king decided he needed more highly educated people living in his country if it was to thrive. He turned to the Catholic Church to provide this education. All cathedrals and monasteries were told to create schools which provided a free education to any boy who had the intelligence and the determination to complete his studies.

Most boys were taught the following: Latin, grammar, rhetoric, logic, astronomy, philosophy and mathematics. Latin was very important since the Bible was written in Latin and the church services were conducted in Latin. As in today's schools, science was also studied. The scientific "facts" that they learned were different than those taught to children today. They were taught Aristotle's idea that women were essentially deformed men. They were taught that some animals, such as hyenas, can change their sex at will. They were taught that an elephant's only fear is of dragons. These students learned more useful and correct scientific information when they left the classroom and talked with farmers, trappers and hunters, who spent their time observing wildlife. The church also encouraged boys to become talented artists and builders. These graduates built some of the finest and most beautiful cathedrals that still stand today as works of art.

Girls weren't allowed to receive a formal education. Some daughters of the rich and powerful were allowed to attend select classes. Most women who learned to read and write, however, did so at home. Sometimes parents taught their daughters themselves. Sometimes they hired tutors to come to their home to teach them. Sometimes tutors were hired to teach their sons and the girls were also allowed to sit in on the lessons. Most of a girl's studies, however, were focused on helping her to become a better wife and mother. There weren't many jobs available for women outside of the home during this time period. To be fair, there weren't many jobs available for men outside of the home, either. During the Middle Ages, most people worked from home.

Universities were also created in some of the larger cities during the Middle Ages. At age 14 or 15, a select number of boys went off to continue their studies at these institutions. Some who continued their education became clergy and some became doctors. As you can see, education during medieval times what quite different from what it is like in modern times.

Write in Your Journal

Materials:
- Your child's journal
- Paper
- Pencil, colored pencils, markers, etc.

Preparation: None

Parent Note: Have your child write down a few key points about what they learned about the church and medieval education. Depending on their age and ability, you can require your child to write one sentence or several paragraphs. You can also let them narrate back to you what they have learned. Then, have them draw a picture or print pictures from the internet to add some more insight to their journal page.

Possible Writing Prompt: Pretend you are a student who is attending school at the local monastery. Write a letter back home telling your family how things are going. As a variation, you might want to write a letter as a female who wishes to beg the local priest for a formal education.

What Did the Students Learn?

Materials: Logic puzzle from companion download

Preparation: Print one copy of the logic puzzle for each child.

Lesson: Four monks were attempting to teach The Lord's Prayer to four different students. Some students were able to learn the prayer more quickly than others. Can you determine who learned the prayer first, what color shirt they were wearing, and how many books they carried?

The Murder of Thomas Becket

Materials:
- Legos or other building blocks

Preparation: None

Lesson: Thomas Becket was the son of a London merchant. When he was a boy, he was said to be prideful, vain and arrogant. Later in life, however, he became one of the most virtuous and committed archbishops of the 12th century.

Although Thomas was a mere merchant's son, he developed an unlikely friendship with a boy named Henry, who later became King Henry II of England. The boys were best friends. They were so close that people often said that they had 'but one heart and one mind.'

Henry became King of England when he was 21 years old. As soon as that happened, he made Thomas his Chancellor. The Chancellor was the second-highest non-royal subject in the land after the Archbishop of Canterbury. Both men worked tirelessly to bring justice and order to Henry's kingdom. It was during this time that 'trial by jury' became a regular practice. The king had judges travel throughout the land helping to ensure that the common law was followed by the people.

The common law was followed by all lay people; however, the church had its own courts and laws. Priests who broke a common law such as murdering or raping could avoid the punishment of the secular court by claiming 'benefit of clergy,' which allowed them to be tried by a high church official instead. Rather than receiving the death penalty or imprisonment, the bishop's harshest sentence involved either administering a severe penance or being expelled from the priesthood.

Unfortunately, during the Middle Ages there were some church leaders who exploited their privileges and committed crimes without punishment. Even though they swore loyalty to the king, and they also insisted that their highest allegiance was to God, they committed some terrible crimes. If their highest loyalty was to God, do you think they would have committed these crimes in the first place?

Even though most church leaders were godly men, the crimes of the few corrupt ones made Henry very angry. When the Archbishop of Canterbury died in 1161, Henry saw his chance to make changes in the church. He appointed his best friend, Thomas, to the post.

When Thomas became the Archbishop of Canterbury, however, his entire outlook on life changed. He had a deep religious conversion, causing him to completely change his life. He began to wear sackcloth. He also deprived himself by eating a sparse diet and drinking only water.

King Henry and Thomas Becket were still good friends; however, they no longer agreed about clerical privilege. Thomas began to take the side of the church in the matter. This made Henry very upset. In 1164, the two friends had a huge quarrel. Angry words were exchanged and Thomas ended up fleeing to France.

Thomas spent six years exiled in France before things calmed down enough for him to return to his post in Canterbury. In 1170, Thomas preached a sermon on Christmas Day in which he had an angry outburst at the pulpit and ended up excommunicating some fellow bishops.

When Henry learned about this, he is said to have uttered the words, "Will no one rid me of this turbulent priest!"

Unfortunately, Henry's words were heard by four of his knights. They took Henry's frustrated words as a summons to action and left for Canterbury immediately. On December 29th, 1170, the knights found Thomas in Canterbury Cathedral. The four men attacked and butchered the Archbishop. It is recorded that they cracked open his skull.

Henry was horrified when he learned of his best friend's death. He felt Thomas's murder was his own fault. As an act of penance, he put on sackcloth and ashes and fasted for three days. What a sad way for these men's close friendship to end!

Thomas Becket was immediately hailed as a martyr and canonized in 1173. His shrine in Canterbury Cathedral became famous throughout Christendom. It was one of the most visited sites for pilgrims during the Middle Ages.

For this activity, you will be designing and building your own cathedral with Legos or other building blocks. You may decide to make your structure look like Canterbury Cathedral or you may decide to come up with an original design.

Literature

Materials:
- The Adventures of Robin Hood by Roger Lancelyn Green

Preparation: None

Parent Note: Read this book aloud and discuss it with your child.

Week Eight – You are a Monk/Nun
Day One

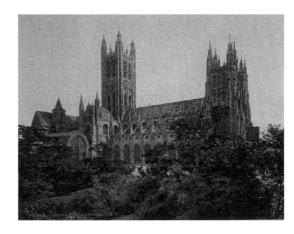

Canterbury Cathedral

Materials: Clip from the supplement section on our website

Preparation: Go to our website and prepare to play the clip designated for this lesson.

Lesson: Canterbury Cathedral has a long and interesting past which begins during the Middle Ages. It is said that Pope Gregory the Great saw some Angle slaves for sale in the marketplace and that he was struck by their beauty. He sent Augustine and a group of monks to England to convert these people to Christianity.

Augustine sailed to England in the year 597AD. When he arrived, he was surprised to find that a local queen, Bertha, was already a Christian. Her husband, King Ethelbert, gave Augustine a church for his use which was called St. Martin of Tours. This church had been built during the Roman occupation of Britain. (That church, seen above, is still in use today.)

Augustine had Canterbury Cathedral built within the Roman city walls of Kent. After the completion of the cathedral, the pope made Augustine the first Archbishop of Canterbury. Since the Middle Ages, there has been a continuous community of believers offering daily prayer to God from Canterbury Cathedral.

The cathedral was badly damaged during Danish raids on Canterbury in 1011. The Archbishop, Alphege, was held hostage by the raiders and eventually killed at Greenwich on April 19, 1012. He was the first of Canterbury's five martyred archbishops.

Canterbury Cathedral was destroyed by fire in 1067, a year after the Norman Conquest. Rebuilding began in 1070 under the first Norman archbishop, Lanfranc. He cleared the ruins and reconstructed the cathedral using stone brought from France.

During the 10th century, the cathedral became home to a formal community of Benedictine monks, which continued until the monastery was dissolved by King Henry VIII in 1540.

There have been many additions to Canterbury Cathedral over the last nine hundred years, but some of the windows and their stained glass date from the 12th century.

Canterbury Cathedral is a beautiful place of worship. For this activity, you will be watching a series of short videos which show the Cathedral in modern times as well as some of the events which take place within its walls.

Exploring the Moon

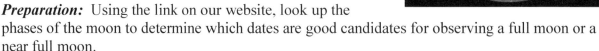

Materials:
- Binoculars
- Paper
- Pencil
- Link to moon calendar on the supplement section of our website
- Link to moon map on the supplement section of our website

Preparation: Using the link on our website, look up the phases of the moon to determine which dates are good candidates for observing a full moon or a near full moon.

Lesson:
1. Choose a clear night with a full or nearly full moon.
2. Set up chairs or a blanket so that you and your children can comfortably view the moon.
3. Use binoculars to look closely at the moon. What features do you observe?
4. Count the number of large craters that you see? Can you see any small craters? Count those as well.
5. You should be able to spot the Tycho crater near the southern pole and Copernicus crater near the equator and slightly west of center. Both of these craters have long, radiating lines which you should be able to see through your binoculars. These rays were caused by material being flung out when the crater was created by a meteor impact.
6. Look for the flat plains called "seas." These seas don't hold water, by the way. The three most visible seas (or maria, as they are often called) are the Sea of Showers near the northern pole, the Sea of Serenity near the equator and to the east, and the Sea of Tranquility, just south of the Sea of Serenity.
7. Draw your own moon map. Start with a large circle. Next, fill in all the craters and seas that you observe.
8. Label the larger features. Use the link on our website or other Moon Maps found on the internet to check your work.

Reading

Parent Note: The read aloud suggestions are intended for you to read to your child. The individual reading suggestions are intended for your child to read aloud to you – or to read on their own. Continue reading each selection throughout the monk/nun weeks until you are finished.

Read Aloud For Younger Children:
Summer Birds: The Butterflies of Maria Merian by Margarita Engle

Read Aloud For Older Children:
Cathedral: The Story of its Construction by David MacCauley

Individual Reading for Grades 2-4:
The Big Book of Knights, Nobles and Knaves illustrated by Adria Fruitos

Individual Reading for Older Children:
Crispin: The Cross of Lead by Avi

Baked Pears

During the Middle Ages, baked pears were thought to have medicinal properties. They were one of the foods often given to sick people during this time period. Feasts also often ended with baked pears as a dessert. Try this recipe and see if you and your family also enjoy them. ☺

Ingredients:
- Pears, cored
- Cinnamon & sugar to taste (optional)

Directions:
1. Place whole, cored fruit in a baking dish or pan. You may also peel them if you desire.
2. Bake at 400° F until the fruit has completely turned a deep brown, about 30 to 45 minutes. *You may choose instead to microwave your pears on HIGH for 6-8 minutes.*
3. ***NOTE:*** In medieval times, they were served plain – but you may want to top yours with cinnamon and sugar before baking.

Marbles

Materials:
- Marbles

Preparation: None

Lesson: As we've learned before, children in the Middle Ages didn't have many toys. One toy that boys sometimes were able to obtain, however, were marbles. Try some of these various marble games and see which ones you enjoy the most.

Bun Hole - A one-foot wide hole is dug in the center of the playing field. Players attempt to get a marble as close as possible to the hole without going in. Whoever's marble comes closest without going in wins a marble from each player. Knocking in your opponent's marble is permitted.

Castles - Each player makes a small pyramid of four of his marbles, three as a base with one on top. Players take turns shooting at these pyramids and they are allowed to keep any marbles they knock out of position.

Conqueror – The first player shoots a marble away from the line of play. The second player shoots at the first player's marble. If he hits it, he keeps both marbles and shoots a new marble to restart the game. If he misses, his marble remains where it stops. Subsequent players may shoot for any marble out on the playing field. If multiple marbles are hit in a chain reaction, the player may keep all of marbles which are struck.

Dobblers - Each player contributes one or more marbles to start the game. The marbles are arranged in a straight line, each marble being exactly twice the width of a marble away from the marbles on either side. Each player then shoots in turn and may keep any marbles he hits. In some variations, a successful hit entitles the shooter to another turn. The player's marble remains where it lies at the end of his turn and subsequent turns are played from where the marble lies. A player whose marble is hit by another marble must add one marble to the line to 'buy back' his shooter.

Week Eight – You are a Monk/Nun
Day Two

The Crusades

Materials: None

Preparation: None

Lesson: The Crusades were a series of battles which took place during the Middle Ages. The majority of the battles were an attempt to regain control of the city of Jerusalem. Jerusalem is a holy city to three different religious groups. Christians revere Jerusalem because it is the place where Jesus was crucified and ascended to heaven. Muslims look up to Jerusalem because it is the place where Muhammad was said to have ascend to heaven. Jews love Jerusalem because it is the site of Solomon's temple and the place where God told them to worship Him.

In the year 600 AD, Muslim Arabs entered Jerusalem and took control away from the Jewish people. For about 400 years, the Arabs allowed Christian and Jewish pilgrims to visit Jerusalem. They even allowed them to live in Jerusalem if they paid their taxes like the rest of the inhabitants.

The problem began around 1095, when a different set of Arabs took control of Jerusalem. They were Islamic Fatimids and they decided to stop allowing Jews and Christians access to the city. When this happened, Pope Urban strongly urged the people to form an army whose goal was to retake control of Jerusalem. The Pope told people that if they died while fighting a holy crusade, they would automatically be welcomed into heaven. About 30,000 men from Europe volunteered for this quest. People were so enthusiastic about this crusade that even children and elderly people wanted to go!

Several of these passionate people set out for Jerusalem before the main army was organized. They believed that God was going to knock down the walls of Jerusalem for them as soon as they arrived, so they didn't bring any weapons with them. Some of them didn't even bring any money or supplies. Most of these groups found that the traveling and fighting were drastically harder than they had imagined. Many of them died on the way. One group decided it was too hard to get to Jerusalem to fight the Fatimids and instead stopped in Germany to fight the Jews. Thousands of Jews were robbed and killed by these Crusaders, just because they were not Christians. Isn't that sad?

While this was going on, the main army continued to organize. Each crusader was given a red cross to wear on their shirt or armor. The red cross was also added to their flags and banners. This helped to unify the army and to remind the men of the holy purpose of their quest.

The journey was hard for the main army as well. They also battled hunger, disease, and freezing weather for about two years in their effort to reach Jerusalem. When they finally arrived, they created a siege around the city which lasted about two months. This caused the Muslims to fall and allowed the crusaders to retake control of Jerusalem.

Less than fifty years after the first crusade, the Muslims returned to again retake Jerusalem. The Pope again called for a crusade to take back control. The Second Crusade lasted from 1147 to 1149 and was unsuccessful. Most of the soldiers were killed as they marched through Turkey. They attacked Damascus and were defeated. The soldiers who remained alive marched home in disgust.

The Third Crusade lasted from 1189 to 1192 and was also unsuccessful. This is the Crusade in which Richard the Lionhearted, the King of England, participated. In fact, the kings of England, France, and Germany all marched to war during this crusade. The German king drowned taking a bath while on the journey to Jerusalem. When this happened, most of the German soldiers marched home. The English and French kings continued on their quest and they did have some success. After defeating the city of Acre and taking 2,700 men prisoner, the French king decided he'd had enough and took his army home. Richard demanded a ransom for the prisoners he had taken. When it wasn't paid by the deadline he had given, he killed the prisoners. Richard's army was unable to defeat the Muslims on his own, so he struck a peace treaty with them instead. Christian pilgrims were again allowed to travel to Jerusalem. Richard returned home to find that the French king had been attacking his possessions in France while he was away.

The Fourth Crusade is when things began to get really complicated and ugly. The crusaders decided to try to attack the Muslims from a different route. Instead of going over land and coming down from the north, they decided to sail to Egypt and come up from the south. In order to have enough boats to get all of their soldiers to Egypt, they needed help from Venice, which was a great sea power. They didn't have enough money to buy the boats, so instead they promised to fight to get back the city of Zara, which had gone to the control of Hungary. Zara was a Christian city; but, this didn't stop the crusaders. When Pope Innocent found out that they had taken control of Zara he excommunicated them.

The crusaders continued on their quest. At this time, they were very low on funds. Alexius Comnenus stepped up to help them. He had been the ruler of Constantinople but had recently been thrown out of the city. He promised the crusaders that if they helped him to regain his throne, he would pay for the rest of the Crusade. They agreed. The crusaders attacked Constantinople and put Alexius back on the throne. They also burned churches and libraries and took valuables such as jewelry, paintings and statues from the people. The crusaders never made it to Jerusalem. They took their loot and instead of using it to fund their quest, they went home.

Amazingly, this wasn't the end. In the year 1212, something called the Children's Crusade occurred. Many thousands of children from France and Germany decided to march to Jerusalem to attack the Muslims. They thought that God would help them with their quest because they were children. Many of them died of hunger or froze to death on their march. When they reached the Mediterranean Sea, they thought that God would part the waters and allow them to pass on dry ground as he had for the Israelites when they escaped from Egypt. When this didn't happen, the children who survived turned around and headed home in defeat.

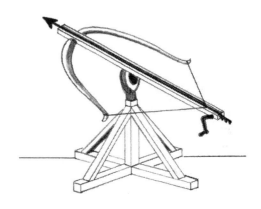

Over the next seventy years, there were several other crusade attempts. At this point, the crusaders were motivated by personal gain and not by any religious purpose. By 1291, European leaders lost interest in the quest to retake Jerusalem. They never admitted defeat, however. They just stopped calling for more crusades.

This was a very complicated time in history. What started as a desire to free a holy city became an excuse to gain riches instead. There is much more to the story of the crusades. If you are interested, you should read some books which can give you many more details about the events which occurred during the crusades.

Literature

Materials:
- The Adventures of Robin Hood by Roger Lancelyn Green

Preparation: None

Parent Note: Read this book aloud and discuss it with your child.

Learn to Draw a Church Bell

Materials:
- Paper
- Pencil with an eraser
- A black marker (optional)
- Colored pencils or crayons (optional)

Preparation: None

Lesson: In this lesson, you will learn to draw a church bell step-by-step.

1. First, draw a half ellipse and then two lines down to make the top of the bell. Next, draw flat oval for the bell opening. Draw an oval with two lines on top for the clapper as shown.

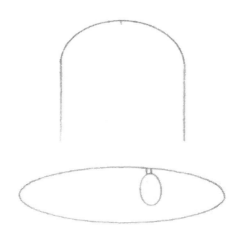

2. Draw two curves to connect the top and the bottom of the bell.

3. Draw a half ellipse on top of the bell. Draw a vertical rectangle on top of the ellipse. Then draw two shapes that look like curvy sevens on either side of the rectangle.

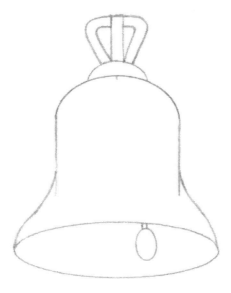

4. Add a few curve details lines as you see below. You may now use the black marker to trace all of the lines you are keeping. Lastly, erase your construction lines. Your church bell should look something like the one below. You may then use the colored pencils or crayons to add color to your drawing if you would like. Great job!

Different Perspectives

Materials:
- Camera (preferably a digital one)
- Printer (optional – makes it easier to print your child's photos but isn't required)

Preparation: None

Lesson: One of the easiest ways to add interest to your photos is to take them from different perspectives. If you take a picture of something which is low to the ground, such as flowers, by standing up and pointing your camera down at the flowers, you will end up with a photo that looks exactly like most other pictures of flowers that you've seen. If you lie on the ground and point your camera straight at or even up at the flowers, you will end up with an exceptional and unique photo.

Another unique way to take photos is to take them at an angle. Be sure that if you do this, you do it in such a way that it looks like you've done it on purpose and not accidentally. You can take pictures of objects or people at an angle.

A third way to show a different perspective on your subject is to zoom in so far that you only have part of the object in the frame. Instead of taking a photo of your brother's entire face, try taking a photo of just his eyes or mouth. Instead of taking a photo of a group of friends, take a photo of just their legs or feet.

For this lesson, try taking several photos which are from a different perspective than you normally take them. You may want to include a few of your better photos in your journal.

Leeches

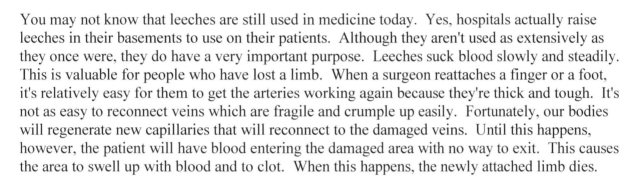

Materials:

- Small container for collecting a water sample
- Microscope or magnifying glass

Preparation: None

Lesson: You might know that leeches have been used in medicine for over 2,500 years. Doctors used to use them often because they thought that most diseases were caused by the patient having too much blood. They were even used for tonsillitis. Can you imagine having a doctor put a leech in your throat?

You may not know that leeches are still used in medicine today. Yes, hospitals actually raise leeches in their basements to use on their patients. Although they aren't used as extensively as they once were, they do have a very important purpose. Leeches suck blood slowly and steadily. This is valuable for people who have lost a limb. When a surgeon reattaches a finger or a foot, it's relatively easy for them to get the arteries working again because they're thick and tough. It's not as easy to reconnect veins which are fragile and crumple up easily. Fortunately, our bodies will regenerate new capillaries that will reconnect to the damaged veins. Until this happens, however, the patient will have blood entering the damaged area with no way to exit. This causes the area to swell up with blood and to clot. When this happens, the newly attached limb dies.

This is where the leeches come in. After the limb has been reattached, leeches are put on the wound to suck off the excess blood. This gives the body time to regenerate those new blood vessels. Leeches also secrete anticoagulants that prevent the blood from clotting.

Leeches aren't used as often in modern medicine as they once were, but in some circumstances, they're still the best option. They are also very inexpensive. One disadvantage, however, is that when they are full they will unattach themselves and try to hide under a patient's blankets. They've just eaten the equivalent of several months' worth of food and they're ready to take a good, long nap.

Activity: For this activity, go to a swamp or pond and collect a water sample. Bring this sample back home and observe the water using either a microscope or a magnifying glass. If leeches are present at the body of water you visit, you may try to gather a specimen for observation as well. If you are interested in this topic, you may decide to order a leech over the internet to study.

Week Eight – You are a Monk/Nun
Day Three

Nun Numbers

Materials:
- Paper and pencil

Preparation: None

Lesson: Nuns also used math to figure out different situations throughout their day. See how well you can solve these problems. The answers are in the companion download.

1. Paula embroidered half as many tapestries as Lilly. Altogether they've embroidered 18 tapestries. How many tapestries did Paula embroider?

2. If you ate a bowl and a half of stew in a day and a half, how many bowls of stew would you eat in seven days?

3. You have blue pants, green pants, a blue shirt, a red shirt, and an orange shirt. How many different combinations of outfits can you make?

4. Four people are equally sharing 48 pennies. How many pennies will each person get?

Exeter Cathedral

Materials:
- Paper and pencil

Preparation: None

Lesson: Exeter Cathedral is considered the finest surviving example of Decorated Gothic, which is a form of architecture that flourished in England from 1270 to 1369. This cathedral has a long history. Before 1050, the main church of Exeter was a Saxon minster dedicated to St. Mary and St. Peter. After that time, the minster became a cathedral when a bishop was placed there to help protect the area from sea raids.

In 1107, William Warelwast, a nephew of William the Conqueror, became the bishop. He decided he wanted a new cathedral built on the site in the Norman style. He began construction in 1112.

Exeter Cathedral was rebuilt in the 13th century as successive bishops decided they wanted to make their cathedral more beautiful and modern. Made entirely of local stone, the new and improved cathedral took less than a century to complete. The Norman towers and some of the nave walls were retained, but the rest was entirely rebuilt in the Decorated Gothic style.

Activity: Gothic architecture is divided into three types: Early English Gothic, Decorated Gothic, and Perpendicular Gothic. For this activity, using any resources available to you, write a paper detailing the differences between these three styles of architecture. Try to find existing buildings which were built in these different styles and include pictures of them in your paper.

Reading

Parent Note: The read aloud suggestions are intended for you to read to your child. The individual reading suggestions are intended for your child to read aloud to you – or to read on their own. Continue reading each selection throughout the monk/nun weeks until you are finished.

Read Aloud For Younger Children:
A Year in a Castle by Rachel Coombs

Read Aloud For Older Children:
Cathedral: The Story of its Construction by David MacCauley

Individual Reading for Grades 2-4:
The Big Book of Knights, Nobles and Knaves illustrated by Adria Fruitos

Individual Reading for Older Children:
Crispin: The Cross of Lead by Avi

Make Your Own Church Bell

Materials:
- Clay or terracotta pot about 5" in diameter
- Clay or terracotta pot which is very small (to use as the clapper)
- 2 large wooden beads (larger than the hole in the bottom of your pots)
- Decorative cord or string
- Paint
- Other embellishments as desired

Preparation: None

Lesson:
1. Decorate the outside of the larger pot with paint as desired. After the paint has dried, you may use any embellishments you desire to further decorate your bell.
2. Cut the cord two feet long.
3. Fold the end over 3 inches and tie in a knot, making a loop. This loop is for hanging the bell from a hook or a nail.
4. Now turn the larger clay pot upside-down. Pass the loose end of the cord down through the hole in the pot.
5. Lay the pot on its side and slide one of the large wooden beads up the cord until it is about 10 inches from the loose end.
6. Now tie the cord around the bead so that the bead cannot slip from its position on the cord. If you have done this correctly, you can lift the pot by the loop.
7. On the loose end of the cord, you are going to attach the small pot in the same way. Slide the small pot up the cord to make it easier to tie the other large wooden bead on the end of the cord.
8. Now when you lift the entire arrangement by the loop, the smaller pot should hang freely inside the larger pot, making a pleasant sound when it claps against the larger pot.
9. Hang your bell in a place where you can enjoy the sound as it sways in the wind.

Odds and Evens

Materials:
- Several buttons, marbles, pennies, or other small objects

Preparation: None

Parent Note: This traditional English game can be quite fun. To play, one child holds a small number of objects in his hands and the other child has to guess whether the total is odd or even. A correct guess wins a token. A wrong guess loses one.

A similar game is called "Eggs in the Bush." In this game, one player holds a number of marbles in one hand and the other players have to guess the number of marbles. Those who guess correctly are paid that number of marbles. Those who guess incorrectly must pay the holder the difference between the number guessed and the number actually held. Players take turns holding marbles.

Week Eight – You are a Monk/Nun
Day Four

The Medieval Stone Mason

Materials: None

Preparation: None

Lesson: The medieval mason was a highly skilled craftsman who was instrumental in building the medieval castles and cathedrals which are still standing today. The actual job of a mason was to shape squared blocks of masonry. These blocks were used for building purposes. Because the Master Mason was in charge of the entire building project, however, masons needed to be able to do many things other than just shaping stones. A mason needed to be part architect, part builder, part craftsman, part designer and part engineer. Using simple tools such as a compass, a set square and a staff or rope marked off in halves, thirds and fifths, the mason was able to construct some of the most amazing structures ever built. Masons had to have a good understanding of proportion and basic geometry to be able to make their beautiful creations. See, math actually is a useful school subject!

Most of the actual construction of these buildings was done during the spring and summer months. This allowed the mortar to set and the laid stones to settle over the winter. Taking a break during the winter also gave the masons a chance to carve more stones which they would use the following summer.

Masons were highly skilled craftsmen. Just like other tradesmen we learned about previously, they also belonged to a guild. Unlike the other tradesmen we learned about, a mason's guild was

202

not linked to just one town. Their guilds were international because members of the mason's guild didn't stay in one place. They were required to move to wherever building was required.

Because masons needed to go wherever their jobs took them, they tended to lead nomadic lives. Other tradesmen could live their entire life in one village as there was usually enough business for their skill to allow them to settle. However, masons had to move on to their next source of employment once a building had been completed - and that could be many miles away.

A mason who was at the top of his trade was called a Master Mason. He had other masons working for him. A Master Mason also had charge over carpenters, glaziers etc. In fact, everybody who worked on a building site was under the supervision of the Master Mason. He worked in what was known as the Mason's Lodge. All important building sites had such a building that served as a workshop and a drawing office from which all the work on the building site was organized.

Many masons had an apprentice working for them. When the mason moved on to a new job, the apprentice moved with him. When a mason felt that his apprentice had learned enough about the trade to go out on his own, he had him examined at a Mason's Lodge. If the apprentice passed this examination of his skill, he was admitted to that lodge as a Master Mason and given a mason's mark that was unique to him. Once given this mark, the new Master Mason put it on any work that he did so that it could be identified as his work.

The free masons were responsible for squaring off the blocks of masonry for the cathedrals and other building projects. These masons were some of the most important workers on the site. They made the blocks and laid the more difficult stretches of wall while most of the building was done by the rough masons. In early Norman times, all masons used a tool similar to the modern fireman's axe for shaping stone. Over time, however, the free masons began using a chisel and mallet for most jobs.

Masons spent a lot of time perfecting their craft. Each stone was made as perfect as possible - even the parts that only God could see. It was a matter of pride for them to present their finest work when erecting these majestic cathedrals.

Quiz Bowl

Parent Note: See how well you and your children can answer questions about the material that has been covered concerning monks and nuns.

1. When a person became a monk or nun, what did two things did they need to do? (Gave up all of their possessions and took a vow to remain poor all of their life)

2. What was the name of the book which guided monks and nuns on how to live? (The Book of Hours)

3. Did monks and nuns do any duties other than worship God all day long? (Yes, many!)

4. During the Middle Ages, what language did most of the priests use for conducting mass? (Latin)

5. Were most people able to read the Bible during the Middle Ages? (No)

6. Since people didn't understand Latin and they couldn't read the Bible, what did priests do to teach Biblical principles to them? (They created Miracle Plays or Mystery Plays)

7. Where were most people educated during the Middle Ages? (At home)

8. For people who attended school outside of the home, where were most of them educated? (In monasteries and churches)

9. Name at least three of the school subjects which were taught during this time. (Latin, grammar, rhetoric, logic, astronomy, philosophy and mathematics)

10. Were girls allowed to receive an education during medieval times? (They weren't allowed to attend school but noble women were often educated at home by their parents or with a tutor.)

11. In the Middle Ages, how old were boys when they attended university? (14 or 15)

12. For which careers did university classes train boys? (Clergy and doctors)

13. What city were the majority of the crusades an attempt to recapture? (Jerusalem)

14. What did the pope tell people would happen to them if they died while fighting in the crusades? (They would automatically be welcomed into Heaven.)

15. Were any of the crusades successful? (Not completely. Jerusalem was retaken for a time - but not permanently. And the crusaders' initial religious motivation turned into a desire for riches.)

16. Did it require much skill to be a medieval stone mason? (Yes! They were responsible for building many of the beautiful cathedrals which are still standing today.)

17. During which seasons did the masons work to build cathedrals? (Spring and summer)

18. What did they do during the winter months? (They carved more stones which they would be able to use on the next summer's buildings)

19. What types of tools did a mason use for shaping stones? (In early medieval times they used an axe. Later on, they switched to a chisel and mallet.)

20. What was the title of the man who was in charge of the entire building site? (The Master Mason)

Literature

Materials:
- The Adventures of Robin Hood by Roger Lancelyn Green

Preparation: None

Parent Note: Read this book aloud and discuss it with your child.

Write in Your Journal

Materials:
- Your child's journal
- Paper
- Pencil, colored pencils, markers, etc.

Preparation: None

Parent Note: Have your child write down a few key points about what they learned about medieval masons. Depending on their age and ability, you can require your child to write one sentence or several paragraphs. You can also let them narrate back to you what they have learned. Then, have them draw a picture or print pictures from the internet to add some more insight to their journal page.

Possible Writing Prompt: Write a journal entry as if you were a medieval mason who has been working on building a cathedral for his entire lifetime. Talk about how you feel knowing that you will never see the completion of the job during your lifetime.

Field Trip to See a Cathedral

Parent Note: This week is a great time to visit a cathedral. If you do a Google search, you should be able to find several Catholic Cathedrals in your area. You may want to call ahead to see if any of them offer architectural or historical tours.

There are also many virtual tours of cathedrals on the internet. These contain some interesting information; but, they won't be as impactful as if you take your child to an actual cathedral. If you happen to live next to an old monastery, nunnery, or abbey, touring one of these is even better! While on the tour, be sure to ask your child questions so that they can compare their experience with what they have learned so far about the life of a monk or nun. And have your child take lots of pictures for their journal.

Week Eight – You are a Monk/Nun
Day Five

Medieval Sundials

Materials:
- Foam or paper plate
- Plastic knife
- Lump of clay or Play-doh
- Small piece of cardboard
- Scissors
- Timer or clock with alarm
- A paperclip

Preparation: None

Lesson: From early Saxon times until the Renaissance, churches alone kept time in most towns and villages throughout Great Britain. Medieval sundials were once commonly found on the walls of churches throughout the country. Some of the earliest examples of sundials were crudely scratched into the wall of the church. These were most likely created by individual priests. There are, however, some fine examples of sundials which were carved by stone masons.

People were able to use sundials to tell time because of the way the earth rotates on its axis. You can see how this works by shining a flashlight on a globe. Spin the globe on its axis and you will see how the "sun" shines on different parts of the earth at different times. Spin the globe slowly and notice that while the "sun" is rising on one continent, it is setting on the previous one. For this lesson, you will be making your own sundial. This lesson needs to be done on a sunny day.

Activity:
1. Give each child a plate and the lump of clay. Have them make a ball with the clay and then flatten it out to make a disc which covers their entire plate.
2. Give each child the cardboard and ask them to cut out a right triangle. The length of the bottom should be ¼" shorter than the radius of your sundial (the length from the edge to the center.)
3. Have your child press one edge of their triangle onto the clay in the center of their plate. The point with the smallest angle should be touching the very center of the disc.
4. Go outside and have your child choose a sunny spot in which to place their sundial.
5. Now it's time to calibrate your sundial. Every hour on the hour, have your child go outside with the knife and press a deep line into the clay where the shadow falls.
6. Using an open paper clip, have your child etch the time of day next to the line.
7. You can continue marking the hours on your sundial until the sun goes down.
8. Leave your sundial undisturbed overnight.
9. The next day, go outside again every hour on the hour to see if your sundial tells you the correct time.

Make Your Own Quill Pen

Materials:
- 1 Quill per child (goose, swan or turkey are best)
- A knife
- A block of wood just slightly larger than the quill

Preparation: If your feathers are fresh, you will need to hollow out their tips before shaping them. This will allow you to remove all oil or fatty tissue from the quill. You will also need to dry the quill. You can do this by sticking the end in hot sand for a few minutes. Most craft stores carry quills which are ready to use without needing to do this step.

Lesson: We've already learned that many people during Medieval Times didn't know how to read or write. For those who did write, however, they used pens made from feathers versus the modern pen and pencils that we use today. These pens were called quill pens. Today, you will be making your own quill pen.

1. Follow the pictures below for cutting the end of your quill into the proper shape. You will be using the block of wood as a cutting block to make forming the quill easier.
2. When you are finished, the tip of your quill should look like the 8th shape below. It is now ready for you to use.

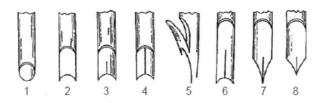

208

Writing with Your Quill Pen

Materials:
- Quill pen from above activity
- Pen or pencil (whichever your child prefers using)
- Washable ink
- Paper towels for blotting and cleanup
- Writing paper
- Small, disposable cup
- Smock to protect your child's clothing
- A timer or clock

Preparation: None

Lesson:
1. Write the alphabet using a modern day pen or pencil. Have someone time you.
2. Pour some of the washable ink into a small cup.
3. Watch your parent demonstrate how to use the quill pen (dipping the tip in the ink, tapping off the extra, and writing on the paper.)
4. Have paper towel ready to blot out any splotches you might make.
5. Write the alphabet again using the quill pen. Have someone time you again.

Parent Note: Discuss the differences in their times. Talk about how improvements in technology have helped writing to become easier. Allow your child to continue writing or drawing with their quill pen as desired. Put a sample of their writing in their journal.

Reading

Parent Note: The read aloud suggestions are intended for you to read to your child. The individual reading suggestions are intended for your child to read aloud to you – or to read on their own. Continue reading each selection throughout the monk/nun weeks until you are finished.

Read Aloud For Younger Children:
See Inside Castles by Laura Parker

Read Aloud For Older Children:
Cathedral: The Story of its Construction by David MacCauley

Individual Reading for Grades 2-4:
The Big Book of Knights, Nobles and Knaves illustrated by Adria Fruitos

Individual Reading for Older Children:
Crispin: The Cross of Lead by Avi

Medieval Adventure, Scene Four

Materials:
- Script from companion download
- Monk and nun clothes which were made/gathered in a previous lesson
- Whatever other props you create during your lessons and/or have laying around the house to add excitement to this adventure.

Preparation:
1. Photocopy the script so that each actor has their own copy.
2. Read through the script a few times so that you know what to expect and can help to direct the kids.

Parent Note: Choose roles for yourself and your children. Remember, the more dramatic you act the more your kids will as well – and the more value they will gain from this assignment. If you are planning to videotape the play, you may want to do it while on your field trip to the cathedral so that the background looks right. ☺

Activity Suggestions for Further Learning and Fun

Below is a list of further suggestions which have not been incorporated into the two weeks of learning that you may also want to try. The more you immerse your child in these types of activities, the more they will learn and enjoy this experience. ***Warning:*** You child will probably most enjoy some of the suggestions are the messiest or the most out of the ordinary! ☺

Lifestyle
- For one day, pray as often as a medieval monk or nun: midnight, 3am, 6am, 9am, noon, 6pm, and 9pm
- Observe silence from 9pm until midnight (or a different 4 hour block of time depending on the age of the child)
- Sort through your toys and give some away to charity
- Give your favorite toy to someone less fortunate

Livelihood
- Volunteer to work in a soup kitchen or homeless shelter
- Visit someone in the hospital
- Practice hospitality by invite a guest to your home
- Create illustrations for one of your favorite books
- Work to earn money – give the money to charity

You are a Baron

in Medieval England

Table of Contents for Baron/Baroness Weeks

Week Nine – You are a Baron/Baroness
Day One

Daily Life of a Baron or Baroness

Materials: None

Preparation: None

Lesson: We learned previously how Medieval England was run as a feudal system. One of the higher positions in that system was that of baron. This week, you will be imagining that you are either a baron or the wife of a baron called a baroness.

A baron is a man who has been given the opportunity to lease land from the king. The section of land he was given was called a manor. The baron was called the Lord of the Manor and he had complete control over his land. He was allowed to create his own laws, mint his own money, and set his own tax rates.

In return for being allowed to rule over his manor, the baron was expected to serve on the royal council, pay rent, and send knights for military service whenever the king asked for them. Barons were also required to provide food and lodging for the king and his court whenever they traveled around the country. This could be extremely expensive as the king traveled with quite a large entourage!

Barons were very rich men. They kept as much of the land as they wished for their own use and divided the rest up among their knights. Like the other people we've learned about in previous weeks, however, their lives were still filled with much activity throughout the day.

Barons and baronesses woke up at dawn. The first thing they did was to hear mass and to say their prayers. Then they had breakfast between 6am and 7am. Breakfast for a lord and lady was a casual event. It might have included white bread, three meat dishes, and three fish dishes. They usually had wine or ale to drink with their meal.

After breakfast, a baron attended to business matters related to his manor. He collected rent money and taxes. He spent time settling legal disputes between the peasants who lived on his land. Much time was also spent having political discussions, listening to complaints from tenants, and other such types of activities. Barons also made it a point to spend some time practicing with various weapons to keep their fighting skills sharp.

Then he had dinner and midday prayers. This meal was eaten between 11am and 2pm. A baron usually had three courses with this meal but each course contained four to six different types of food. The food usually included various meats, fish, wine and ale. This was a tremendous amount of food and it is likely that only small parts of each dish were actually eaten. Quite a lot of this food was thrown away – although the baron's servants salvaged some of this food for themselves if the baron wasn't paying attention.

In the afternoon, the baron turned to activities such as hunting, hawking, or inspecting his estate. Evening prayer and supper took place between 6pm and 7pm. This meal was similar to the midday meal; however, it also included some slightly more unusual dishes such as pigeon pie, woodcock, and sturgeon. Again, wine and ale were available at this meal.

After supper, there was frequently entertainment. Minstrels, troubadours, and jesters entertained the people who lived at the manor with music, dancing, juggling, acrobatics, and jokes. When the baron was ready to retire for the evening, the rest of the manor retired as well. Bedtime prayers were the last thing the baron or baroness did before they went to sleep for the night.

For the next two weeks you will pretend to be a baron or a baroness living in medieval England. You will get to experience some of the responsibilities and pleasures that a baron or a baroness experienced. As you complete these activities and go about your day, try to imagine what it would have been like to do these things all day, every day of your life.

Literature

Materials:
- <u>The Canterbury Tales</u> by Geoffrey Chaucer (retold by Geraldine McCaughrean)

Preparation: None

Parent Note: Read this book aloud and discuss it with your child.

NOTE: The Canterbury Tales are extremely funny. There are a few tales which are a bit bawdy in nature. This adaptation is cleans them up considerably; however, you may want to read them in advance if you have younger children or are concerned about content. I think that Geraldine does a good job of making these classic tales suitable for children. Reading these tales will definitely educate your family about what it was like to be on a pilgrimage during medieval times.

Write in Your Journal

Materials:
- Your child's journal
- Paper
- Pencil, colored pencils, markers, etc.

Preparation: None

Parent Note: Have your child write down a few key points about what they learned about the daily life of a baron or baroness. Depending on their age and ability, you can require your child to write one sentence or several paragraphs. You can also let them narrate back to you what they have learned. Then, have them draw a picture or print pictures from the internet to add some more insight to their journal page.

Possible Writing Prompt: Imagine you are a powerful baron. Write a journal entry at the end of a long, hard day. Describe the various tasks you had to perform. How does it feel to have so much power over so many people? Does it feel invigorating? Is it exhausting?

Medieval Music

Materials: Clip from the supplement section on our website

Preparation: Go to our website and prepare to play the clip designated for this lesson.

Lesson: As we learned about in a previous week, music was important to people during medieval times. It was used during festivals as well as during daily life. For this lesson, you will be able to listen to and gain an appreciation of a variety of medieval songs.

Creating a Baron or Baroness Costume

Materials for Baron Costumes (Pick and choose as desired):

- A red, blue, brown or black shirt made of velvet, silk, cotton, taffeta or satin damask. These fabrics were considered luxurious and were suitable for the rank of baron.
- Clothes could be trimmed with any fur but sable, which was reserved for royalty
- Barons also wore tights or leggings.
- A hood with a wide collar which covered the shoulders, back and chest.
- Pointed shoes.
- A pouch to be used as a coin purse.

Materials for Baroness Costumes (Pick and choose as desired):

- Long, trailing dress with puffy sleeves in red, blue, brown or black. Velvet, silk, cotton, taffeta, or satin damask were appropriate materials for a baroness.
- A cloak.
- Pointed Shoes.
- An elaborate headdress or braided hair.
- A hood with a wide collar which covered the shoulders, back and chest.
- A broach to hold the cloak or collar in place.

Parent Note: For this activity, we are going to create an outfit to wear while acting in the drama as well as while completing their other lessons if your child so desires.

You can make this activity as simple or as elaborate as you and your children would enjoy. There are many sites on the internet which give you ideas on sewing medieval costumes. We are going to show you simple ways in which you can gather costumes – but you are welcome to take the time to make more elaborate costumes if that is something which interests you.

An easy and inexpensive way to gather the clothing items we recommend is to check out secondhand stores and garage sales. Feel free to improvise! The most important thing is that your child feels the part – not that they are completely authentic.

Week Nine – You are a Baron/Baroness
Day Two

Hadrian's Wall

Materials:
- Paper and pencil
- Internet or library

Preparation: None

Lesson: When Rome occupied England, they knew that they were quite a distance from their home base and that it would be hard for them to defend their new conquest from future invaders. Because of this, they decided to build two walls across Great Britain. The first wall was begun in 122 AD and was called Hadrian's Wall since Hadrian was the Roman Emperor at the time. The second wall was called Antonine Wall. Hadrian's Wall is better known today because more of it still exists.

Hadrian's Wall was the most heavily fortified border in the Roman Empire. In addition to its use as a military defense, it is thought that many of the gates in the wall were places where soldiers could impose taxes on travelers. Much of Hadrian's Wall still survives today and can be followed on foot or bicycle.

For this activity, you need to research Hadrian's Wall and write a few paragraphs on the information that you find. You may choose any aspect about the subject which interests you such as modern tourism because of the wall, Roman conquest of Great Britain, or the bike trail which currently follows the wall. You may want to include some internet photos with your paragraphs as well. Be sure to include your completed report in your journal.

Matthew Paris

Materials:
- Paper and pencil

Preparation: None

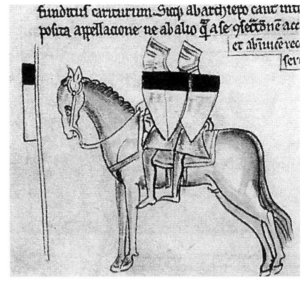

Lesson: Matthew Paris, or Matthew the Parisian, is one of the earliest English artists about whom we know something. Despite his name, he was English. It is thought that he was educated in Paris hence giving him his name.

Matthew was a Benedictine monk who traveled, created sculpture, drew illuminations and wrote books. Some of his books were written in Latin and some were in Anglo-Norman or French. His reputation as a writer and historian grew and important people visited him, no doubt hoping that he would say good things about them in his records. Those who visited him included King Henry III. Even though Henry spent quite a bit of time working with him on his writings, Matthew still disagreed with Henry's policy of appointing foreign advisers and he was often very critical of the king in his books. Writing things in opposition to the king was an extremely dangerous thing to do!

As well as being a talented English writer, Matthew was a gifted English artist, and in the margins of his books he illustrated the text with drawings and paintings. Although he has been criticized for relying too much on rumor and gossip and being prejudiced against foreigners and friars, Matthew Paris is considered to be one of the most important artist/historians of the medieval period. He died in 1259 AD.

Activity: For this activity, you will try to draw an illustration similar to something Matthew Paris might have drawn. You may use the horse or elephant drawings above or a different work you are able to find in a book or on the internet. Depending on your artistic ability, you may want to trace one of Matthew's works instead.

Plan the Manor

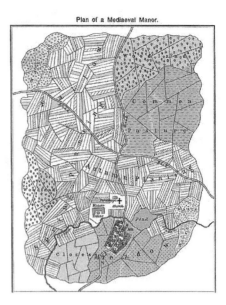

Plan of a Mediaeval Manor.

Materials:
- Graph paper
- Construction paper (use multiple colors that you see in nature – green, brown, tan, yellow, etc.)
- Pencil, pen, or markers
- Glue stick
- Scissors

Preparation:
1. Cut ½ inch strips of construction (this can be done by your child, depending on their ability)

Lesson: Some peasants owned the land on which they worked; but, many of them did not. Much of the land on a manor belonged to the baron or lord. These barons doled out land in small strips to different tenants, or people who worked their land for them. Because much of the farmland was divided into strips, this became known as strip farming.

Activity: Today, you are going to map out the land around your castle for your tenant's crops. Try to map out the manor in a way that will be efficient and will allow many different peasants to live comfortably on the land.
1. Start with a sheet of graph paper and draw a rectangle that is 1" x 2" in the middle. This represents the baron's castle or large manor house.
2. Draw some areas of forest.
3. Draw a pond and a river or two.
4. Draw some pasture land on which your livestock can graze.
5. Draw an area of fallow land, an area where spring planting will take place, and an area where autumn planting will take place.
6. Now lay out the strips of paper that represent the crops of your tenants. (See example above illustration of the plan of a medieval manor for some ideas.)

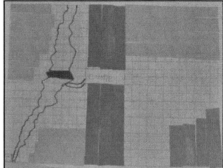

Reading

Parent Note: The read aloud suggestions are intended for you to read to your child. The individual reading suggestions are intended for your child to read aloud to you – or to read on their own. Continue reading each selection throughout the baron/baroness weeks until you are finished.

Read Aloud For Younger Children:
You Wouldn't Want to be a Medieval Knight by Fiona MacDonald

Read Aloud For Older Children:
Shakespeare Can Be Fun: Much Ado About Nothing for Kids by Lois Burdett

Individual Reading for Grades 2-4:
Knight at Dawn (A Magic Treehouse book) by Mary Pope Osborne

Individual Reading for Older Children:
The Book of Three by Lloyd Alexander

Relay Tag

Materials:
- A stick or jump rope to make a start/finish line
- Objects such as a Frisbees or balls to use as batons

Preparation:
- Identify a convenient turnaround point such as a tree or bush.
- Split the children into two teams.
- Choose which team will start.

Lesson: You've probably noticed that medieval children used to play lots of different running games. This was because these types of activities didn't require much equipment and could be played at a moment's notice. Today, you will be playing a game called relay tag.

1. When the first player on team two says "go", the first player from team one should attempt to race from the start line, around the turnaround point, and back across the finish line without being tagged by player one on team two. As soon as he crosses the finish line, player one on team one will pass the baton to player two on team one.
2. Player two on team one will then attempt to race from the start line, around the turnaround point, and back across the finish line without being tagged by player two on team two. As soon as he crosses the finish line, player two on team one will pass the baton to player three on team one.
3. This continues until all members of team one have successfully crossed the finish line.

Week Nine – You are a Baron/Baroness
Day Three

The Peasant's Revolt

Materials: None

Preparation: None

Lesson: Punishment in medieval times was very severe and was usually enough of a deterrent to keep people from causing trouble. There were also soldiers stationed at most of the castles in England. Even with these measures, several revolts took place in medieval England. The most serious of these was called the Peasants' Revolt. It took place in June of 1381.

There were several reasons why the peasants were angry enough to revolt. After the Black Death, many of the baron's were left with a shortage of workers. They relied on peasants to work their land and as you already learned many peasants died from this terrible epidemic. To encourage the peasants to stay on their manor and continue working, many of the barons gave the peasants their freedom and began to pay them to work the land. The peasants started to fear that these new privileges would be taken away and they were prepared to fight to keep them.

The peasants were also angry because they were being forced to work on church land without any pay. Some of them worked for the church up to two days a week! This made it extremely hard for them to be able to support their families with the time that they had left. The peasants decided they were tired of this burden which was contributing to them staying poor.

Another reason the peasants were angry was because of costly taxes. England had been at war with France for a long time, causing King Richard II to create a new tax. This was called the Poll Tax and it was the king's attempt to pay for the war. Peasants were furious about this tax because it was one more burden they didn't feel they could afford. They decided to ignore the king's demands for this additional tax.

In May 1381, a tax collector arrived in Fobbing, Essex to find out why the people hadn't paid their poll tax. The villagers threw him out. In June, soldiers arrived at Fobbing to force the people to pay the tax. They were also thrown out of the village.

By this time, many other villages in Essex had joined the peasants' movement. A large group of villagers marched from Kent and Essex to London to plead their case to the king. One man emerged as the leader of the peasants. His name was Wat Tyler. As the peasants marched to London, they destroyed all tax records and registers along the way. They burned down any buildings they passed which contained government records. The people of London opened the gates and let them into the city. King Richard was only 14 at this time. In spite of his age, he agreed to meet the peasants at a place called Mile End. Can you imagine how scared he must have been?

On June 14th, the king met the peasants at Mile End. At this meeting, Richard II agreed to all of the peasants' demands and asked them to go home peacefully. Some of them did. Others returned to the city and did something which no one had ever done before. They took over the Tower of London. They also murdered the archbishop and the king's treasurer – they cut off their heads on Tower Hill near the Tower of London. King Richard II spent the night in hiding fearing for his life.

On June 15th, Richard met the peasants again at Smithfield outside of London's walls. This was done to get the rebels out of the city. Most of the buildings in medieval London were wooden and the streets were cramped. Any attempt to put down the rebels in the city could have ended up with a significant part of the city being burned to the ground. It also allowed many of the peasants to vanish and hide within the city.

At this meeting, the peasants' leader, Wat Tyler, was killed. The details of what happened aren't known; but, with the death of Tyler and with Richard promising yet again to give the peasants what they asked for, the peasants headed back home.

By the summer of 1381, the peasants' revolt was over. King Richard did not keep any of his promises claiming that they were made under duress and were therefore not valid under the law. Other leaders from both Kent and Essex were hanged. The poll tax was withdrawn but the peasants were forced back into their old way of life - under the control of the lord of the manor.

Everything didn't go badly for the peasants, however. There was still a shortage of labor and many peasants found that they could earn more money than they had been able to previously because their work was still in high demand. The peasants asked the barons for more money and the lords didn't have any choice other than to give it to them.

Literature

Materials:
- The Canterbury Tales by Geoffrey Chaucer (retold by Geraldine McCaughrean)

Preparation: None

Parent Note: Read this book aloud and discuss it with your child.

NOTE: The Canterbury Tales are extremely funny. There are a few tales which are a bit bawdy in nature. This adaptation is cleans them up considerably; however, you may want to read them in advance if you have younger children or are concerned about content. I think that Geraldine does a good job of making these classic tales suitable for children. Reading these tales will definitely educate your family about what it was like to be on a pilgrimage during medieval times.

Learn to Draw a Horse

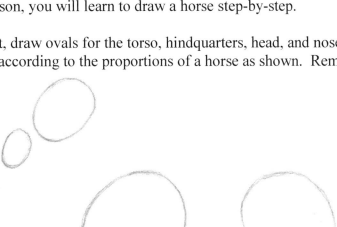

Materials:
- Paper
- Pencil with an eraser
- A black marker (optional)
- Colored pencils or crayons (optional)

Preparation: None

Lesson: In this lesson, you will learn to draw a horse step-by-step.

1. First, draw ovals for the torso, hindquarters, head, and nose. Try to space them out according to the proportions of a horse as shown. Remember to draw lightly!

2.   Next, connect the ovals to make the head, neck, and body of the horse.

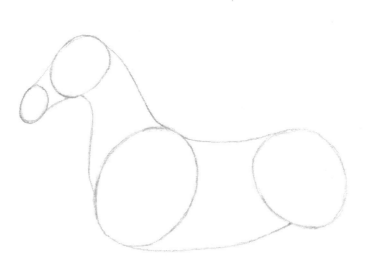

3.   Next, draw the ears, eye, and nostril. Draw the legs and hooves. You'll want to make the legs a tiny bit longer than the thickness of the chest.

4.   Now, trace the lines you are keeping with your black marker. Erase construction lines as shown.

5. Lastly, draw the mane and tail. Now you can add shadows and give your horse the details that will make it look more realistic. You may also use the colored pencils to color in your horse if you'd like. Great job!

Making a Comet

Materials:

- 2 cups of water
- 2 cups dry ice (frozen carbon dioxide)
- 2 spoonfuls of sand or dirt
- A dash of ammonia
- A dash of organic material (dark corn syrup works well)
- An ice chest
- A large mixing bowl (plastic if possible)
- 4 medium-sized plastic garbage bags
- Work gloves
- A hammer, meat pounder, or rubber mallet
- A large mixing spoon
- Paper towels
- Safety goggles

Parent Note: Dry ice is available from ice companies and grocery stores in most cities (look under "ice" in the Yellow Pages for a local source.) Day-old dry ice works best, so you might want to buy it the afternoon before you do the activity. Keep the dry ice in an ice chest when transporting it and in your refrigerator's freezer compartment overnight. Most ice companies have a minimum on the amount of ice they will sell (usually 5 pounds.) Having extra dry ice on hand will be useful, however, because some will evaporate and also because it is advisable to practice this activity at least once before doing it with your child.

Lesson: During the Middle Ages, comets were known as "hairy stars." Symbols of comets were often used on coins during medieval times. They were often represented with crude and irregularly shaped symbols such as combs, bars, pyramids, etc. In 1066, William the Conqueror used his sighting of Halley's Comet that year as his omen for victory over Harold II of England. A comet was also depicted on the Bayeux Tapestry (see the above illustration.)

Did you know that you can make your own comet? The ingredients for a comet are not difficult to find and watching a comet being "constructed" is something that you will remember for a long time.

Activity:
1. Cut open one of the garbage bags and use it to line your mixing bowl.
2. Have all of the ingredients and utensils arranged in front of you.
3. Place the water in the mixing bowl.
4. Add the sand or dirt and stir well.
5. Add a dash of ammonia
6. Add a dash of organic material (e.g. corn syrup.) Stir until well mixed.
7. Place the dry ice inside the remaining 3 garbage bags which have been placed inside each other. ***Be sure to wear gloves while handling dry ice to keep from being burned.***
8. Crush the dry ice by pounding it with the hammer.

9. Add the dry ice to the rest of the ingredients in the mixing bowl while stirring vigorously.
10. Continue stirring until the mixture is almost totally frozen.
11. Lift the comet out of the bowl using the plastic liner and shape it as you would a snowball.
12. Unwrap the comet as soon as it is frozen hard enough to hold its shape.

Now you can place the comet on display for your child to watch during the day as it begins to melt and sublimate or change from a solid to a gas. Your comet will do this as it sits at room temperature. Comets which are in space also do this as they are heated by the sun.

It is best to have a spoon or a stick to use while examining the comet. As it begins to melt, you may notice small jets of gas coming from it. These are coming from areas where the carbon dioxide gas is escaping through small holes in the frozen water. These jets can also be seen on real comets. The jets can sometimes push out enough gas to make small changes in the comet's orbit.

After several hours, the comet will become filled with craters. Each time a real comet passes the sun, it also becomes filled with craters due to all of the escaping gas. Eventually, old comets may break into several pieces or even completely fall apart. In some cases, the comet may have a solid, rocky core that will continue to travel in its same orbit as an asteroid.

Baron Business

Materials:
• Paper and pencil

Preparation: None

Lesson: Barons used math extensively to figure out different situations throughout their day. See how well you can solve these problems. The answers are in the companion download.

1. Ben gave Jen ½ of his acorns. Jen ate half of her acorns and gave the rest to Kyle. Kyle kept 8 of the acorns and gave the last 10 to Kim. How many acorns did Jen eat?

2. It takes 6 bricks to build a staircase with 3 steps. How many bricks would it take to build a staircase with 11 steps?

3. James ate half of a bowl of soup for dinner. The next morning, he ate another 1/3 of the bowl for breakfast. What fraction of the original bowl does he have left for lunch?

4. Jared has 50 marbles in a bag. 20% of the marbles are blue. How many marbles are blue?

Week Nine – You are a Baron/Baroness
Day Four

Choose a Site for Your Village

Materials:
- Colored pencils
- Paper
- Relief map of England from the supplement section on our website
- Map of England detailing waterways from the companion download
- Map of England with castles from the companion download

Preparation: Go to our website and print a copy of each of the maps designated for this lesson.

Lesson: In this activity, you will use several maps to try to logically determine the best place in which to establish a new village. Here are several things you will want consider when choosing your site:

1. It was always a good idea to locate a village near an existing castle. This gave good protection against thieves and attackers.
2. The next best thing to positioning yourself near a castle was to build the new village on high ground. This gave a good view of the surrounding area and gave the villagers a better chance of spotting attackers with as much advance notice as possible. High ground is also easier to defend than are lower positions.
3. An invaluable natural resource is water. Be sure you build your village near some sort of water supply – either a lake, a river, a pond, etc. Remember, in medieval times people had to fetch fresh water daily so you don't want to have it too far away from the village.
4. Wood is another natural resource it was hard to live without. Be sure to choose a building site which will have an abundant supply of wood for constructing the houses, shops, and other necessary buildings in your village. Wood also comes in handy when you're making a fire either for staying warm or for cooking.
5. Be sure there is some open land nearby as well for growing your crops. There are many great locations from which to choose. After you have chosen a location, draw your village site. You may do this by using the actual location you have identified or by making up an ideal location on your own. Be sure to include your drawing in your journal.

Design Your Sword

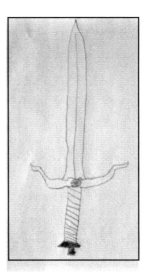

Materials:
- Paper and pencil

Preparation: None

Lesson: Medieval sword smiths were highly skilled tradesmen who required a good understanding of mathematics and proportion. They made different types of swords, depending on their purpose. Some swords were made for thrusting into the gaps in armor. These had a sharp, reinforced point. The edges of these swords may not have been sharp at all. Some swords were made for cutting through flesh, clothing, leather armor, and mail armor.

Swordfights you see in the movies are very different than those which occurred in real life. In the movies, swordfights are intended to help bring more excitement and drama to the movie. They are long, very highly choreographed fights. In real life, sword fights were much shorter, more brutal, and quieter. Swordsmen wouldn't have hit sword upon sword as often as what they do in the movies. That dulled their blades and was avoided.

For this lesson, you will be learning about the different parts of a sword. After learning the part names and functions try designing a sword of your choice. First, decide the use of your sword. Next, draw the sword however you like. Be sure to put a copy of your sketch in your journal.

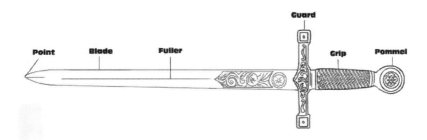

Point - The tip of the sword's blade.

Blade - The section of the sword, which is not part of the hilt.

Fuller - A groove down the center of a blade, used to both lighten a sword, and conserve sword steel (making a wider blade possible with less material). Often, this is mistakenly called a "Blood Groove."

Guard - The section of the sword hilt whose purpose is to protect the wielder's hand. It may take of the shape of a simple bar, a steel basket, a flat disc, or several other forms.

Grip - The part of the hilt held by the user (the handle).

Pommel - A counter-weight at the end of a sword's hilt, used to balance the sword. Also may be used as a striking implement.

Reading

Parent Note: The read aloud suggestions are intended for you to read to your child. The individual reading suggestions are intended for your child to read aloud to you – or to read on their own. Continue reading each selection throughout the baron/baroness weeks until you are finished.

Read Aloud For Younger Children:
You Wouldn't Want to be a Crusader by Fiona MacDonald

Read Aloud For Older Children:
Shakespeare Can Be Fun: Much Ado About Nothing for Kids by Lois Burdett

Individual Reading for Grades 2-4:
Knight at Dawn (A Magic Treehouse book) by Mary Pope Osborne

Individual Reading for Older Children:
The Book of Three by Lloyd Alexander

Pickaback Relay

Materials:
- 2 jump ropes or sticks

Preparation: Use the ropes to form a starting line and a turnaround line.

Lesson: Players should divide into two teams. The lightest person on each team is the "burden." At the starting signal, the first person on each team carries the burden on his back to the turnaround line and back to the start, where the next person takes the burden and repeats the course. The first team to have all players except the burden race the course with the burden on their back wins. If the burden ever touches the ground, the team must start over. If this doesn't sound tough enough, there's an Ancient Egyptian tomb painting which shows children playing this game where the burden has to juggle! Feel free to try doing that as well if you would like. ☺

Rope Making and Braiding

Materials:
- Twine, jute, or sisal yarn
- A pencil

Preparation: None

Lesson: In rope making, there are four basic steps: preparing the fiber, spinning the fibers together to form yarn, twisting the yarn in bunches to form strands, and winding the strands into rope.

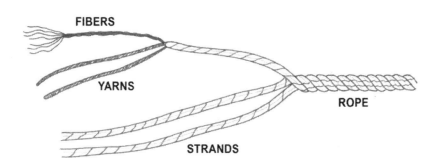

During the Middle Ages, people used to make their own ropes. Rope making was a manual process which was done without the use of tools. It could be done alone, or by two people working together.

Some countries braided their ropes; but, the majority of the people in Europe twisted their ropes. It was one of the daily chores of the children on the farm to make rope. They were used as animal lead ropes, belts, clotheslines and bucket handles. They were used to binding wheat sheaves and to tie herbs, etc.

If two people worked together, one person held the two strands, one of them in his hand and the other tied to his big toe, while his companion standing some distance away twisted them together. If done alone, the rope was clamped onto the open barn door. When children had extra time they also twisted skipping ropes and braided friendship bracelets.

Activity: For this activity, you will be twisting your own rope. If you want to be able to use your rope as a jump rope, you'll want to make it twice as long as the distance from your armpit to the floor.

1. Cut your twine into three pieces a little more than twice the length you want the rope to end up being.
2. Tie off each end of the string with an overhand knot (see picture on the right.)

235

3. Secure one end of each piece of twine to the pencil.
4. Holding the pencil in one hand, stretch the twine with your other hand to be sure that all three threads have equal tension on them
5. Begin spinning the twine clockwise. Keep twisting until you feel the rope start to pull really tight when under moderate tension.
6. Stick your finger right in the middle of the string and bring your end to the secured end, slowly letting rope twist together.
7. Tie an overhand knot securing the ends together so it will not unravel.

After you've created your rope, try using it for something. If you've made it long enough, you can use it to play jump rope if you like.

Week Nine – You are a Baron/Baroness
Day Five

The Magna Carta

Materials: None

Preparation: None

Lesson: As time went on, the kings of England gained more and more power. The people of England didn't mind this fact too much as long as they were being ruled by a good king, such as William the Conqueror or Henry II. But when King Richard died in 1199 and his younger brother John became king, this was no longer the case.

King John was a tyrannical king who didn't care about his country as much as he did about himself. The first thing he did that upset people is he lost almost all of the land in France which had been controlled by England. This made his country much weaker than it had been. Then, he made everyone who owned land in England pay extra taxes which upset the people even more. He also got into fights with the Pope about who should control the Catholic Church in England. King John's fight with the Pope got so bad that the Pope excommunicated him at one point.

Because they felt that King John was out of control, a group of earls, dukes, and counts decided to try to get back some of the power from the king. In 1215, they wrote a letter saying that everyone in England must have certain rights that the king shouldn't have the power to take away from them anymore. They insisted that even the king should have to obey the law. This was not a new idea. Roman emperors were supposed to obey the law – even though quite often they didn't. Early medieval kings were chosen by the powerful men of their kingdom and knew they could be removed if they behaved badly. But as the English kings gained more and more power others in nobility felt they needed to push

237

back in order to keep their rights.

After writing this document, these noblemen forced King John to sign it unless he wanted to start a civil war. Their intention at the time was only to protect their own rights as aristocrats. They didn't care so much about the poor peasants who had even less rights than they did. Nevertheless, over time, the rights established by this letter, which was later known as The Magna Carta or 'The Great Charter', were also extended to common people.

Most of the rules that were in the Magna Carta aren't even laws anymore today. Of the 63 clauses in the Magna Carta only three of them are still followed. One law still in force guarantees the liberties of the English church. The second law which remains in existence confirms the privileges of the City of London and other towns. The third and most famous law which is still valid is called habeas corpus, which means "Do you have the body?" in Latin. This law means that the government can't keep people in jail secretly. They have to tell the public if someone has been arrested or is being held for any reason. Habeas corpus protects people from being kidnapped by the government without having a just cause.

The Magna Carta was an important document because it was the first time that an English king put any limits on royal authority. Through listing various freedoms, its goal was to prevent the king from taking advantage of his power in impulsive ways. It made it clear that the king was subject to the law, not above it. It is the first document that guaranteed the rights of the average citizen from being taken away by the king of England. The Magna Carta set the groundwork for English common law and later for the U.S. Constitution and the Bill of Rights.

In the Village

Materials: Logic Puzzle from the companion download

Preparation: Print a copy of the logic puzzle page for each child.

Lesson: Arthur, Brad, Clarissa, and Donna, whose last names are Elmhurst, Ford, Gustave, and Harper, live in four houses in a row in the local village. Solve this logic puzzle by determining each person's full name and house position (with house number one, or the first house, being at the far left.)

Literature

Materials:

- The Canterbury Tales by Geoffrey Chaucer (retold by Geraldine McCaughrean)

Preparation: None

Parent Note: Read this book aloud and discuss it with your child.

NOTE: The Canterbury Tales are extremely funny. There are a few tales which are a bit bawdy in nature. This adaptation is cleans them up considerably; however, you may want to read them in advance if you have younger children or are concerned about content. I think that Geraldine does a good job of making these classic tales suitable for children. Reading these tales will definitely educate your family about what it was like to be on a pilgrimage during medieval times.

Write in Your Journal

Materials:

- Your child's journal
- Paper
- Pencil, colored pencils, markers, etc.

Preparation: None

Parent Note: Have your child write down a few key points about what they learned about the Magna Carta. Depending on their age and ability, you can require your child to write one sentence or several paragraphs. You can also let them narrate back to you what they have learned. Then, have them draw a picture or print pictures from the internet to add some more insight to their journal page.

Possible Writing Prompt: Imagine you are either King John or one of the noblemen who forced him to sign the Magna Carta. Write a journal entry describing how you feel after this momentous day.

Strawberries in Snow

Ingredients:
8 Egg whites
1 pint Whipping cream
1/2 cup Sugar
1-2 Tbsp. Rose water
2 pints Strawberries
1 cup Red wine
1/4 cup Sugar
1/2 tsp. Cinnamon
1/4 tsp. Ginger
Shortbread cookies (optional)

Directions:
1. Whip the cream and set it aside.
2. Beat the egg whites until they form soft peaks.
3. Add the egg whites to the whipped cream and whisk them together.
4. Add the rose water and sugar - adding a little sugar at a time. When it's ready it will have a consistency something like whipped cream.
5. Clean the strawberries and place them into a bowl.
6. Mix the red wine, sugar, cinnamon, and ginger.
7. Pour the mixture over the strawberries and let them marinate for an hour or so.

Serve "snow" with strawberries on top. You can also serve with a couple of shortbread cookies on the side if desired.

Week Ten – You are a Baron/Baroness
Day One

The City of London

Materials: Map of London's Square Mile from companion download

Preparation: Print one copy of London's Square Mile for each child

Lesson: London is a very old city; however, it has not always been the large urban center that it is today. It is thought that the area currently occupied by the city was a collection of scattered, rural settlements long ago. Spear heads and weapons have been found around the Thames, the large river which flows through London. In 2002, an archaeological dig discovered evidence of a possible wooden bridge across the Thames which was about 3,000 years old.

The Romans are the ones who built London. In 43 AD, they invaded Britain and founded a city named Londinium. The original Roman city was fairly small. In 60 AD, Queen Boudica of the Iceni tribe rose up against the Romans and caused them to flee. They then burned the city to the ground. However, the Romans eventually regained control and rebuilt London. This time, they added a Forum (market) and a Basilica (a business center.) They also slowly built a wall around the city to protect it from future invasions. The area inside this defensive wall is now known as "The Square Mile" or "The City" and it is the financial center of the United Kingdom. There is quite a bit of archaeological evidence remaining of the Roman city of Londinium. Often, when new buildings are built, archaeological artifacts are made!

When the Roman Empire crumbled in the 5th century, the Romans abandoned London for good leaving it largely deserted. Britain was then invaded by the Angles, the Saxons and the Jutes. (Remember, we have already discussed this in detail.) These "Anglo-Saxons" were farmers and tended to live outside big towns. We know very little about what happened to London during this period.

By the beginning of the 7th Century, the city had become important enough to justify the building of a cathedral - St Paul's Cathedral. We know very little about London for the next few hundred years, although during the 9th and 10th Centuries there were many attacks by the Vikings.

Soon afterwards, the Normans invaded from France and William the Conqueror

241

took control. He quickly began to build the Tower of London as a stronghold to guard London from future attacks. During William's reign, the city of London grew. It remained within the original Roman walls, however, which were repaired and built up. Houses were made of wood and plaster and were crowded together very tightly.

In modern times, the entire city of London covers about 700 square miles. If you go to the Square Mile today, you will find streets such as Pudding Lane, Bread Street and Milk Street. These roads have been in existence since medieval times. Other ancient roads are called Threadneedle Street, Ropemakers Square, Silk Street, and Poultry Street. Can you imagine what types of occupations were located on these streets in the Middle Ages?

There are also a number of streets with "gate" in their name, such as Bishopsgate or Moorgate. These were where the original gates were located in the defensive wall which allowed people to enter or exit the city.

For this activity, you will be familiarizing yourself with a map of the Square Mile. See if you can find the various street names which mark where ancient gates were located. Notice some of the interesting street names. If you see the name of a person, feel free to Google that name to try to find out more about them.

Eyeglasses or Spectacles

Materials:
- Glass jar
- Water
- Something to read

Preparation: None

Lesson: In 1268, Roger Bacon was the first person we have record of using lenses to help people to see well. Magnifying lenses inserted in frames were used for reading both in Europe and China at this time. We aren't sure who first came up with the idea. Imagine a baron having poor eyesight during medieval times. What a relief it must have been to be able to see well enough to read again!

Activity: For this activity, you will see how reading glasses actually work.
1. Fill the jar with water.
2. Hold the reading material close to the jar and read it through the water-filled jar. Notice that the print appears larger.
3. Because the glass is curved, the light enters the jar on a slant and changes direction as it goes through the water. This causes the print to appear larger. This is the same reason why a magnifying glass works.
4. Hold various objects and print up to your jar to see what difference the magnification has on them.

Manor House Design

Materials:
- Paper and pencil
- Internet or library

Preparation: None

Lesson: The term "manor house" can be loosely applied to a whole range of buildings, but it generally refers to the house of a local lord or landowner. In strict architectural terms a manor house is a late medieval country house. The design of a manor house had its beginnings in the Saxon hall, which was a simple rectangular building used as a community gathering place for eating, sleeping, and conducting business. Servants slept around an open fire in the center of the hall, while the lord and his family occupied a raised platform at one end of the hall. This simple Saxon design was incorporated into early Norman castles with the hall concept occupying the entire first floor of the castle keep.

By the 13th century the fortified manor house emerged. These houses were not quite castles, yet they were more advanced than a Saxon hall. Early fortified manors were built with brick or stone and had a wooden roof. The fire was still open and the hall was still the living place for the servants; however, now another room called the solar was added. The solar was a private room for the lord and his family, usually on the first floor, and was entered from the raised platform at one end of the hall. The space beneath the solar was often used for storage.

At the other end of the hall from the solar was the kitchen area, usually separated from the main hall by wooden screens. Over time the kitchen became a totally separate room. The main entrance of the manor was at the kitchen end. A good example of this type of manor design can be seen at Stokesay Castle in Shropshire, England (see picture on the right.) Window space was at a minimum in the fortified manor, and outer defenses may have included a moat with a gatehouse that could be reached by a drawbridge.

In the 14th century, more elaborate rooms were added to the manor house. The buttery, or food storage area, appeared between the kitchens and the main hall. Above the buttery was a guest room. Porches were added at the entrance. Galleries were included for musicians. Most manor houses were still built with stone; however, those who could afford it began to use brick as well.

By the early 15th century there wasn't as much need for fortified manor houses. Conditions were more peaceful and defense was no longer the highest priority when building a house. At this point, people desired homes with more comfort than fortifications. The drawbridge became a fixed bridge over the moat. The gatehouse became a grand entry rather than a foreboding barrier. The upper floor of the gatehouse was often used as a chapel.

The manor house began to be arranged around a central courtyard. With more space devoted to comfort, private bedrooms and reception rooms became common, as well as family areas like the solar. All lords liked to impress other members of the nobility and the grander their manor the more self-important a lord might feel. Even the entrance to the manor was designed to make a statement about their importance.

Activity: For this activity, you have your choice of either of the following:
1. Look at a variety of manor houses on the internet to notice and appreciate their different architectural features.
2. Design your own manor house. Decide whether you will create a fortified house or if you would rather design a house with comfort in mind. You may either draw your design on paper or create a model of your house using whatever materials you have on hand. The choice is yours!

Reading

Parent Note: The read aloud suggestions are intended for you to read to your child. The individual reading suggestions are intended for your child to read aloud to you – or to read on their own. Continue reading each selection throughout the baron/baroness weeks until you are finished.

Read Aloud For Younger Children:
Don't Forget the Knight Light by Tina Gagliardi

Read Aloud For Older Children:
Shakespeare Can Be Fun: Much Ado About Nothing for Kids by Lois Burdett

Individual Reading for Grades 2-4:
Knight at Dawn (A Magic Treehouse book) by Mary Pope Osborne

Individual Reading for Older Children:
The Book of Three by Lloyd Alexander

Shove the Groat

Materials:

- 20 Heavy coins (50 cent piece, silver dollar, etc)
  OR 20 Large washers
- Piece of poster board

Preparation:

1. Make the game board (see illustration below.)
2. Divide the poster board into ten horizontal sections. Each section should be the same size, which is at least 1 ¼ times as wide as the coins which are being used. The larger you make the sections the easier the game will be.

Lesson: Shove the Groat is a gambling game that Vikings played on long sea-voyages to pass the time. The traditional playing pieces were groats which were large, heavy coins.

Players take turns placing 10 coins in the section closest to them. Using either their thumb and middle finger, or the heel of their palm, players strike their coins (or shove their groats) into the different sections of the game board. To score, a coin must lie completely within a section without touching a line. Subsequent coins may knock a coin into or out of scoring position.

There are two variations of the game. In the first variation, each section is given a point value based on its distance from the player. A coin landing in that section, scores that point value. A coin leaving the board incurs a negative penalty score. The first player to reach a predetermined score wins.

The second version requires twice as many coins. For this version, a player must score exactly twice in every section. Additional coins in the same section score for the opponent if they still need points in that section. Subsequent scores in that section are ignored. There is no penalty for a coin leaving the board. The first player to score twice in every section wins.

Week Ten – You are a Baron/Baroness
Day Two

The Hundred Years War

Materials: None

Preparation: None

Lesson: Previously, we talked about how William the Conqueror took control of England in 1066. Because William had been a powerful French lord in Normandy, which is in France, when he became the King of England he claimed much of France as his kingdom as well. As William's descendants took the throne in England, they also maintained their right to rule parts of France. As time went on, the French people resented this more and more.

In 1152 AD, King Henry II of England married Eleanor of Aquitaine, who was the heiress to much of southwest France. This gave the English king control over even more land in France than the French king!

In 1328 AD, the king of France died without leaving a direct heir. The king of England, Edward III, was the grandson of the now deceased French king. This made him the rightful successor to the French throne, which would have allowed him to rule both England and France.

The resentment against English rule had been gaining strength in the hearts of the French people. They didn't want to be ruled by the English any longer. A Frenchman named Philip of Valois, who was the nephew of the deceased king of France, began to make preparations for war with England. This war, called the Hundred Years War, lasted from 1337 - 1453.

Partly because of the Black Death, neither side could really end the war. Under their new young king Henry V, the English won an especially big battle at Agincourt in 1415, where Henry used a new weapon called a cannon to help him win the battle.

The English managed to take over almost all of France. But Henry V died young in Paris. After he died, the French started to win again under a woman named Joan of Arc, who recaptured the towns of Orleans and Reims, among other places, for her king, Charles VII.

Even though the English eventually captured Joan and burned her alive in Rouen in 1431, the French continued to win the war. In 1453, the English king Henry VI gave up his claim to rule France. Henry VI lost all his land in France except the port at Calais.

The Hundred Years War greatly strengthened France, while weakening England. Following the war, England began a period of civil war that lasted for another 30 years.

Literature

Materials:
- The Canterbury Tales by Geoffrey Chaucer (retold by Geraldine McCaughrean)

Preparation: None

Parent Note: Read this book aloud and discuss it with your child.

NOTE: The Canterbury Tales are extremely funny. There are a few tales which are a bit bawdy in nature. This adaptation is cleans them up considerably; however, you may want to read them in advance if you have younger children or are concerned about content. I think that Geraldine does a good job of making these classic tales suitable for children. Reading these tales will definitely educate your family about what it was like to be on a pilgrimage during medieval times.

Learn to Draw a Medieval Archer

Materials:
- Paper
- Pencil with an eraser
- A black marker (optional)
- Colored pencils or crayons (optional)

Lesson: In this lesson, you will learn to draw a medieval archer step-by-step.

1. First, draw an ellipse for the head. Now, draw construction lines for the body. Think of how an archer stands and what the position of his arms would be for him to shoot a bow and arrow.

2. Next, draw the archer's eyes, nose and mouth. Remember that an archer closes one eye when shooting a bow. Now, draw the helmet, bow, and hands as shown.

3. Next, start drawing clothes on the archer's upper body. Try to think of how clothes should fit on his arms and shoulders. Use the construction lines as a guide.

4. Now, draw the archer's legs, boots, belt, and the bottom of his shirt as shown.

5. Using the black marker, trace all of the lines that you will be keeping. Then you can erase your construction lines.

6. Lastly, draw the quiver with arrows, the bow string, and the arrow that he's holding as shown. Add wrinkles in his clothes, shading, and any other details you would like to make it your own. You may also use the colored pencils to color in your archer if you like. Great job!

Horizontal or Vertical? Framing Your Subject

Materials:
- Camera (preferably a digital one)
- Printer (optional – makes it easier to print your child's photos but isn't required)

Preparation: None

Lesson: When taking a picture, you need to make some decisions. Where will the edges of a picture be? Should you hold the camera horizontally or vertically? Unless you have an artistic reason for doing otherwise, you should let the subject of your picture dictate which way you hold the camera. If your subject is vertical, hold the camera vertically. If your subject is horizontal then hold it horizontally. Otherwise, your picture will have empty space that doesn't add anything to the picture.

Notice in the pictures above, how the first picture looks better with horizontal framing because that way the entire car is pictured in the background. The second picture looks better with vertical framing because it is a close-up of just the boys.

For this lesson, try taking several photos holding the camera vertically as well as horizontally. If you've never held the camera vertically before, try ONLY holding it that way so you can get used to moving the camera into that position. You may want to include a few of your better photos in your journal.

What is Wind?

Materials:
- Baby powder
- A lamp with the shade removed

Preparation: None

Lesson: Air is made up of molecules that are moving constantly. As air warms up, the molecules vibrate and bump into each other which increases the space around each molecule. As the space around the molecules increases, the air expands and becomes less dense. This means it also becomes lighter. As the warm air becomes lighter, it rises.

The opposite effect happens as air cools. As the air temperature drops, molecules move more slowly taking up less room. The amount of space the air takes up shrinks and becomes more dense. This means it also becomes heavier. As the cold air becomes heavier, it sinks.

When warm air rises, cold air moves in replacing the warm air. This movement of air is what we call wind. In this activity, you will get to create some wind yourself.

Activity:
1. Put the lamp on the floor or another surface which can be cleaned later. Keep it turned off.
2. Sprinkle some baby powder near the light bulb.
3. Notice what happens to the powder. (It should sink slowly down through the air.)
4. Turn on the lamp and allow the light bulb to heat up for a few minutes. *Parents Note*: The higher the wattage of the light bulb, the better this experiment will work.)
5. Sprinkle a little more of the powder near the lamp.
6. Notice what happens to the powder. (It should rise through the air – or at least sink at a slower rate.) Why does this happen?

Week Ten – You are a Baron/Baroness
Day Three

Knight Conundrum

Materials:

- Paper and pencil

Preparation: None

Lesson: As we already learned, barons and knights used math to figure out different situations throughout their day. See how well your child can solve these problems. The answers are in the companion download.

1. The local baron has 75 knights who will defend his land for him. Each knight is responsible for rounding up 23 peasants to help in the fighting. How large will this baron's fighting force become once all of the peasants have been rounded up?

2. The attacking forces have 5,000 soldiers. ¼ of these soldiers are on horseback. How many of the soldiers are on horseback?

3. William's army has 3 trebuchets which are each capable of knocking down 12 feet of castle wall an hour. After 8 hours, how many feet of castle wall will have been knocked down?

4. The best archer in the fighting force can accurately shoot 10 enemy archers every 15 minutes. If there are 250 archers on the city walls, how long will it take the archer to shoot them all?

Bath, England and Mosaics

Materials:
- Flour
- Salt
- Food Coloring (optional)
- A bag of dried black beans
- A bag of various colored beans
- Varnish (optional)
- Possible designs from companion download (optional)

Preparation: (do right before using so the dough will be soft while completing this activity.)
1. Make salt dough by mixing 3 parts flour to one part salt.
2. Add water and mix until the dough has a similar consistency to Play-doh.
3. Food coloring can also be added if desired.
4. Print the designs from the companion download if desired

Lesson: Bath, England is an ancient city which contains three natural hot springs. These hot springs gush water which is 114.8 degrees Fahrenheit or 46 degrees Celsius. That is hotter than you probably bathe in at home.

The original inhabitants of England, the Celts, are said to have built a shrine on these hot springs. In 835BC, the legendary King Bladud was said to have built the first baths on this location.

When the Romans invaded England, they constructed a temple and a large bathing complex on this location. This complex contained swimming pools, changing rooms and toilets. All of the buildings had roofs with high ceilings. The walls were painted and the floors contained beautiful mosaics. People used to visit the baths for leisure. Sick people also came because they thought that if they swam in the waters they would be cured.

The baths were also important during the Middle Ages. Around 500AD, King Arthur is said to have defeated the Anglo-Saxons at this location. Like all legends, no one knows for sure whether this is true. Sick people still came to see if the waters would cure their ills.

The water in the Great Bath is now green and looks dirty. This is because the water is filled with algae. During Roman times, the bath buildings had roofs which stopped the growth of algae. Now that the site is in ruins, that is no longer the case.

For this activity, you will be creating a mosaic like the kind found on the floor of these famous baths. The mosaic tile you create can be used as a trivet in the kitchen, if desired, or simply for decoration.

Activity:
1. Decide which design you would like to complete. Either use a design from the companion download or come up with your own.
2. Press your portion of salt dough flat, into whatever shape you desire.
3. You may decide to use black beans to outline your design – or you might use different colors for different sections of your design. Press the beans into the soft salt dough. Be sure to press them in firmly so that they remain in place once the dough dries.
4. Fill in the design with the other colorful beans.
5. Allow your mosaic to dry.
6. Coat your project with varnish if desired. Be sure to do this step in a well ventilated area.

Gunpowder During the Middle Ages

Materials: Video clip from the supplement section on our website

Preparation: Go to our website and prepare to play the clip designated for this lesson.

Lesson: Did you know that gunpowder had been invented already prior to medieval times? It wasn't called gunpowder, yet, since guns hadn't been invented. But black powder was invented in China before 492 AD. Black powder was created by mixing sulfur with saltpeter.

The Chinese used to mix these two substances with an herb called birthwort, which created carbon. This mixture was created for medicinal purposes. There are descriptions coming from ancient China about alchemists who heated this mixture and ended up burning their hands, their faces, and sometimes even burning down the houses where they were working.

Once the explosive power of black powder was discovered, the Chinese created a large variety of weapons including flamethrowers, rockets, bombs, and land mines. Did you realize that these types of weapons existed during ancient times?

Black powder didn't come to Europe until later in the Middle Ages. Roger Bacon talked about the military uses of gunpowder in his book, *De nullitate magiæ* where he said, "By only using a very small quantity of this material much light can be created accompanied by a horrible fracas. It is possible with it to destroy a town or an army." He also described using gunpowder as creating "artificial lightning and thunder."

Gunpowder eventually played an important role in European warfare. It was popular because it was easy to use, light to carry, and cheap to make. This brought about some changes to medieval life. No longer did men have to train for years in order to be skilled in battle. Castle walls were no longer as impenetrable.

Cannons also began to appear in the 14th century. The Bombard was the most primitive form of cannon. It consisted of a simple tube. It was especially effective firing against castle walls, where an assault could now be successful in a matter of days. England used cannons against the Scots in 1327. They were also used by both the French and the English during the Hundred Years' War (1337-1453.)

Because gunpowder is so dangerous, we won't be making any on our own. We will, however, be watching a video of someone else making gunpowder and setting it on fire. After watching the video, you'll understand why having an explosive substance such as this changed warfare as we know it today.

Quoits, Dobblers and Horseshoes

Materials:
- A stick or rope for the starting line
- A target to throw towards – a stick pushed into the ground, a ball, or other object of your choice
- Frisbees, pool rings, or other objects to toss

Preparation: Set up the target and the starting line.

Lesson: The National Horseshoe Pitchers Association says that the game of horseshoes dates back to the Roman Empire. While modern play sets may never have been near a horse, actual horseshoes were used in tournament play right up until 1909. The game may have started with blacksmith's children playing with old worn out and cast off shoes.

Quoits is played with fully closed rings. Horseshoes is played with U-shaped open rings. The Encyclopedia Britannica states that modern quoits evolved from the Greek throwing of the discus. The rules for quoits and horseshoes are virtually identical. Only the shape of the projectile is different. While we tend to think of all horseshoes being U-shaped, this is not the case. Some horseshoes are closed rings, either to better conform to a specific breed of horse or to help protect a hoof injury. In some parts of England, quoits are still referred to as "shoes," and horseshoes are thought of as the "rustic" version of quoits.

Dobbers is the indoor version of quoits. The usual target is a six-inch wooden peg at the center of a one-foot circle within a two-foot circle. Most 'dobbers' used today are either rubber or plastic.

For this activity, see how closely you can throw your object toward the target. Whoever gets the closest to the target wins.

Reading

Parent Note: The read aloud suggestions are intended for you to read to your child. The individual reading suggestions are intended for your child to read aloud to you – or to read on their own. Continue reading each selection throughout the baron/baroness weeks until you are finished.

Read Aloud For Younger Children:
The Sunflower Sword by Mark Sperring

Read Aloud For Older Children:
Shakespeare Can Be Fun: Much Ado About Nothing for Kids by Lois Burdett

Individual Reading for Grades 2-4:
Knight at Dawn (A Magic Treehouse book) by Mary Pope Osborne

Individual Reading for Older Children:
The Book of Three by Lloyd Alexander

Week Ten – You are a Baron/Baroness
Day Four

The Daily Life of a Baroness

Materials: None

Preparation: None

Lesson: We've already learned that women in medieval times didn't have very many rights. This is also true for women who were as high up the social ladder as a baroness. When she married, the law gave her husband full rights over her. She was considered to be his property. She was subservient to her husband.

This doesn't show the full picture of her life, however. A baroness also had quite a bit of power. She was an authority figure and her word was law when her husband was absent, which was quite often. Barons had to travel frequently in service to the king. They could be gone for many months at a time. Whenever he was gone, the baroness was responsible for running the manor, which included collecting rent, supervising the farming, and settling disputes.

A baroness was responsible for ensuring that adequate provisions were available at the manor. She purchased expensive materials and spices. She was also expected to assist or supervise the preparation of various foods. Her most important role, however, was to provide children for the lord of the manor.

A baroness received an education of sorts. At a very young age, girls of nobility were sent to the households of other nobility to be taught the skills necessary for her to perform her future duties. Sometimes these girls were also sent to nunneries to be educated. Some noble women were even taught to read and write. This was done more in an effort to keep them busy than to give them useful skills. If young girls had too much time on their hands, it was a concern that they might fall into sinful behaviors.

When a girl of nobility was between twelve and fourteen years old she entered society. This was a time when her parents were looking for a husband for her. Boys were allowed to marry at age 14 and girls at age 12. Can you imagine getting married at that age? Marriages were more about wealth and alliances than love – so the women wouldn't have had any say in who they married.

A baroness was also called a "Lady of the Manor." Manors were typically between 1200 – 1800 acres. The baron was required to support himself and his household. The rest of this land on the manor was allotted to the peasants who were his tenants. A manor typically included a manor house, a village, a church, and lots of farming land for the peasants.

The manor house was typically set apart from the village and farms where the peasants lived. Manor houses varied in size depending on the wealth of their owner. They generally consisted of a great hall, a solar, a kitchen, storerooms, and servants' quarters. Sometimes there was even a chapel attached to the house. As you can imagine, barons and baronesses lived in houses which were much more opulent than those of their tenants.

Quiz Bowl

Parent Note: See how well you and your children can answer questions about the material that has been covered concerning barons and baronesses.

1. True or False - A baron was allowed to create his own laws, mint his own money, and set his own tax rates. (True)

2. What was a baron required to provide for the king as he traveled around the country? (Food and lodging)

3. How early did barons wake up in the morning? (At dawn)

4. What are the first two things a baron did after waking up in the morning? (Hear mass and say his prayers)

5. Why was Hadrian's Wall built? (To help the Romans defend their new conquest against future invaders.)

6. What was the name of the most serious revolt to take place in medieval England? (The Peasant's Revolt)

7. Name at least one reason why the peasants were angry enough to revolt? (Fear that they would lose their freedom, anger from having to work on church land, and costly taxes.)

8. Who emerged as the leader of the peasants during the revolt? (Wat Tyler)

9. Why did the noblemen feel that they needed to create the Magna Carta? (Because King John was out of control and thought he was above the law.)

10. What important law, which originated in the Magna Carta, is still a law today? (Habeas Corpus - Doesn't allow the government to keep people in jail secretly. They have to tell the public if someone has been arrested or is being held for any reason.)

11. Why was the Magna Carta so important? (It was the first time that any limits were put on royalty. It made it clear that the king was subject to the law not above it.)

12. In what famous place is a comet depicted? (On the Bayeux Tapestry)

13. When planning a medieval village, what are two things you want to consider for choosing your site? (Proximity to existing castles, if it's on high ground, access to natural resources such as wood and water, and open land for growing crops)

14. What new weapon was used during the Hundred Years War to help the English to win some important battles? (A cannon)

15. Who was the famous French hero during the Hundred Years War? (Joan of Arc)

16. Did a medieval baroness have many legal rights? (No. Her husband had full rights over her.)

17. Did that mean that she didn't have any power? (No, she had quite a bit of power. She was in charge of the manor whenever her husband was away on business, which was quite often.)

18. What was a baroness's most important responsibility? (To provide children for the lord of the manor)

19. Did a baroness receive an education? (Yes. They were either sent to the households of other nobility or to nunneries to be educated.)

20. At what age were the nobility allowed to marry? (Boys at age 14 and girls at age 12)

Literature

Materials:

- The Canterbury Tales by Geoffrey Chaucer (retold by Geraldine McCaughrean)

Preparation: None

Parent Note: Read this book aloud and discuss it with your child.

NOTE: The Canterbury Tales are extremely funny. There are a few tales which are a bit bawdy in nature. This adaptation is cleans them up considerably; however, you may want to read them in advance if you have younger children or are concerned about content. I think that Geraldine does a good job of making these classic tales suitable for children. Reading these tales will definitely educate your family about what it was like to be on a pilgrimage during medieval times.

Write in Your Journal

Materials:
- Your child's journal
- Paper
- Pencil, colored pencils, markers, etc.

Preparation: None

Parent Note: Have your child write down a few key points about what they learned about the daily life of a baroness. Depending on their age and ability, you can require your child to write one sentence or several paragraphs. You can also let them narrate back to you what they have learned. Then, have them draw a picture or print pictures from the internet to add some more insight to their journal page.

Possible Writing Prompt: Imagine you are a baroness whose husband has been absent for several months. Write a letter to your husband telling him how things are going around the manor. You may decide to be honest with him or you might decide to only tell him about the positive things that have been happening. The choice is up to you!

Field Trip to a Manor House and/or Horseback Riding

Parent Note: This week is a great time to visit a manor house in your area. If there aren't any manor houses nearby, you might want to take your child horseback riding instead. Riding a horse was a daily activity of many people in Medieval England. Whichever field trip you choose, be sure to ask your child questions so that they can compare their experience with what they have learned so far about the life of a baron or baroness. And have your child take lots of pictures for their journal.

Week Ten – You are a Baron/Baroness
Day Five

Making a Hydrometer

Materials:
- A ruler with centimeter marks
- A permanent marker
- A straight straw
- Three glasses
- Water
- 1 Tbsp salt
- 1 Tsp dishwashing liquid
- A small piece of clay or Play-doh
- A measuring cup
- 1 or 2 small, light nails which are small enough to slip inside the straw

Preparation: None

Lesson: Leonardo da Vinci was extremely curious. He knew that solid objects of the same size, such as a block of wood and a block of concrete, weighed different amounts due to their differing densities. Leonardo wondered if this was also true for liquids. He held a cup of honey and a cup of water and observed that they weighed different amounts. Leonardo wanted to invent a way to measure the density of liquids in relation to each other.

Leonardo invented something called a hydrometer, which was based on a scientific principle explained by Archimedes, who was an ancient Greek scientist. Archimedes said that a solid suspended in a liquid will be buoyed up by the force equal to the weight of the liquid displaced. In other words, the lower the density of the liquid, the lower the object will sink.

If you've ever had real maple syrup, you've eaten something which was made with the help of a hydrometer. Maple syrup comes from maple sap, a liquid which is collected from maple trees in the early spring. Maple sap is made up mostly of water. In fact, if you want to make a gallon of maple syrup you need at least 40 gallons of maple sap to do so. To make the sap, the extra water must be boiled off. To know that the sap has been boiled long enough, syrup makers float a hydrometer in the finished product. If the sugar-to-water ratio is 66 percent, then the syrup is ready.

For today's activity, we will be making our own hydrometer.

Activity:

1. Using the marker, draw half centimeter marks on the straw to create a scale.
2. Plug the bottom of the straw with a tiny piece of clay which is big enough that no water leaks into the straw – but small enough that it doesn't add much weight.

265

3. Drop 1 or 2 small nails into the straw, one on top of the other, so that they sit at the bottom against the clay. (You may need to experiment to see if 1 nail works better or 2 – depending on the size of your nails.)
4. Take your three glasses and fill them with an equal amount of warm water.
5. Leave one glass with plain water. Add the salt to the second glass and stir. Add the dish detergent to the third glass and stir.
6. Gently place your hydrometer in each glass, noting where the mark on the hydrometer is in relation to the top of the glass. Which liquid is the most dense? Which liquid is the least dense? How can you tell?

Crack the Whip

Materials: None

Preparation: None

Lesson: No one knows how old this game is. Any number of kids can play. Someone is chosen as the "leader." Players form a line behind the leader and hold tightly to the belt or garment of the person in front of them. Sometimes players hold hands instead.

The "leader" quickly changes pace and speeds up or slows down. Sometimes the leader goes in circles and moves very fast - the other players try to hold on. The leader attempts to get those holding on to let go. If they do, they must drop out of the game.

Parent Note: If varying ages of children are playing this game, tell the older ones to take it easy on the younger ones so that no one gets hurt! Sometimes it helps to have the younger kids be near the front of the line. ☺

Make a Medieval Flail

Materials:
- Empty paper towel roll
- Newspaper
- Masking tape
- Scissors
- Black and/or silver spray paint
- A couple of sheets of printer paper or craft foam
- String
- Hole punch

Preparation: None

Lesson:

1. Loosely wrap some newspaper into a ball. You don't want to make the ball too tight or the mace could be dangerous. Crunch it up loosely and then wrap some masking tape around it. It helps to add one sheet of newspaper at a time until you get the ball to be the size you want.

2. Wrap your string around the mace ball. Wrap it in different spots and at least 4 times. With a varied wrap like this the string will not come off the ball. Tie a knot after each wrap.

3. Take another piece of string which is about 12" long and attach it to the string which is around the mace ball.

4. Completely wrap the mace ball with masking tape. Try to make it as smooth as possible because you will be painting this ball later.

5. Now let's make the pointy cones that will attach to the mace ball. Using your masking tape as a template, draw 6 circles on a sheet of paper or the craft foam. Cut these circles out.

6. Fold each circle in half and form it into a cone.

7. Tape the cones to the mace ball in a random pattern. Don't fill them with newspaper or anything because we want them to collapse rather than hurting anyone if the mace is used on a sibling. ☺

8. Attach the mace ball to the handle by making a few holes in one end of the paper towel roll and tying the other end of the string to it.

9. Paint your mace a combination of silver or black as desired.

10. After your mace dries, you may gently use it in battle. It is probably more suitable as a decoration, however. A well constructed mace can be quite dangerous so we have purposefully made ours on the fragile side to prevent injury.

Reading

Parent Note: The read aloud suggestions are intended for you to read to your child. The individual reading suggestions are intended for your child to read aloud to you – or to read on their own. Continue reading each selection throughout the baron/baroness weeks until you are finished.

Read Aloud For Younger Children:
Max's Castle by Kate Banks

Read Aloud For Older Children:
Shakespeare Can Be Fun: Much Ado About Nothing for Kids by Lois Burdett

Individual Reading for Grades 2-4:
Knight at Dawn (A Magic Treehouse book) by Mary Pope Osborne

Individual Reading for Older Children:
The Book of Three by Lloyd Alexander

Medieval Adventure, Scene Five

Materials:
- Script from companion download
- Costumes which were made/gathered in a previous lesson
- Whatever other props you create during your lessons and/or have laying around the house to add excitement to this adventure.

Preparation:
1. Photocopy the script so that each actor has their own copy.
2. Read through the script a few times so that you know what to expect and can help to direct the kids.

Parent Note: Choose roles for yourself and your children. Remember, the more dramatic you act the more your kids will as well – and the more value they will gain from this assignment.

Activity Suggestions for Further Learning and Fun

Below is a list of further suggestions which have not been incorporated into the two weeks of learning that you may also want to try. The more you immerse your child in these types of activities, the more they will learn and enjoy this experience. ***Warning:*** You child will probably most enjoy some of the suggestions are the messiest or the most out of the ordinary! ☺

Baron
- Wake up at dawn
- Try to settle a dispute between friends or siblings
- Field trip to a courtroom
- Practice with weapons (sword, archery, etc.)
- Field trip to observe a falconer

Baroness
- Wake up at dawn
- Try running a household for a day or a week (i.e., make a chore chart, menu, grocery list, etc.
- Serve your father or brothers – practice being completely subservient
- Attend a fancy dance or party – get really dressed up!

You are a King

in Medieval England

Table of Contents for King/Queen Weeks

Week Eleven – You are a King/Queen
Day One

Pastimes of a Medieval King

Materials: None

Preparation: None

Lesson: You might think that you would have loved to have been a medieval king. After all, who wouldn't want to have that kind of fame, money, and power?!? A king had many responsibilities, too, however. Some were pleasant and some were not so pleasant.

First, a medieval king got out of bed around dawn. This meant that his servants had to be awake much earlier than that in order to get everything prepared for him. The first thing the king did was to get dressed and washed for the day. His attendants helped get his clothes ready. His grooms dressed him and styled his hair.

Next, the king went to get his queen who had her own bedroom. Then, together, they attended a morning church service called mass.

Next, the king ate breakfast. It featured several courses and also some sort of entertainment. Court jesters, jugglers, musicians, and acrobats attempted to amuse the king and his guests after they were done with their meal.

After breakfast, the king was busy with his many responsibilities. If the country was at peace, his daily schedule was filled with many important tasks, such as:

- Communicating with lords, foreign leaders, and his advisors
- Passing judgment in disputes

- Traveling around his kingdom to be "seen" by his subjects
- Laying hands on sick people (Kings were thought to have the power to heal certain illnesses.)
- Presiding over knighthood ceremonies and feasts
- Planning for the maintenance and demolition of old buildings as well as for the building of new ones
- Anything else necessary for overseeing his kingdom

If his country was at war, the king still had to do all of the above tasks, although he might decide to leave a steward behind to run things in his absence. Some kings chose to ride out with their troops to take part in battles. Some chose to move to a fortified castle or other residence in order to better protect themselves.

As you can see, a king had lots of responsibilities. Many days, however, he also had some leisure time. Kings participated in a variety of recreational activities such as reading, playing card or dice games, hunting, practicing horsemanship skills, listening to music, etc. If a king was serious about his faith, he also took time out of each day to pray.

A king had servants prepare him for bed. They ran the dogs out of the room, got his bed ready by checking it for fleas, started a fire in his fireplace, and helped him to undress. Once the king was in bed, the servants closed the curtains around his bed and prepared to sleep nearby in the room in case they were needed in the night.

For the next two weeks you will pretend to be a king or a queen living in medieval England. You will get to experience some of the responsibilities and pleasures that a king or a queen experienced. As you complete these activities and go about your day, try to imagine what it would have been like to do these things all day, every day of your life.

Write in Your Journal

Materials:
- Your child's journal
- Paper
- Pencil, colored pencils, markers, etc.

Preparation: None

Parent Note: Have your child write down a few key points about what they learned about the daily life of a medieval king. Depending on their age and ability, you can require your child to write one sentence or several paragraphs. You can also let them narrate back to you what they have learned. Then, have them draw a picture or print pictures from the internet to add some more insight to their journal page.

Possible Writing Prompt: Imagine you are a king whose advisors aren't dependable and who doesn't trust his wife. Write a journal entry which details how alone you feel without anyone you can trust.

Creating a King or Queen Costume

Materials for King Costume (Pick and choose as desired):
- A long coat or jacket in a vibrant color
- Fancy pants or hose
- Bright piece of fabric to use as a cape
- Anything with fur or velvet
- A crown (we will be making one later)

Materials for Queen Costume (Pick and choose as desired):
- Long, trailing dress with long or puffy sleeves – in a vibrant color
- Pointed shoes
- Anything with fur or velvet
- Crown with veil over hair (We will be making a crown later)

Parent Note: For this activity, we are going to create an outfit to wear while acting in the drama as well as while completing their other lessons if your child so desires.

You can make this activity as simple or as elaborate as you and your children would enjoy. There are many sites on the internet which give you ideas on sewing medieval costumes. We are going to show you simple ways in which you can gather costumes – but you are welcome to take the time to make more elaborate costumes if that is something which interests you.

An easy and inexpensive way to gather the clothing items we recommend is to check out secondhand stores and garage sales. Feel free to improvise! The most important thing is that your child feels the part – not that they are completely authentic.

Literature

Materials:
- <u>Arthur High King of Britain</u> by Michael Morpurgo

Preparation: None

Parent Note: Read this book aloud and discuss it with your child.

Frutours

In the Middle Ages frutours, or fried apple slices, was a recipe found in the cookbooks of the nobility. Give them a try – they're delicious!

Ingredients:
1 apple
1 cup flour
1 egg
1/2 cup beer
1 Tbsp. powdered sugar (optional)
oil (for frying)

Directions:
1. Peel, core, and slice the apples.
2. Mix the flour, egg, beer and sugar together to make a thick batter.
3. Coat the apple slices in the batter and deep fry in oil until golden.
4. Serve hot, dusted with powdered sugar.

Week Eleven – You are a King/Queen
Day Two

Make a Crown

Materials:

- A wide piece of lace long enough to go around your child's head
- Tacky glue
- Metallic gold or silver spray paint
- Acrylic sealer
- Scissors
- Glitter (optional)
- Wax paper

Preparation: None

Activity:

1. Use the lace to measure around your child's head. Try to match the pattern in the lace leaving a ½ inch overlap.
2. Glue the lace into the crown shape and allow it to dry.
3. Place the crown on the wax paper. Spray the crown with the spray paint. Be sure to cover the inside and outside of the crown. Optionally, you may sprinkle the crown with glitter while it is still wet.
4. Allow the paint to dry.
5. Spray the crown with the acrylic sealer and allow it to dry again. That's it! You may now wear your beautiful and unique looking crown.

Reading

Parent Note: The read aloud suggestions are intended for you to read to your child. The individual reading suggestions are intended for your child to read aloud to you – or to read on their own. Continue reading each selection throughout the king/queen weeks until you are finished.

Read Aloud For Younger Children:
The King of Capri by Jeanette Winterston

Read Aloud For Older Children:
Castle by David MacCauley

Individual Reading for Grades 2-4:
The Sword in the Tree by Clyde Robert Bulla

Individual Reading for Older Children:
Tuesdays at the Castle by Jessica Day George

Make a Medieval Castle from Cardboard

Materials:

- Scissors
- Masking tape
- Gray or silver spray paint
- Slightly darker gray paint (optional)
- Tiny sponge (optional)
- A variety of boxes (regular box, rectangular tissue box, upright tissue box)
- Empty Pringles cans or empty paper towel rolls
- A piece of cardstock
- Newspaper

Preparation: None

Lesson:

1. First, make the main structure, or the keep, of your castle. To do this, choose a large enough box to allow any action figures your child might have to fit inside them comfortably. We used an 11x10x6 box for our castle.
2. Reinforce any seams with masking tape.
3. Cut windows, doors, and a drawbridge.
4. Cut the rectangular tissue box in half to make two turrets. Cut arch windows in both halves.
5. Cut strips from the card stock. Make these strips into crenellations and tape them to the top of the towers.
6. Decide where you'd like doors and windows in your towers (Pringles cans or paper towel rolls) and cut them out.
7. Using the tape, attach the towers to the castle.
8. Feel free to add other boxes to your castle to create more rooms or structures.
9. Cut more crenellations from the cardstock and tape them to the back of the castle.
10. When you are finished, cover all of the joints with masking tape.
11. Take your castle outside, put it on some newspaper, and spray paint it gray or silver. Allow the paint to dry. The paint will transform your castle in an amazing way!
12. Optionally, once the paint has dried, you may decide to use the sponge and the darker gray paint to add some "bricks" to your castle.

Be sure to save this castle until sometime next week when we will be attempting to storm it using a catapult that we make. ☺

Battling Tops

Materials:

- One top per child

Preparation: None

Lesson: The origin of "tops" is unknown. A variety of different types of top shapes can be used for this game. While some tops are spun by pulling a string wrapped around the top - larger tops can be "whipped" in order to keep them spinning. Another type of top makes use of a spindle to hold it in place while a string is pulled. The aim of each player is to attempt to have his top spin longer than any other top. While the tops spin, a player hopes that his top will keep spinning and also stop other tops from spinning - hence, the name of the game.

Coat of Arms

Materials:
- Crayons, colored pencils, markers, etc.
- Coat of arms template from companion download
- Coat of arms information sheet from companion download

Preparation:
1. Print a blank coat of arms for each child.
2. Print at least one coat of arms information sheet for reference.

Lesson: Coat of arms first came about in the early twelfth century. This is the time when knights began to wear helmets and other armor. With knights being almost completely covered up in battle, it was extremely difficult to tell people apart. This caused men to start wearing a coat of arms on their shields, tunics, and saddle blankets. The designs on the coat of arms functioned sort of like team uniforms. At first, knights were the only ones who wore them. Over time, however, they began to be used by priests, by women, and even by towns and cities. Because few people could read or write, having these symbols posted everywhere was an easy way for people to communicate with each other.

For this lesson, you will be creating your own coat of arms. Use the information sheet about the various symbols as a guide.

Activity:
1. Design your very own coat of arms.
2. When you are finished, you may want to display your coat of arms on the door or wall of your bedroom.

Week Eleven – You are a King/Queen
Day Three

Daily Life of a Medieval Queen

Materials: None

Preparation: None

Lesson: Medieval queens woke up at dawn. The first thing she did in the morning was to have her ladies-in-waiting help her get dressed. Then she attended mass with the king. After mass, she had breakfast with the king.

A queen was raised from birth for her eventual position. She was taught to be a queen and was told that the purpose of her life was to be in service to the king and his kingdom. She learned to be graceful and respectful. She was also raised to have a strong faith in God.

A medieval queen wouldn't have had many friends. She was closest to her ladies-in-waiting and others who lived in the castle. A queen stayed in her area of the castle for the majority of the day. She was in charge of supervising the servants who prepared the meals. In her leisure time she was able to embroider, sew, mend clothes, oversee the education of her daughters, pray, and practice her dancing skills.

Most queens went days or even weeks without seeing the king. Quite often, she was married because of her noble position and was counted on to have children. The king and queen weren't usually in love with each other. Having said that, a queen was still one of the king's most trusted allies. She was one of the only people who ever spent time alone with the king. She was counted on to help him strategize and analyze the meaning behind the words and actions of others.

Not only was it important for a queen to have children, it was important that she produce a male heir. This was to help secure the king's hold on the throne and the empire. Queens were greatly pressured to have a healthy, male baby. If she was unable to perform this task, the king might have shunned her, divorced her, or even killed her. Imagine how stressful this was for the poor queen!

During times of peace, a queen also acted as a socialite and a hostess. She planned many feasts, balls, and seasonal parties. She also accompanied the king when he was invited to celebrations thrown by other nobility throughout the kingdom.

Because kings were often called away from the castle to handle their responsibilities, queens were sometimes left in charge. This was rare, however. If there was any male relative available to be in charge instead, they did this rather than putting a woman in charge. Even if the male was extremely young, they would have found putting him in charge to be preferable to having a woman in charge.

Being a queen during medieval times also had its perks. Imagine being able to live in the castle, having the admiration of all of the women in the kingdom, and having ladies-in-waiting at your beck and call. Once she had produced a male heir, her life would have been one of extreme leisure compared to that of most other women during medieval times.

Literature

Materials:
- Arthur High King of Britain by Michael Morpurgo

Preparation: None

Parent Note: Read this book aloud and discuss it with your child.

Medieval Music

Materials: Audio clips from the supplement section on our website

Preparation: Go to our website and prepare to play the clips designated for this lesson.

Lesson: We learned previously that music was very important to people during Medieval Times. For this activity, you will get a chance to listen to some medieval music. Try to listen for instruments which sound different than what you're used to hearing. Be sure to listen to a variety of songs.

Who Won the Games?

Materials: Logic puzzle from companion download

Preparation: Print one copy of the logic puzzle for each child.

Lesson: One quiet, winter evening four knights were competing in backgammon and chess tournaments. Your job is to determine the ages of the men and their positions in the each game.

What is Hard Water?

Materials:
- Chalk
- Powdered soap (such as laundry soap)
- A stone
- 3 jars with lids
- Water
- A handkerchief
- 1 Tbsp. washing soda or borax

Preparation: Using the stone, grind the piece of chalk into a powder.

Lesson: I'm sure you know how important clean drinking water is to people no matter what time period they live in. But, did you know that there is hard water and soft water? Have you ever seen water that is hard? You might be surprised to hear that you have. The water in our homes is quite often classified as "hard" unless it has been conditioned with a water softener to make it "soft."

The term "hard water" came about during the Civil War. When soldiers tried to cook their beans in certain water, they found that their beans remained hard. When they left that area, they left signs that said, "Hard Water."

Hard water doesn't mix well with soap. Do you have hard water? Try this experiment to see whether the water in your house is hard or soft.

Activity:

1. Fill one of the jars with water.
2. Add the powdered chalk to that jar and stir.
3. Filter the water by pouring the water/chalk mixture through a handkerchief. Pour half of the mixture into the empty jar so that you have two identical jars with the same mixture. *Parent Note*: Some of the water will be absorbed by the handkerchief.)
4. Add the washing soda or borax to ONE of the jars and stir.
5. Fill the third jar with regular tap water.
6. Add a spoonful of powdered soap to all three jars.
7. Put the lids on the jars and shake them.
8. You should see that the chalky water to which you added the washing soda or borax produces more suds than does the regular chalky water. That is because the washing soda or borax "softened" the water allowing it to mix more easily with the soap.

9. Compare the amount of suds in the regular tap water with chalky water in the other two jars. Do you think your water is hard water or soft water? Why?

Week Eleven – You are a King/Queen
Day Four

Chemical, Biological, and Psychological Warfare during Medieval Times

Materials:
- A clear glass jar
- ½ - 1 cup lemon juice
- 1 Tbsp baking soda
- 1 tsp liquid dish soap
- Small baking pan

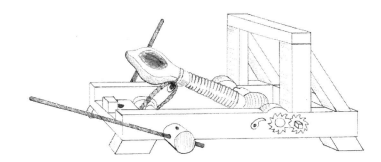

Preparation: None

Lesson: If you've studied modern warfare, you know that some of the most insidious and heinous weapons known to man are chemical, biological, and psychological weapons. When countries use these tactics, they are generally condemned by all of civilized society as fighting unfairly. Were you aware that these types of weapons were also used in the Middle Ages? Unfortunately, there was much fighting during medieval times - and many weapons were dreamt up to try to gain the upper hand.

One of these chemical weapons was called Greek Fire. Fire had long been used as a method for attacking wooden homes and villages. As a defense, people began using wet animal hides to put out the flames. Because these hides were so effective, people tried to develop forms of fire which wouldn't be put out so easily.

The formula for making Greek Fire was a closely guarded secret and it remains a mystery today. It was used in naval battles because it burned on water. Men were known to flee their posts rather than to face Greek Fire. If used on land, sand was used to put out Greek Fire. Otherwise, it was almost impossible to stop the burning. Imagine the terror that this type of weapon caused with the enemy forces!

Another form of chemical weapon in use was poisoned spears and arrows. Many of these poisons were made by using scorpion or snake venom. They used many other chemical weapons as well. Armies mixed several elements together to produce a "choking gas." They threw poisonous herbs into their enemy's water supply. They threw quicklime, or calcium oxide, at their enemies which caused them to go blind.

Medieval soldiers also used to use rudimentary biological weapons. They catapulted dead and diseased animals into a well defended fortress in the hopes that they could spread the disease among their enemies. They threw poisonous snakes onboard enemy ships. They pretended to befriend their enemy and gave them items which were infected with smallpox and the Black Death.

Psychological warfare was also common. Some soldiers wore armor which was several times larger than what they needed in an attempt to appear larger and inflict fear. They made loud noises to scare their enemies. They catapulted the severed heads of their captured enemies back into their camps.

An ingenious psychological attack was to prop up dummies beside the walls to make it look like they had more defenders than they really did. They might also throw food from the wall to try to show their besiegers that their provisions were more plentiful than they really were. Sometimes attackers removed their dead from the battlefield so that it wouldn't look like there had been any casualties.

As you can see, even during this time when chivalry was supposed to be utmost in everyone's mind, there was quite a bit of underhanded and sneaky fighting that took place. As bad as we view chemical, biological, and psychological warfare today, it is unfortunately not anything new.

Activity: For this activity, you will be working with a less dangerous chemical called lemon juice.

1. Put the jar inside of the baking pan.
2. Add the baking soda to the jar.
3. Add the dish soap on top of the baking soda. Try to spread it out while it is dripping into the jar.
4. Add the lemon juice and see what kind of reaction occurs. You may want to record your observations in your journal.

Learn to Draw a Princess

Materials:
- Paper
- Pencil with an eraser
- A black marker (optional)
- Colored pencils or crayons (optional)

Preparation: None

Lesson: In this lesson, you will learn to draw a princess step-by-step.

1. First, draw about half of an oval. Then draw her eyes, eyelids, nose and mouth as shown.

2. Next, draw her hair by first making an upside down V shape to create her bangs. Then, make an ellipse from the left side of her face going up to make the top of her hair. Draw a crown on the ellipse. Now, draw another curved line to finish the back of her head. Add a bun, her ear and curvy lines to finish this step as shown.

3. Next, draw her neck by making two curvy lines coming down from her face. Make one line by her chin and the other by her ear. Connect the neck lines with a half circle to make the neckline of her dress. To make the rest of her dress, make shoulder puffs, and upper body, waist, and bottom of the dress as shown. You can make her have curves or more straight whichever you choose.

4. Next, draw her arms. You want them to end up just below the waistline. It also helps to add gloves to make her look more elegant. Add detail to her waist, as shown, to separate the top of the dress from the bottom. This also adds dimension.

5. Lastly, add a pearl necklace and ear rings using tiny circles. Draw small half ellipses for her feet. In this step, you can get as creative as you want with her dress, crown, and hair. Have fun making your very own princess. If you'd like, you can trace your princess with the black marker and use the colored pencils to color her in. Great job!

Reading

Parent Note: The read aloud suggestions are intended for you to read to your child. The individual reading suggestions are intended for your child to read aloud to you – or to read on their own. Continue reading each selection throughout the king/queen weeks until you are finished.

Read Aloud For Younger Children:
The Queen of Style by Caralyn Buehner

Read Aloud For Older Children:
Castle by David MacCauley

Individual Reading for Grades 2-4:
The Sword in the Tree by Clyde Robert Bulla

Individual Reading for Older Children:
Tuesdays at the Castle by Jessica Day George

Leap Frog

Materials: None

Preparation: None

Lesson: This is a game for two teams. Normally, the same teams have the same number of players. One team is the first at being the "frogs." Each player on the "frog" team gets in a line and crouches down on the ground. The second team lines up and quickly tries to run and jump over all of the "frogs." A "frog" may make this difficult by arching his back or shifting position.

At the end of a run, the teams change positions. Points are given to each team for each player on the team who successfully leaps over all the frogs of the other team. Depending upon the players, points may be deducted from a team for a player who "lands" on a "frog" or knocks him over.

What is the United Kingdom?

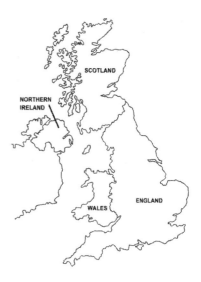

Materials:
- Tracing paper (optional)
- Pencil
- Colored pencils
- Map from companion download

Preparation: Print one copy of the map for each child.

Lesson: In modern times, if you hear the term United Kingdom or UK, the countries that are being referred to are England, Wales, Scotland, and Northern Ireland. During the majority of the medieval era, these were all separate countries with their own sense of identity, their own history, and their own language. In fact, these countries even fought each other frequently for control of the land. There was no such word as British. People were English, Scottish, Welsh, or Irish. So, how did these four separate countries ever become one united country?

Between 1535-1542, near the end of the Middle Ages, England and Wales were united. Scotland and Ireland remained their own, separate kingdoms with their own parliaments and laws until much later in history.

James VI became the King of Scotland at the age of thirteen months, after his mother, Mary, Queen of Scots, was compelled to give up the throne to him. Four different regents governed while he was a child. He gained full control of his government in 1583.

In 1603, King James VI of Scotland also became James I of England. He succeeded the last Tudor monarch of England and Ireland, Elizabeth I, who died without having had any children. James very much wanted to be considered the King of Great Britain. James was the king of all three kingdoms for 22 years, a period of time known as the Jacobean era. In 1652, Scotland and England were united together through force by Oliver Cromwell. The Scots were very upset by this action and never accepted it.

In 1707, Scotland lost her Parliament and her independence and became part of the country known as the Kingdom of Great Britain. In 1801, the Irish Parliament voted to join the union making it the United Kingdom of Great Britain and Ireland. In 1922 the name changed to the United Kingdom of Great Britain and Northern Ireland when most of the southern counties in Ireland chose to be Independent. Currently, Scotland is again discussing their independence.

The name United Kingdom makes up what were once four independent countries. They are now considered countries within a country. The capital of England is London. The capital of Scotland is Edinburgh. The capital of Wales is Cardiff. The capital of Northern Ireland is Belfast. The capital of the United Kingdom is London.

Another term with which you should become familiar is Great Britain. If you hear that term, the three countries of England, Scotland, and Wales are what they are referring to.

Activity: For this activity, you will be tracing a map of the United Kingdom of Great Britain and Northern Ireland. Either use tracing paper or use regular paper and hold the map up to a window to trace. Color the four countries within a country separate colors using the colored pencils.

Week Eleven – You are a King/Queen
Day Five

Manners at a Medieval Feast

Materials: None

Preparation: None

Lesson: There was definitely an unusual set of rules followed by people who attended a medieval feast. First, it was extremely important to make sure enough deference was shown to the king. He must be addressed as "Your Majesty" at all times.

At the beginning and the end of the meal, servants brought around a bowl filled with scented water and napkins so that guests could wash their hands. No napkins were used during the meal, however. There were no forks - only spoons and knives. And knives were used to spear objects rather than to cut them as we do today. Many foods were picked up and eaten with hands. When people's fingers inevitably got covered with food, it was perfectly acceptable for them to wipe their hands on their bread.

Guests were served in their order of importance to the host. Common dishes were served to all of the guests; however, some of the most rich and exotic foods were only served to the host and to highly distinguished guests. The salt shaker was placed directly before the king. He passed it to his guests whenever the fancy struck him. The guests never asked for it to be passed to them. Can you imagine what it would be like to want some salt on your food and not to be able to ask for it?

Feasts usually started with foods which were considered easier to digest, such as soups and salads. Foods which were more difficult to digest, such as meats, were served later in the meal.

When meat was eaten, it was usually followed with cheese. When fish was served, it was followed with nuts. The doctors of the day recommended this practice because they believed it helped the guests digest their food. Meals usually ended with sweet fruits, cakes, and spiced wines.

Meals were usually arranged in separate courses. Royal feasts broke the courses up with something called a subtlety, which contained elaborate decorations made from food. These were quite often made from sugar and could have been anything from models of saints to heroes to intricately decorated castles complete with wine fountains, musicians, and food.

Music was played throughout the meal. Oftentimes, jugglers, jesters, minstrels and others entertained the dinner guests throughout the meal as well.

A medieval feast was a very merry and satisfying time for the stomachs, the eyes, the ears, and the noses of the guests. And the guests were even allowed to throw the empty bones on the floor. Imagine how much fun that would have been!

Which Dog When?

Materials: Logic puzzle from companion download

Preparation: Print one copy of the logic puzzle for each child.

Lesson: Solve this logic puzzle by determining each of the dogs' name and the order in which Albert had them.

Make your own Trencher

Materials:
- 1 flat piece of focaccia bread per child (**Parent Note**: You can buy a long piece of French bread instead and slice it into thick, wide wedges.)

Preparation: Slice or scoop the bread to make it the shape of a trencher.

Lesson:
1. Toast your bread at 250 degrees for 20 minutes or until it becomes crispy.
2. Use your trenchers to eat a meal today. You may want to save it for the feast activity which is planned for this day as well. Remember that you are royalty this week. Peasants may have eaten their trenchers at the end of the meal but royalty would have given it to the servants or thrown it to the dogs! ☺

Literature

Materials:

- <u>Arthur High King of Britain</u> by Michael Morpurgo

Preparation: None

Parent Note: Read this book aloud and discuss it with your child.

Medieval Feast

Materials:

- White tablecloth
- Lots of candles
- Wooden plates (optional)
- Trencher made earlier today
- Medieval costumes made previously

Preparation:

1. Have the whole family dress up in medieval costumes. Be sure someone dresses up as the king.
2. To spice up the feast, you might want to secretly tape a note of treason underneath someone's chair. During the feast, the king can discover the note and condemn the traitor to death. ☺
3. There are many recipes for medieval style food on the internet. These recipes include such foods as turkey legs, herb salad, pork pot pies, and non-alcoholic spiced wine. Choose several recipes that will suit your family's tastes and prepare them in advance.

Lesson: Using the information you just learned about medieval feasts, throw a feast for your family. A good medieval feast should last several hours and include several courses. After enjoying your meal, you might want to follow it up with music and dancing.

Week Twelve – You are a King/Queen
Day One

Write in Your Journal

Materials:
- Your child's journal
- Paper
- Pencil, colored pencils, markers, etc.

Preparation: None

Parent Note: Have your child write down a few key points about what they learned about a medieval feast. Depending on their age and ability, you can require your child to write one sentence or several paragraphs. You can also have them draw a picture or print pictures from the internet as well.

Possible Writing Prompt: Imagine you are either a court jester or a regular dinner guest at a medieval feast. Describe the sights and sounds and tastes. How did it feel to be in attendance? Were you in awe of the royal family?

You Can Lift Your Parent!

Materials:
- A large, wooden block or a brick
- A plank which is at least 1in. thick and at least 4ft. long

Preparation: None

Lesson: People during medieval times knew all about simple machines. In fact, they used simple machines quite often in their daily lives. There are six simple machines: pulley, lever, wedge, screw, wheel and axle, and inclined plane. For today's lesson, we are going to use a simple machine called a lever for you to easily lift your parent into the air!

1. First, make a lever by placing the plank on top of the wooden block, which is the fulcrum. *Parent Note*: You'll want to set this up near something that you can hang onto because you're going for a ride!)
2. Be sure the fulcrum is closer to the end of the plank where the parent will stand.
3. Have the adult stand on their end of the plank.
4. Have the child step onto their end of the plank.
5. What happens? The adult should be lifted off of the ground. If it doesn't work, move the fulcrum even closer to where the adult is standing and try again – or try using a longer plank.

Decorate Your Own Grail

Materials:
- 1 plastic goblet per child
- Plastic adhesive gems
- Metallic puffy fabric paint (optional)
- Transparent paint (optional)

Preparation: None

Lesson: The Holy Grail is a very important relic according to the legend of King Arthur. Many knights have gone on quests to try to find the Holy Grail. Archaeologists and treasure hunters have searched for the Holy Grail for centuries. So what exactly is the Holy Grail?

The grail is said to be the cup that Jesus drank from during the Last Supper. It is also supposed to be the cup which caught his blood when he was on the cross. According to legend, if you were able to drink from the grail, all of your wounds would be healed and you would become immortal. You can imagine why people have searched for the grail all of these years if they really believed that the grail had that kind of power!

According to one legend, Joseph of Arimathea brought the cup to Glastonbury, England when he traveled there as the first Christian missionary to that region. In 1906, a blue bowl claimed by some to be the grail was found there. Since then, at least four other cups have been said to be the grail. How would we ever know if we did find the grail? I'm sure it wouldn't be engraved with the words "Cup of Christ." How could we tell it apart from a regular cup from that same time period?

Activity: For this activity, let your child decorate their own grail. Use the gems and the paint to try to turn their goblet into a Holy Grail. Be sure they leave the rim of their goblet free of decoration so that there's enough space for drinking.

Reading

Parent Note: The read aloud suggestions are intended for you to read to your child. The individual reading suggestions are intended for your child to read aloud to you – or to read on their own. Continue reading each selection throughout the king/queen weeks until you are finished.

Read Aloud For Younger Children:
A Medieval Feast by Aliki

Read Aloud For Older Children:
Castle by David MacCauley

Individual Reading for Grades 2-4:
The Sword in the Tree by Clyde Robert Bulla

Individual Reading for Older Children:
Tuesdays at the Castle by Jessica Day George

Kitty in the Corner

Materials:
- 4 Frisbees, pieces of rope, or other items for marking the bases

Preparation: None

Lesson: This game is for five players and requires four bases or "corners" laid out in a square. Four players each stand on a base. The fifth player, who is "Kitty", stands in the center of the square. He calls out three times "Kitty in the corner". After the third call, all five players race for a different corner at random. The first player to reach a corner keeps it. The player who is left without a corner becomes "Kitty" for the next game.

NOTE: *If you are playing with a smaller group of children, make your game area a different shape and lower number of corners to one less than the number of children who are playing.*

Week Twelve – You are a King/Queen
Day Two

<u>Different Types of Castles</u>

Materials:
- 9 craft sticks (the wider, tongue depressor style)
- 4-6 rubber bands
- 1 plastic spoon
- Several mini marshmallows

Preparation: None

You or your child should read this lesson aloud.

Lesson: When you think of a castle, a picture probably comes to mind of a large, stone structure with crenellated walls. Did you know that castles were actually built in five distinct styles and that the very first castles were made of dirt and wood?

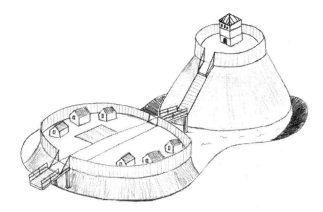

The Motte and Bailey Castle was the very first type of European castle. At least 500 of them were built in England beginning in the 10th century. They began being built in Normandy and were introduced into England by William the Conqueror following his invasion.

This type of castle consisted of a mound of dirt which was surrounded by a Bailey or a courtyard which is surrounded by a wall or fence. These castles were relatively easy and cheap to build. First, two circular ditches were dug. The soil that was removed from the ditches was used to build the motte and to form a berm around the ditches. Then, a stockade fence was built around the outside. The keep was built on top of the motte.

In the 11th century, people began to build castles with a stone keep. The first of these was built with the rectangular shape with which we are familiar today. The Tower of London is an example of this type of castle. These stone castles were definitely an improvement over the motte and bailey structures; however, they were so heavy that they couldn't be constructed on top of a motte.

The rectangular stone keep castles were surrounded by curtain walls which were also made of stone. Also, the only entrance to these castles was often on the second story, making it difficult for enemies to gain entrance.

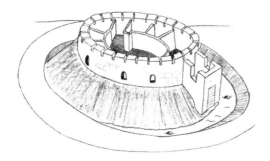

In the 13th century, people began to build castles with a shell keep, which was a circular or semi-circular stone wall with various buildings built inside of it.

The Concentric Castle began being built shortly after this.
It was a

combination of a shell keep and a rectangular keep. This type of castle had multiple defensive walls built in concentric circles. Often, they were also surrounded by moats for an additional line of defense.

One of the important improvements in castle design at this point was the change from rectangular buildings to circular ones. Round towers were much stronger and more able to withstand attack. Square towers had corners which were more vulnerable to attackers digging beneath them causing them to collapse. Square towers also had angles which formed blind spots allowing attackers to hide.

Activity: For this activity, we will be making a catapult.
1. Take 7 of the craft sticks and tie a rubber band tightly around one end.

2. Tie a rubber band around the opposite end of the sticks as well.

3. Take the remaining 2 craft sticks and tie a rubber band tightly around one end of them as well. Try to do this near the edge of the sticks.

4. Insert the 7 sticks banded together through the 2 stick bundle.

5. Tie a rubber band in a cross fashion joining the two pieces. The closer the 7 stick bundle gets to the edge, the more leverage the catapult will have.

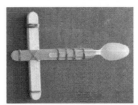

6. Use a few rubber bands to attach the plastic spoon to the end of the 2-stick bundle.
7. Stick a marshmallow on the spoon, pull the spoon down, and let the marshmallow fly! That's it. You have a working catapult.

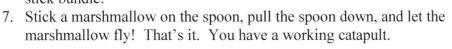

Now that you have finished, use your catapult to storm the cardboard castle you made previously. Use the marshmallows and have a great time! ☺

Literature

Materials:
- <u>Arthur High King of Britain</u> by Michael Morpurgo

Preparation: None

Parent Note: Read this book aloud and discuss it with your child.

King Arthur and the Knights of the Round Table

Materials:
- Paper and pencil

Preparation: None

Lesson: If you've been reading the book *Arthur High King of Britain*, as we suggested, you've been learning a lot about the legend of King Arthur. You may also have heard many other snippets about King Arthur in the past. He is definitely a legendary figure! There is also a chance that he was a real king – or that the stories about him were based on the life of one or more real kings.

For this lesson, try rewriting the story of the Sword and the Stone from someone else's viewpoint. You might decide to write as an unseen observer in the woods. For a very interesting story, try writing from the point of view of the sword or the stone! You may want to put your completed story in your journal.

Make your own Henin (princess hat)

Materials:
- Colored poster board
- Colored cardstock or felt
- 16" piece of string
- Pencil
- Scissors
- Tape – packing tape works great
- Tacky glue
- ½ yard of light netting, chiffon, streamers, or fabric ribbons
- Stick-on jewels or plastic flowers
- Elastic or elastic string

Preparation: None

Lesson:
1. Draw a quarter circle with a radius of about 16 inches on the posterboard. An easy way to do this is by using a pencil tied to a string.
2. Cut out the quarter circle.
3. Trim off a little bit from the tip or pivot point of your quarter circle.

4. A princess cone hat usually has a trailing veil or streamers at the tip. To make one for your hat, you can use netting, chiffon, or streamers.
5. If using netting or chiffon, fold the material lengthwise and gather the material along the folded edge. This will be the edge that attaches to the hat. Decorate the veil with flowers or stick-on jewels.

6. If using streamers or fabric ribbons, cut 5 to 6 long strips of streamer or ribbon. You can curl the ribbons if you like.
7. Tape the trailing veil or streamers onto the tip of your quarter circle. Be sure to tape it securely as it will be easier to do that now than to try to fix it later.

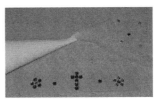

8. Roll the quarter circle into a cone and secure the entire seam with tape.
9. Cut out decorations from the cardstock or felt and either staple or glue them onto the henin. Flowers, diamonds, stars, and fleur-de-lis shapes work well. Be sure to add decoration to the bottom of the henin as well, to frame your child's face.

10. Cut the elastic to be the right size to hold the henin onto your child's head. Either punch holes into the sides of the hat to attach the elastic chinstrap or staple it into place.
11. Your child is now ready to use her princess hat. Have fun!

Magic Colors

Materials:
- Small piece of white cardstock
- Yellow paint, crayon, or marker
- Blue paint, crayon, or marker
- String
- Scissors
- 2 washers or nuts (optional)

Preparation: None

Lesson: You may think that people always wore dull and drab clothing during medieval times; but, that is not necessarily the case. People during this time period knew how to boil plants from the garden to make many colorful dyes: purples, blues, yellows, reds, and even some greens. Clothing was sometimes left its natural color. More often than not, however, it was either bleached or dyed.

Most people during the Middle Ages wore clothing made from linen and wool. Linen turns white if it is left out in the sun and it isn't easy to dye. So linen was quite often left white. Linen was often used for underclothes.

Wool accepts dye very well and was often used for outer clothing. People didn't often use soft pastel colors during medieval times. If they were going to dye their clothing they usually used bright colors. They dyed their fabrics in pots over open fires. They didn't have timers or temperature gauges; so, they used as much dye as possible to try to give color to the cloth.

For this lesson, we are going to do an experiment with color.

Activity:
1. Cut a circle from your piece of cardstock.
2. Using the scissors, punch a hole in the center of the circle
3. Divide the circle into alternating segments of blue and yellow by coloring them with paint, markers, or crayons. You may want to experiment with the sizes for each of these segments. We found that making the yellow segments larger than the blue ones seemed to work best.
4. Thread a piece of string which is about 12" long through the hole in the center of the circle.
5. Optionally, you may want to tie a knot of either side of the circle and thread a small washer or nut onto each side of the cardboard to help stabilize the circle when it's spinning.
6. When you spin the circle, the two colors should blend together into one which is more of a greenish color. The reason this happens is that your brain mixes the two colors together when the circle is spinning rapidly. This occurs because your eyes continue to see each color for a short time after the color has disappeared – so your brain combines the two colors to form a third color.

Week Twelve – You are a King/Queen
Day Three

London Bridge

Materials:
- Craft sticks
- Tacky glue

Preparation: None

Lesson: If you visited London today, you would be able to see London Bridge. This is not, however, the same bridge which existed during medieval times. The story of the original bridge is actually quite fascinating. The earliest references to a wooden bridge on the site were from the late 900s.

Wooden bridges weren't intended to be permanent. The people knew they would fall down, burn down, and require periodic replacement. Have you heard of the nursery rhyme "London Bridge is Falling Down?" This rhyme is believed to have been inspired by a Norseman named Olaf who was sailing up the Thames River. Norsemen believed that rivers were highways and they didn't appreciate the barriers that bridges formed; so, he tied the piers of the bridge to his ship and rowed downstream tearing down the bridge.

In 1176, they started building a permanent stone bridge to take the place of the wooden one. Peter Colechurch was the builder. The bridge was paid for by a tax on wool products which was levied by Henry II. This bridge had nineteen piers in the river – all placed asymmetrically. The bridge was completed in 1209.

This London Bridge was the first stone bridge in the world and was known as one of the wonders of the world for a time. It stood for over 600 years until it was demolished in 1821. The bridge was 20 feet wide. Only three years after its completion, people began to build buildings on top of the bridge. At the entrance to the bridge, they built something called Traitors' Gate, where the heads of traitors were displayed on tall spikes as a deterrent for going against the king.

For this activity, you are going to build a bridge of your own. Using the craft sticks, try to construct a bridge which will hold as much weight as possible. You may want to look up different bridge designs (such as truss, arch, suspension) on the internet – or you may want to come up with your own designs.

Build your bridge, let the glue dry, and then test it out using various weights to see how strong of a design you've built.

Reading

Parent Note: The read aloud suggestions are intended for you to read to your child. The individual reading suggestions are intended for your child to read aloud to you – or to read on their own. Continue reading each selection throughout the king/queen weeks until you are finished.

Read Aloud For Younger Children:
The Wide-Awake Princess by Katherine Paterson

Read Aloud For Older Children:
Castle by David MacCauley

Individual Reading for Grades 2-4:
The Sword in the Tree by Clyde Robert Bulla

Individual Reading for Older Children:
Tuesdays at the Castle by Jessica Day George

The Tower of London

Materials: Video clips from the supplement section on our website

Preparation: Go to our website and prepare to play the clips designated for this lesson.

Lesson: The Tower of London was built shortly after the year 1066, after William the Conqueror came to Britain from France and defeated the English at the Battle of Hastings. Some of the stone used to build the White Tower was obtained from Normandy in France, where William was born. Many other towers have been added over several hundred years.

The Tower of London is made up of lots of different parts, including The White Tower, The Bloody Tower and the Waterloo Barracks where the famous Crown Jewels are stored. During its life, the Tower of London has had many uses. It is well-known as a prison but it has also been used for many other purposes. It has been a royal residence, a place for executions, a royal mint, an armory, a storehouse, a cannon factory, and a royal menagerie or zoo.

People who were taken to the Tower as prisoners usually arrived by boat along the Thames and enter by a very scary looking wooden gate called Traitors Gate. This can still be seen if you are travelling along the River Thames. Many prisoners never left the Tower of London and ended their days there. Beheading was one of the most common punishments; several of these were carried out on Tower Green. The heads were then displayed on spikes around the castle grounds or taken to London Bridge.

Three English Queens were condemned to death in this way: Anne Boleyn, Catherine Howard and Lady Jane Grey who at 16 years old was only the queen for nine days. Some people were executed in front of the public but others came to their end in private with only a selected few present.

For this lesson, you will be watching an interesting video about the Tower of London.

Learn to Draw the Tower of London

Materials:
- Paper
- Pencil with an eraser
- A black marker (optional)
- Colored pencils or crayons (optional)

Preparation: None

Lesson: In this lesson, you will learn to draw the Tower of London step-by-step.

1. Start by drawing two sides of a cube with the left side being higher. If you extend the top lines out until they touch it will help you with details later on.

2. Next, draw a cylinder in the middle as shown.

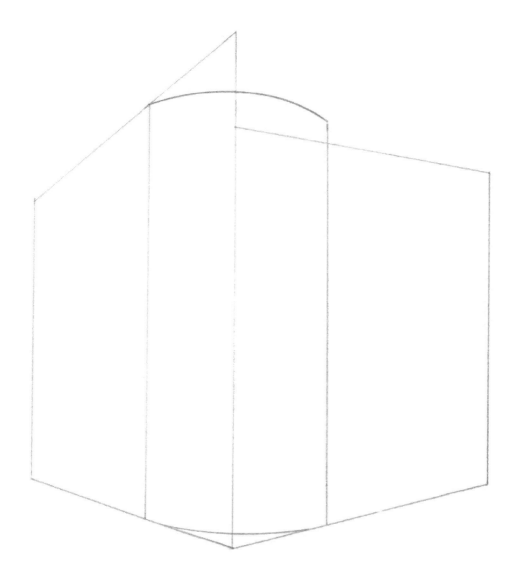

3. Erase the construction lines around the cylinder as shown. Next, draw two rectangular towers on the left and one cylindrical tower on the right.

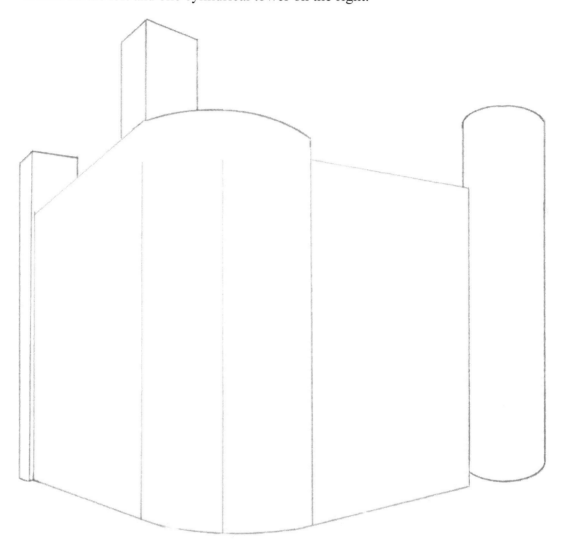

4. Draw the tops of the towers with the details as shown. Now, draw thin brick column details. Extend the column details to the right to wrap around the cylindrical column.

311

5. Next, draw the crenellations in the top of the walls. Draw the windows.

6. Lastly, finish the tower by tracing all of the lines you are keeping with the black marker. Then, erase your construction lines. Add window, brick, and roof details. Have fun adding as many details as you'd like. You may then use the colored pencils to color in your drawing if you would like. Great job!

Touch Tag

Materials: None

Preparation: None

Lesson: Who has not played a game of tag at some time in their life? There are many versions of the game of tag, and *Touch Tag* is just one of these. This game can be played indoors in a large room as well as outdoors. Any number of people can play. Someone is chosen to be IT. All the players scatter. Whoever is IT chases the other players and tries to touch one of them. The player who is touched becomes IT, and the game begins again.

Week Twelve – You are a King/Queen
Day Four

The Domesday Book

Materials:
- Local Area Survey sheet from companion download
- A pencil or pen
- Graph paper (optional)

Preparation: Print one copy of the survey for each child

Lesson: After William conquered England in 1066, he confiscated most of the land from the Anglo-Saxon nobility and divided it up between Norman barons and the church. Shortly afterward, William decided that he needed to do a survey of his land to find out how much tax he could expect to collect from his people as well as how many soldiers he could expect the lords to press into service if needed.

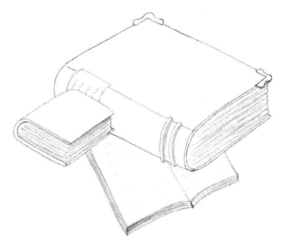

To find out this information, he appointed groups of officials and sent them out to nearly every hamlet in the country. Their job was to count every pig, every person, every farm, and every rooster in the kingdom. It was the first census that had been taken since Roman times.

The officials reported their findings back to King William. Their reports were entered in a book that the people called the Domesday Book. Dome (pronounced doom) means judgment. The survey was so thorough that William's subjects compared the "inquisition' of having to answer these invasive questions with that of God's judgment at the end of the world.

The survey revealed that much had been destroyed when William became king. Most of the land owned by Saxon landlords in 1066 had become the property of Norman lords by 1086. Two hundred Normans now controlled the land which had previously been owned by 2,000 Saxons. This meant that each new Norman baron was much more powerful than had been the previous Saxon owners since each one controlled much more land.

Today, the Domesday Book is important because it tells us a great deal about the people of England during medieval times. The survey reveals what areas of the countryside were worked as plowed farm land, pasture, meadow or woodland. It also tells us something about the people who held or worked the land. As one Anglo-Saxon chronicler wrote, "not one ox nor one cow nor one pig which was there left out and not put down in his record." Because it took 20 years to complete, Domesday also tells of how the landscape changed as a result of William's activities, such as castle building, which were intended to protect Norman England.

Activity: For this lesson, we are going to complete a Domesday Book-like survey.
1. Take a short walk around your neighborhood. If you live in an unpopulated place, you may want to drive to a small town or city to complete this project. Be sure to bring your survey forms with you.
2. While walking, complete your survey form.
3. When you are finished with your walk, discuss the results. What would a historian learn from your survey results? Optionally, you may want to compile your results into a graph. Be sure to include your survey in your journal.

Literature

Materials:
- <u>Arthur High King of Britain</u> by Michael Morpurgo

Preparation: None

Parent Note: Read this book aloud and discuss it with your child.

Make Your Own Barometer

Materials:
- A quart sized, wide mouth canning jar or a large can
- Two straws
- A 9"-12" balloon or a latex glove
- Two rubber bands
- Glue or tape
- Small piece of cardstock
- Piece of paper
- Marker

Preparation: None

Lesson: The barometer wasn't invented until after the Middle Ages. Knowing how important crops were to peasants, however, imagine how helpful it would have been for them if they had had barometers to help them to know what kind of weather was headed their way.

The simplest of barometers are merely jars filled with air. When a barometer is first made, the air pressure inside of the jar will be the same as the air pressure outside of the jar. As the weather changes, however, the air pressure outside of the jar will change. If clear, sunny weather is developing the outside air pressure will rise. This will push down on the balloon because the air pressure outside of the jar will be greater than the air pressure inside of the jar. As the balloon is pushed down upon, the lever on top of the barometer will move, causing the arrow attached to it to go up.

If a storm is developing the outside air pressure will drop. This will cause the balloon to bulge outward because the air pressure outside of the jar will be lower than the air pressure inside of the jar. As the balloon bulges up, the lever on top of the barometer will move, causing the arrow attached to it to go down.

Activity:
1. Cut the balloon like the picture on the right. If you are using a glove instead, cut a big piece of latex out of the hand.
2. Stretch the balloon over the mouth of your container. Secure it as tightly as you can.
3. Wrap a couple of rubber bands around the balloon, making a tight seal on the jar. You don't want air to be able to leak out.
4. Cut a small arrow from the cardboard. Insert it into the end of one of the straws.
5. Insert one of the straws into the other, making your barometer's arm longer. This will increase its accuracy.
6. Put a drop of glue in the center of the stretched balloon. Put the end of the straw onto the glue dot then apply a piece of tape over it. The tape will hold the straw in place until the glue can dry.

317

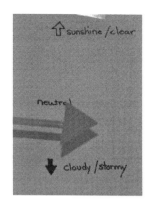

7. Draw a gauge on the paper similar to the one seen in the picture on the right – with a neutral line as well as with arrows for clear weather and stormy weather.

8. Put your barometer near a wall and tape up your gauge so that the arrow points to the neutral line.

9. As the barometric pressure changes you will see the arrow move up and down. As that needle goes up it means the weather is clearing. And as that needle goes down it means there is a storm moving in. You might want to mark lines on your gauge as the needle moves up and down so that you can better track its movement.

10. Observe your barometer a couple of times a day for a week or two. Record the changes in barometric pressure that you detect in your journal. You should also note the specific weather that is occurring at the time. Your barometer should help you to be able to make fairly accurate predictions about the weather.

Write in Your Journal

Materials:
- Your child's journal
- Paper
- Pencil, colored pencils, markers, etc.

Preparation: None

Parent Note: Have your child write down a few key points about what they learned about the Domesday Book. Depending on their age and ability, you can require your child to write one sentence or several paragraphs. You can also let them narrate back to you what they have learned. Then, have them draw a picture or print pictures from the internet to add some more insight to their journal page.

Possible Writing Prompt: Imagine you were just visited by the king's agents and were interviewed for the Domesday Book. How did it feel to describe all of your worldly goods to someone who had recently overtaken your country? Were you cooperative? Describe the encounter with as much detail as possible.

Field Trip to a Castle

Parent Note: This week is a great time to visit a castle in your area. You might be surprised at how many castles exist around the globe. Some of these castles are larger and more elaborate than others. Some of them are private houses; however, many of these castles are either part of universities. Many of them are available to visit at least part of the year.

Touring a castle will be a unique experience for your child. If you are able to arrange a more detailed tour such as exploring the secret passageways, eating a meal in the castle, or any other type of activity that will only help to enhance the experience for your child. You might be surprised at the varied activities that are possible. Be sure to ask your child questions so that they can compare their experience with what they have learned so far about the life of a king or queen. And have your child take lots of pictures for their journal.

Week Twelve – You are a King/Queen
Day Five

Wars of the Roses

Materials:
- Edward III's Family Tree from companion download
- Link for creating a family tree from supplement section of our website

Preparation: Print at least one copy of the family tree to study while reading the lesson

Parent Note: Be sure to follow along on the family tree as you read this lesson as the royal family relationships get complicated.

Lesson: Can you imagine wanting to be the king so badly that you were willing to fight your cousins for the privilege? That's exactly what happened during the Middle Ages. The Wars of the Roses were a series of battles between two rival branches of the same family. It was between the houses of Lancaster and York. The family was warring over which of its cousins would sit on the throne of England. The House of Lancaster was represented by a red rose and the House of York was represented by a white rose which is how these battles got their name.

The cause of the Wars of the Roses began during the reign of Edward III. It all started with a power struggle between his sons after his death. The four eldest sons of Edward III (1312 - 1377) were Edward the Black Prince (heir to the throne), Lionel of Antwerp (Duke of Clarence), John of Gaunt (Duke of Lancaster), and Edmund of Langley (Duke of York).

Edward III died in 1377. His eldest son, Edward the Black Prince, had died of the plague in 1376. Because of this, his grandson, Richard, aged ten and son of the Black Prince, became king. Because Richard II was only ten years old, his uncle, John of Gaunt, Duke of Lancaster, ruled the country for him. As Richard grew older he rebelled against his uncle and made decisions that were not popular with the most powerful men in the country.

320

In 1399, John of Gaunt died and Richard II confiscated the land his uncle had owned. John of Gaunt's son, Henry, raised an army and attacked Richard II. When Richard surrendered Henry became king and was known as Henry IV. Henry imprisoned his cousin, Richard, in Pontefract castle where Richard mysteriously died in February 1400.

Henry IV established the House of Lancaster when he became king. He also faced a number of challenges to his place on the throne because he was not the natural successor to Richard II. With the death of Richard II, the crown should have passed to Edmund Earl of March, great grandson of Lionel, Duke of Clarence. Somehow, Henry managed to remain the king. When he died in 1413, the country was at peace and his son, Henry V, took over the throne without any opposition from the rightful heir.

Henry V was a strong leader. He ordered the execution of Richard, Earl of Cambridge for plotting to put someone from the House of York on the throne. He then invaded France where he won many battles including the Battle of Agincourt in 1415. Henry V conquered Normandy and Rouen for England. In 1420, when Henry married the daughter of the king of France, it was agreed that their children would be the heirs of both the English and the French throne. When Henry V died in 1422 from dysentery his son, Henry VI, became the only king to be crowned king of England and France at the same time.

Henry VI was only four months old when he became king and his uncles ruled England and France in his place. France was soon lost when Joan of Arc raised an army against the English and restored the French monarchy. As Henry grew older it became apparent that he was a weak king. He was completely dominated by his French wife, Margaret of Anjou. He was also prone to bouts of insanity. His cousins from the House of York began plotting to take his place on the throne.

The first official battle of the Wars of the Roses took place at St. Albans on May 22, 1455. The House of York, led by Richard, Duke of York, easily defeated the King's army. Henry VI was injured and taken prisoner. In 1455, Henry VI suffered another bout of insanity and Richard, Duke of York was made protector of England. In 1456, Henry recovered and retook the throne. There were further battles and in 1459, Richard was killed at the Battle of Wakefield.

In 1461, Richard's son Edward, Earl of March, defeated Henry VI's army and took the King prisoner. He then made himself King Edward IV. Henry's wife, Queen Margaret, took her son and fled to Wales where they were taken in by the king's half-brother, Jaspar Tudor. In 1470, Henry regained the throne. In 1471, he was defeated by Edward's army at the Battle of Tewkesbury and taken prisoner. Henry's son, Edward, Prince of Wales was killed during the battle. With no other heir from the House of Lancaster to challenge him, Edward IV remained king until his sudden death in 1483.

Edward IV had two sons, Edward and Richard. Edward was the heir to the throne. Before he could be given the crown, however, other family members declared his father's marriage to his mother to be illegitimate. Their uncle Richard, Duke of Gloucester, was given the crown instead. Richard ordered that the two princes be taken to the Tower of London and held prisoner. In the summer of 1483, they mysteriously disappeared. It is believed that their uncle murdered them. Richard was crowned Richard III. He was not a popular king and he faced many challenges to his place on the throne, notably from Henry Tudor.

Henry's main claim to the English throne came from his mother through the House of Beaufort. Henry's mother, Lady Margaret Beaufort, was a great-granddaughter of John of Gaunt who was the son of Edward III.

Henry Tudor raised an army from the House of Lancaster to go up against Richard III. At the Battle of Bosworth Field in 1485, Richard was killed and the House of York was defeated. It is said that Henry found Richard's crown on the battlefield and placed it on his own head. Henry VII was crowned king and married Edward IV's daughter, Elizabeth of York. This was a wise move that not only cemented his place as king; but, it also ended the Wars of the Roses by joining the two houses in marriage.

Activity: I'm sure you saw how helpful it was to follow along on the family tree while reading the above lesson. Families can get very complicated! Even if your family isn't currently fighting for a throne, it is probably complex as well. For this activity, you will be creating a family tree of your own.
1. Go to the link on the supplement section of our website.
2. Enter as much information for your family as you are able. Be sure to pick your parents' brains about their extended families.
3. If you are interested, you might want to go to the closest library in your area which has census information on microfilm. Do some genealogy research to see how much information you can find out about your ancestors. Genealogy is a fascinating hobby! Be sure to include your findings in your journal.

Follow the Leader

Materials: None

Preparation: None

Lesson: This is another very ancient game that is still played today on city streets, in public parks and playgrounds, and in rural areas. No one knows how old this game is. Any number of children can play. Someone is chosen to be the leader. Players form a line and try to duplicate the movements of the leader.

The leader may lead the players in a line or just stand still and only move arms and legs. The leader might do both at the same time. Sometimes the leader might do something quite difficult such as climbing or engaging in some physical feat.

The leader attempts to force players to drop out of the game by quickly changing movements and speeding up or slowing down. The player who can't "follow the leader" must drop out of the game!

Quiz Bowl

Parent Note: See how well you and your children can answer questions about the material that has been covered concerning kings and queens.

1. When did a medieval king get out of bed? (Dawn)

2. True or False: A medieval king led a life of leisure with no real responsibilities. (False)

3. For what did king's servants check his bed before he went to sleep? (Fleas)

4. Why did knights start putting a coat of arms on their shields? (So that it was easier to tell them apart while they were in their armor.)

5. How long might a queen go without seeing the king? (Days or even weeks)

6. What was a queen's most important responsibility? (To have a male heir)

7. Was a medieval queen ever left in charge during a king's absence? (Yes, but they would have tried to find any other male to put in charge, even an extremely young one, if at all possible.)

8. Name one chemical weapon used during the Middle Ages. (Greek Fire, poisoned spears, poisoned arrows, choking gas, quicklime)

9. Name one biological weapon used during the Middle Ages. (catapulting dead and diseased animals, throwing poisonous snakes, giving items infected with smallpox or Black Death)

10. Name one psychological weapon used during the Middle Ages. (Wearing armor which was too big, loud noises, catapulting severed heads, using dummies, throwing food, removing their dead from the battlefield)

11. What countries are included in the United Kingdom? (England, Wales, Scotland, and Northern Ireland)

12. How were hands washed before a medieval feast? (A bowl of scented water and a napkin)

13. If your hands got dirty during a medieval feast, should you wipe them on a napkin? (No, you should wipe them on your bread.)

14. Name at least two things for which the Tower of London has been used. (A prison, a residence, a place for executions, a royal mint, an armory, a storehouse, a cannon factory, and a royal menagerie or zoo)

15. Who ordered the information for the Domesday Book to be gathered? (William the Conqueror)

16. What does Dome mean? (Judgment)

17. What caused the Wars of the Roses? (Cousins fighting for the throne)

18. Which two "houses" were fighting for the throne? (The House of Lancaster and the House of York)

19. What were the names of the two princes who were imprisoned in the Tower of London and later disappeared mysteriously? (Edward and Richard)

20. What finally ended the Wars of the Roses? (The marriage between Henry VII from the House of Lancaster and Elizabeth from the House of York.)

Reading

Parent Note: The read aloud suggestions are intended for you to read to your child. The individual reading suggestions are intended for your child to read aloud to you – or to read on their own. Continue reading each selection throughout the king/queen weeks until you are finished.

Read Aloud For Younger Children:
Blueberries for the Queen by John and Katherine Paterson

Read Aloud For Older Children:
Castle by David MacCauley

Individual Reading for Grades 2-4:
The Sword in the Tree by Clyde Robert Bulla

Individual Reading for Older Children:
Tuesdays at the Castle by Jessica Day George

Medieval Adventure, Scene Six

Materials:
- Script from companion download
- Costumes which were made/gathered in a previous lesson
- Whatever other props you create during your lessons and/or have laying around the house to add excitement to this adventure.

Preparation:
1. Photocopy the script so that each actor has their own copy.
2. Read through the script a few times so that you know what to expect and can help to direct the kids.

Parent Note: Choose roles for yourself and your children. Remember, the more dramatic you act the more your kids will as well – and the more value they will gain from this assignment.

Activity Suggestions for Further Learning and Fun

Below is a list of further suggestions which have not been incorporated into the two weeks of learning that you may also want to try. The more you immerse your child in these types of activities, the more they will learn and enjoy this experience. **Warning:** You child will probably most enjoy some of the suggestions are the messiest or the most out of the ordinary! ☺

King

- Let someone else help you get dressed
- Let someone style your hair
- Play dice or a card game
- Go hunting – use a hunting dog if possible
- Go horseback riding
- Have everyone address you as "Your Majesty" and bow when they see you

Queen

- Let someone else help you get dressed
- Let someone style your hair as elaborately as possible
- Embroidery
- Sew something – you might want to try sewing on a button or mending some socks
- Practice your dancing skills

Materials List – Supplies for Each Day

Regular school items such as paper, pencils, cardstock, tracing paper, staplers, glue, tape, scissors, hole punch, ruler, markers, brads, string, paint, crayons, chalk, camera, printer, etc. will not be listed below. This list contains items which are not normal school supplies.

Week One – Day One
- Items to make peasant costumes such as:
  - Loose fitting pants, such as black or brown sweatpants with long socks pulled up to the knees
  - OR dark jeans rolled up to just below the knees
  - A long-sleeved shirt (possibly baggy)
  - A long handkerchief tied at the waist
  - Tall, black boots or bare feet
  - Long dress made of a simple fabric – usually one color
  - OR a baggy, white blouse paired with a long, full skirt – usually one color
  - Ballet slippers
  - Unmarried girls usually wore their hair loose – but you may want to wrap her head in a handkerchief

Week One – Day Two
- One bucket or bowl per child
- Craft sticks
- Hot glue
- Straw, long grass, or thin twigs (You can use pipe cleaners if necessary)
- Drinking straws
- Duct tape
- A bucket
- Dirt
- Clay
- Sand

Week One – Day Three
- Bean seeds
- Disposable, plastic cups of different colors (must be transparent)
- Disposable, plastic cups that are clear
- Potting soil, seed starter, or dirt
- Packing tape
- Graph paper (optional activity for older kids)

Week One – Day Four
- Light cardboard or card stock
- Weaving material (construction paper, raffia, pipe cleaners, yarn, ribbons, field grasses, metallic wire, fabric, burlap, etc.)
- Something to use for the bowling pins (i.e., empty 2-liter pop bottles)
- A ball (be sure this is soft if you'll be playing indoors)

Week One – Day Five
- A glass jar with a wide mouth (a ½ pint canning jar or an empty baby food jar would work well)
- Extra virgin olive oil
- A fire source – it will be much easier if you use a propane fire starter versus a match
- Hot pad
- A glass or plate which is larger than the opening of your jar for snuffing out the fire
- Graph paper (optional)

Week Two – Day One
- Five three-ounce disposable cups
- Two straws
- Pin
- Timer (optional)
- A hammer (the bigger the better – if you happen to have a sledge hammer, that would be perfect)
- Ingredients for Frumenty (see lesson)

Week Two – Day Two
- Eight Oreo cookies per child
- Plastic knife (optional)

Week Two – Day Three
- 3 or 4 radish seeds
- 2 clear, disposable cups
- Potting soil
- Photos from the past two weeks

Week Two – Day Five
- Two buckets
- Two large cups or bowls
- An outdoor source of water

Week Three – Day One
- Items to make tradesman and/or tradeswoman costumes such as:
  - A long vest or shirt which can be worn as a tunic
  - A long-sleeved, baggy shirt
  - Tights or leggings
  - Long, trailing dress with puffy sleeves
  - OR a baggy, white blouse paired with a long, full skirt – usually one color
  - Pointed shoes
  - An elaborate headdress or braided hair

Week Three – Day Two
- A bar of soap (Ivory or another soap without additives works well)
- Either a jackknife or a popsicle stick (depending on the age and skill of your child)
- Newspaper
- Paper towel
- 2 jump ropes (optional)
- Ingredients for a Medieval Apple Pie (see lesson)

Week Three – Day Three
- Checkerboard (would have been played on a 100 square board if you can find one. Modern day checkers is played on a 64 square board)
- 12 colored discs per player
- A disposable cup which is slightly wider at the top than the opening of the jar
- A jar
- A craft stick
- A pin
- A digital clock, watch with a second hand, or timer

Week Three – Day Four
- Small bead
- Markers, glitter and sequins (optional)
- Small bells (optional)

Week Three – Day Five
- 2 disposable cups
- Food coloring (you pick the color)
- 1 tsp. borax powder (available at most large grocery stores near the laundry detergent)
- A plastic spoon (for stirring)
- A tablespoon (for measuring)

Week Four – Day One
- Telescope or binoculars (optional)
- Ingredients for Waffles (see lesson)
- A blindfold

Week Four – Day Two
- Aluminum foil
- Items for obstacle course (see lesson)

Week Four – Day Three
- Small metal can (an empty vegetable can works well)
- Salt
- Measuring spoon
- Crushed ice
- A box of toothpicks
- A bag of mini marshmallows
- A lotion bottle or some other object with which to prop up your creation until it hardens

Week Four – Day Four
- Wooden clothespins with springs
- Cardboard
- Yarn
- Black felt
- Hot glue
- Embellishments such as ribbon, lace, bells, etc. (optional)

Week Four – Day Five
- Heavy, Styrofoam plate
- Newspaper
- Ink pad(s) – You can use multiple colors of inkpads if you would like
- Football
- 1 Handkerchief per child (optional)

Week Five – Day One
- Boxes of sugar cubes
- Craft sticks for making a portcullis, drawbridge, ladders
- Piece of plywood or thick cardboard for the base of the castle (2'x2')
- Cardboard or construction paper for making turrets, arrow slots etc.
- Items to make knight and/or lady-in-waiting costumes such as:
  - A long vest or shirt which can be worn as a tunic. Knights quite often had a red cross on their tunic. (We will be making a tunic later in the week.)
  - A long-sleeved, baggy shirt
  - A sword and shield
  - A belt to wear over the tunic
  - Boots
  - Sword and shield (We will be making these later on as well.)
  - Long, trailing dress with puffy sleeves
  - OR a baggy, white blouse paired with a long, full skirt – usually one color
  - Pointed shoes
  - Braided hair covered with a veil or wimple

Week Five – Day Two
- Plaster of Paris
- Giotto black line artwork from companion download
- Disposable cup
- Plastic fork
- Plastic or aluminum plate with at least a half inch well
- Acrylic glaze or varnish
- 1 Pool noodle
- 1 PVC pipe with a ½" diameter
- 1 ½" PVC caps (the kind that slides on, not screws on)
- 1 Sheet of thick craft foam
- Hack saw (or other saw for cutting the pipe and the pool noodle)
- Colored duct tape (optional)

Week Five – Day Three
- Dictionary
- 1 yard of felt or flannel (whatever color you prefer)
  OR ½ yard for a shorter tunic
- 1 smaller piece of felt or flannel (of a different color)
- Tacky or fabric glue
- Clay (optional)

Week Five – Day Four
- A pan (optional)
- Wooden spoons (optional)
- Paper bowl (optional)
- Dried beans (optional)
- Swimming noodles to use as a lance (or something else soft like a cardboard wrapping paper tube)

Week Five – Day Five
- 4 cardboard tubes
- Small box
- Gray spray paint (optional)

Week Six – Day One
- A big bowl (glass works great)
- A glass cup which is at least 1'' shorter than the sides of the bowl
- Clear plastic wrap
- Small rock or weight
- A handful of dirt
- Push pin
- Stick or straw
- Ingredients for Gyngerbrede (see lesson)

Week Six – Day Two
- Large piece of cardboard per child
- 2 colors of duct tape or spray paint
- Candle in a holder
- Match
- Glass jar such as a quart canning jar (narrow mouthed jar)

Week Six – Day Three
- A stick, jump rope, or some other way of marking the start line
- A measuring tape OR small sticks for marking each child's jump distance

Week Six – Day Five
- Large dowel approximately 1/2 inch thick and 3 feet long
- Cardboard
- Box cutter or sturdy scissors
- Hot glue gun
- Metallic silver spray paint
- Paper plate

Week Seven – Day One
- A glass jar
- A squeeze bottle with a small nozzle (empty glue bottle, etc)
- Food coloring (several colors)
- Liquid dish soap
- A paper plate to use as a palette
- Black Puffy Paint (optional)

Week Seven – Day Two
- An empty 2-liter pop bottle
- Newspaper
- Aluminum foil
- Craft sticks
- Tissue paper
- Flour
- Monk and Nun costumes such as:
  - A long robe with a hood – brown or black is best
    - OR a long, black garbage bag with a head hole cut in the bottom
  - A rope to use as a belt
  - Sandals or bare feet
  - Long dress or robe – white, brown, or black would be best
  - Full apron worn over dress
  - Huge cross necklace (can make this with cardboard and string if desired)
  - Head covered with a long veil or wimple (long piece of fabric)
- A sidewalk, driveway, or other hard surface
- One stone per player

Week Seven – Day Three
- String
- Plastic protractor
- Straw
- Weight (washer, rock, or fishing weight)

Week Seven – Day Four
- Waterproof or archival pen (optional)

Week Seven – Day Five
- Legos or other building blocks

Week Eight – Day One
- Binoculars
- Ingredients for Baked Pears (see lesson)
- Marbles

Week Eight – Day Two
- Small container for collecting a water sample
- Microscope or magnifying glass

Week Eight – Day Three
- Clay or terracotta pot about 5" in diameter
- Clay or terracotta pot which is very small (to use as the clapper)
- 2 large wooden beads (larger than the hole in the bottom of your pots)
- Decorative cord or string
- Several buttons, marbles, pennies, or other small objects

Week Eight – Day Five
- Foam or paper plate
- Plastic knife
- Lump of clay or Play-doh
- Small piece of cardboard
- Timer or clock with alarm
- A paperclip
- 1 Quill per child (goose, swan or turkey are best)
- A knife
- A block of wood just slightly larger than the quill
- Washable ink
- Paper towels for blotting and cleanup
- Writing paper
- Small, disposable cup
- Smock to protect your child's clothing
- A timer or clock

Week Nine – Day One
- Items to make baron and/or baroness costumes such as:
  - A red, blue, brown or black shirt made of velvet, silk, cotton, taffeta or satin damask. These fabrics were considered luxurious and would have been suitable for the rank of baron.
  - Clothes could be trimmed with any fur but sable, which was reserved for royalty
  - Barons also wore tights or leggings.
  - A hood with a wide collar which covered the shoulders, back and chest.
  - Pointed shoes.
  - A pouch to be used as a coin purse.
  - Long, trailing dress with puffy sleeves in red, blue, brown or black. Velvet, silk, cotton, taffeta, or satin damask would have also been appropriate materials for a baroness.
  - A cloak.
  - Pointed Shoes.
  - An elaborate headdress or braided hair.
  - A hood with a wide collar which covered the shoulders, back and chest.
  - A broach to hold the cloak or collar in place.

Week Nine – Day Two
- Graph Paper
- Construction Paper (use multiple colors that you would see in nature – green, brown, tan, yellow, etc.)
- A stick or jump rope to make a start/finish line
- Objects such as a Frisbees or balls to use as batons

Week Nine – Day Three
- 2 cups dry ice (frozen carbon dioxide)
- 2 spoonfuls of sand or dirt
- A dash of ammonia
- A dash of organic material (dark corn syrup works well)
- An ice chest
- A large mixing bowl (plastic if possible)
- 4 medium-sized plastic garbage bags
- Work gloves
- A hammer, meat pounder, or rubber mallet
- A large mixing spoon
- Paper towels
- Safety goggles
- 2 jump ropes or sticks

Week Nine – Day Four
- Twine, jute, or sisal yarn

Week Nine – Day Five
- Ingredients for Strawberries in Snow (see lesson)

Week Ten – Day One
- Glass jar
- 20 Heavy coins (50 cent piece, silver dollar, etc)
- OR 20 Large washers
- Piece of poster board

Week Ten – Day Two
- Baby powder
- A lamp with the shade removed

Week Ten – Day Three
- Flour
- Salt
- Food Coloring
- A bag of dried black beans
- A bag of various colored beans
- Varnish (optional)
- A stick or rope for the starting line
- A target to throw towards – a stick pushed into the ground, a ball, or other object of your choice
- Frisbees, pool rings, or other objects to toss

Week Ten – Day Five
- A permanent marker
- A straight straw
- Three glasses
- 1 Tbsp salt
- 1 Tsp dishwashing liquid
- A small piece of clay or Play-doh
- A measuring cup
- 1 or 2 small, light nails which are small enough to slip inside the straw
- Empty paper towel roll
- Newspaper
- Black or silver spray paint
- A couple of sheets of printer paper or craft foam
- String

Week Eleven – Day One
- Items to make a king and/or a queen costume such as:
    - A long coat or jacket in a vibrant color
    - Fancy pants or hose
    - Bright piece of fabric to use as a cape
    - Anything with fur or velvet
    - A crown (we will be making one later)
    - Long, trailing dress with puffy sleeves – in a vibrant color
    - Pointed Shoes
    - Anything with fur or velvet
    - Crown with veil over hair (We will be making a crown later)
- Ingredients to make Frutours (see lesson)

Week Eleven – Day Two
- A wide piece of lace long enough to go around your child's head
- Tacky glue
- Metallic gold or silver spray paint
- Acrylic sealer
- Glitter (optional)
- Wax paper
- Gray or silver spray paint
- Slightly darker gray paint (optional)
- Tiny sponge (optional)
- A variety of boxes (regular box, rectangular tissue box, upright tissue box)
- Empty Pringles cans or empty paper towel rolls
- Toy top

Week Eleven – Day Three
- Powdered soap (such as laundry soap)
- A stone
- 3 jars with lids
- A handkerchief or small towel
- 1 Tbsp. washing soda or borax

Week Eleven – Day Four
- A clear glass jar
- ½ - 1 cup lemon juice
- 1 Tbsp baking soda
- 1 tsp liquid dish soap
- Small baking pan

Week Eleven – Day Five
- 1 flat piece of focaccia bread per child (Note: You can buy a long piece of French bread instead and slice it into thick, wide wedges.)
- White tablecloth
- Lots of candles
- Wooden plates (optional)

Week Twelve – Day One
- A large, wooden block or brick
- A plank which is at least 1in. thick and at least 4ft. long
- 1 plastic goblet per child
- Plastic adhesive gems
- Metallic puffy fabric paint (optional)
- Transparent paint (optional)
- 4 Frisbees, pieces of rope, or other items for marking the bases

Week Twelve – Day Two
- 9 craft sticks (the wider, tongue depressor style)
- 4-6 rubber bands
- 1 plastic spoon
- Several mini marshmallows
- Colored poster board
- Colored cardstock or felt
- 16" piece of string
- Tape – packing tape works great
- Tacky glue
- ½ yard of light netting, chiffon, streamers, or fabric ribbons
- Stick-on jewels or plastic flowers
- Elastic or elastic string
- String
- 2 washers or nuts (optional)

Week Twelve – Day Three
- Craft sticks
- Glue

Week Twelve – Day Four
- A quart sized, wide mouth canning jar or a large can
- Two straws
- A 9"-12" balloon or a latex glove
- Two rubber bands

Suggested Reading List

Peasant Weeks

Read Aloud For Younger Children
- Don't Let the Barber Pull Your Teeth: Could You Survive Medieval Medicine? by Carmen Bredeson

Read Aloud For Older Children
- Adam of the Road by Elizabeth Janet Gray

Individual Reading for Grades 2-4
- Roland Wright: Future Knight by Tony Davis

Individual Reading for Older Children
- Dragon Slippers by Jessica Day George

Literature to Read Aloud to All Ages
- Aesop's Fables for Children illustrated by Milo Winter
- OR The Classic Treasury of Aesop's Fables illustrated by Don Daily

Tradesman/Tradeswoman Weeks

Read Aloud For Younger Children
- Who Was Leonardo da Vinci by True Kelley and Roberta Edwards

Read Aloud For Older Children
- The Door in the Wall by Marguerite De Angeli

Individual Reading for Grades 2-4
- The Adventures of Sir Givret the Short by Gerald Morris

Individual Reading for Older Children
- Dragon Spear by Jessica Day George

Literature to Read Aloud to All Ages
- Stories from Shakespeare by Geraldine McCaughrean

Knight/Lady-in-Waiting Weeks

Read Aloud For Younger Children:
- The Princess and the Three Knights by Karen Kingsbury
- The Hero Beowulf by Eric A. Kimmel
- How to Become a Perfect Knight in Five Days by Pierrette Dubé
- Sir Ryan's Quest by Jason Deeble
- Saint George and the Dragon by Geraldine McCaughrean

Read Aloud For Older Children:
- Shakespeare Can Be Fun: Hamlet for Kids by Lois Burdett

Individual Reading for Grades 2-4:
- The Dragon in the Sock Drawer by Kate Klimo

Individual Reading for Older Children:
- The Squire's Tale by Gerald Morris

Literature to Read Aloud to All Ages
- Beowulf as told by Michael Morpurgo

Monk/Nun Weeks

Read Aloud For Younger Children:
- You Wouldn't Want to Work on a Medieval Cathedral : a Difficult Job that Never Ends by Fiona Macdonald
- Marguerite Makes a Book by Bruce Robertson
- Summer Birds: The Butterflies of Maria Merian by Margarita Engle
- A Year in a Castle by Rachel Coombs
- See Inside Castles by Laura Parker

Read Aloud For Older Children:
- Cathedral: The Story of its Construction by David MacCauley

Individual Reading for Grades 2-4:
- The Big Book of Knights, Nobles and Knaves illustrated by Adria Fruitos

Individual Reading for Older Children:
- Crispin: The Cross of Lead by Avi

Literature to Read Aloud to All Ages
- The Adventures of Robin Hood by Roger Lancelyn Green

Baron/Baroness Weeks

Read Aloud For Younger Children:
- You Wouldn't Want to be a Medieval Knight by Fiona MacDonald
- You Wouldn't Want to be a Crusader by Fiona MacDonald
- Don't Forget the Knight Light by Tina Gagliardi
- The Sunflower Sword by Mark Sperring
- Max's Castle by Kate Banks

Read Aloud For Older Children:
- Shakespeare Can Be Fun: Much Ado About Nothing for Kids by Lois Burdett

Individual Reading for Grades 2-4:
- Knight at Dawn (A Magic Treehouse book) by Mary Pope Osborne

Individual Reading for Older Children:
- The Book of Three by Lloyd Alexander

Literature to Read Aloud to All Ages
- The Canterbury Tales by Geoffrey Chaucer (retold by Geraldine McCaughrean)

King/Queen Weeks

Read Aloud For Younger Children:
- The King of Capri by Jeanette Winterston
- The Queen of Style by Caralyn Buehner
- A Medieval Feast by Aliki
- The Wide-Awake Princess by Katherine Paterson
- Blueberries for the Queen by John and Katherine Paterson

Read Aloud For Older Children:
- Castle by David MacCauley

Individual Reading for Grades 2-4:
- The Sword in the Tree by Clyde Robert Bulla

Individual Reading for Older Children:
- Tuesdays at the Castle by Jessica Day George

Literature to Read Aloud to All Ages
- Arthur High King of Britain by Michael Morpurgo

Made in United States
Orlando, FL
07 October 2023

37672587R00191